THE SOUND OF MUSIC

THE TRAPP FAMILY SINGERS

Maria Augusta was sent as a young novice to look after the large family of the widowed Baron von Trapp. She brought with her little besides her guitar and the gift of happiness. With the zest inherited from her native Tyrol, she quickly transformed the gloomy restraint of the house outside Salzburg into a place of bubbling musical activity centred round the festivals of the church year. The children became her close friends, and when the Baron fell in love with her she married him with the blessing of the convent.

Maria von Trapp's optimism and determination carried the family through many trials. When their fortunes crashed, the musical training she had given the children enabled them to earn their living on the concert platform. After a miraculous escape from Nazi-occupied Germany, she led them to the start of a new and outstandingly successful life in the U.S.A. But above all, this wonderful true story—which gave rise to the musical and the film *The Sound of Music*—is one of a close-knit family whose happiness and success were based on a joyous foundation of love and faith.

The Sound of Music

is based on the story of
The Trapp Family
Singers

by

MARIA AUGUSTA TRAPP

Collins
FONTANA BOOKS

First published by Geoffrey Bles 1953
First issued in Fontana Books 1965
Second Impression, May 1965
Third Impression, September 1965
Fourth Impression, September 1965
Fifth Impression, November 1965
Sixth Impression, January 1966
Seventh Impression, August 1966
Eighth Impression, September 1966
Ninth Impression, November 1966
Tenth Impression, December 1966
Eleventh Impression, June 1967
Twelfth Impression July 1967
Thirteenth Impression August 1967
Fourteenth Impression November 1967
Fifteenth Impression September 1958
Sixteenth Impression November 1968
Seventeenth Impression April 1969
Eighteenth Impression August 1969
Nineteenth Impression March 1970

© Maria Augusta Trapp, 1953
Printed in Great Britain
Collins Clear-Type Press
London and Glasgow

CONTENTS

PART ONE: AUSTRIA

PART TWO: AMERICA

CONTENTS

Foreword

About fifteen years ago my family and I were on a visit in the Tyrol. Our hostess was a famous writer.

"Isn't it funny," she said one day, "I never wrote a word in my life until after I was forty!"

"That's quite incredible," we mused.

The next day we all went into a picturesque valley. On the way we saw a chapel greeting us from one of the wooded slopes.

"Let's climb up there," said our hostess. "That's an interesting place." And so it was. The ancient building was of quaint architecture. Through the roof came a rope dangling down, which belonged to the bell in the little steeple. Playfully I took the rope to try out the sound of the bell.

Looking at our friend, I said: "I wish I could become a writer, too, after I'm forty!" I meant that as a joke, and felt a little embarrassed when she didn't smile.

She looked at me rather queerly and said: "Did you know the story?"

I let the rope go and asked: "Which story?"

"Well," she said, "people say that once in a hundred years it happens if someone rings this bell while pronouncing a wish, that wish, whatever it may be, will come true, provided the person is unaware of the legend. The people of this valley call it the ' wishing bell.' "

"No—I didn't know that story," I said.

This was fifteen years ago.

While working on this book and writing down the memories of a family, it amazed me to see how much love—genuine, real love—was stored up in one short lifetime; first, God's love for us His children, the guiding, protecting love of a Father; and, as all real love calls forth love in return, it couldn't be any different in our case.

As we are singers, this story turned into a canticle. "Sing unto the Lord a new song," sings King David in one of his Psalms. "The Story of the Trapp Family Singers" is introduced as a canticle of love and gratitude to the Heavenly Father in His Divine Providence.

Cor Unum
Stowe, Vermont
Pentecost Sunday, 1949

PART ONE: AUSTRIA

I. Just Loaned

Somebody tapped me on the shoulder. I looked up from the exercise books of my young pupils, which I was just correcting, into the lined, kindly face of a little lay sister.

"Reverend Mother Abbess expects you in her private parlour," she whispered.

Before I could close my mouth, which had opened in astonishment, the door shut behind the small figure. Lay sisters were not supposed to converse with candidates for the novitiate.

I could hardly believe my ears. We candidates saw Reverend Mother Abbess only from afar in choir. We were the lowest of the low, living on the outskirts of the novitiate, wearing our black mantillas, waiting with eager anticipation for our reception into the novitiate. I had just finished the State Teachers' Course for Progressive Education in Vienna and had to get my diploma before the heavy doors of the enclosure would shut behind me—for ever.

It was unheard of that Reverend Mother Abbess should call for a candidate. What might this mean? Her private parlour was far at the other end of the old Abbey, and I chose the longest detour to go there, in order to gain time for examining my conscience. I was the black sheep of the community; there was no doubt about that. I never meant anything bad, but my upbringing had been more that of a wild boy than that of a young lady. Time and again I had been warned by the Mistress of Novices that I could not race over the staircase like that, taking two and three steps at a time; that I definitely could not slide down the banister; that whistling, even the whistling of sacred tunes, had never been heard in these venerable rooms before; that jumping over the chimneys on the flat roof of the school wing was not fitting for an aspirant to the novitiate of the holy Order of Saint Benedict. I agreed whole-heartedly each time, but the trouble was, there were so many *new* trespasses occurring every day.

What was the matter now, I thought, slowly winding my way down the two flights of old, worn steps, through the ancient coble-stoned kitchen yard, where the huge crucifix greets one from the wall, and where the statue of Saint Erentrudis, founder of our dear old Abbey, rises above a fountain. Slowly I entered the cloister walk on the other side of the kitchen court.

Troubled as I was, I still felt again the magic of this most beautiful place on earth. Twelve hundred years had worked to make Nonnberg, the first Abbey of Benedictine Nuns north of the Alps, a place of unearthly beauty. For a moment I had to pause and glance again over the grey, eighth-century cloister wall before I ascended the spiral stairway leading to the quarters of Reverend Mother Abbess.

Shyly I knocked on the heavy oaken door, which was so thick that I could hear only faintly the " Ave," the Benedictine equivalent of " Come in."

It was the first time I had been in this part of the Abbey. The massive door opened into a big room with an arched ceiling ; the one column in the middle had beautifully simple lines. Almost all the rooms in this wonderful Abbey were arched, the ceilings carried by columns ; the windows were made of stained glass, even in the school wing. Near this window there was a large desk, from which rose a delicate, small figure, wearing a golden cross on a golden chain around her neck.

" Maria dear, how are you, darling? "

Oh this kind, kind voice! Big rocks fell from my heart when I heard that tone. How could I ever have worried? No, Reverend Mother was not like *that*—making a fuss about little things like whistling—and so a faint hope rose in my heart that she might perhaps talk to me now about the definite date of my reception.

" Sit down, my child. No, here near me. "

After a minute's pause she took both my hands in hers, looked inquiringly into my eyes, and said: " Tell me, Maria, which is the most important lesson our old Nonnberg has taught you? "

Without a moment's hesitation I answered, looking fully into the beautiful, dark eyes: " The only important thing on earth for us is to find out what is the Will of God and to do it. "

"Even if it is not pleasant, or if it is hard, perhaps very hard?" The hands tightened on mine.

Well now, she means leaving the world and giving up everything, I thought to myself.

"Yes, Reverend Mother, even then, and whole-heartedly, too."

Releasing my hands, Reverend Mother sat back in her chair.

"All right then, Maria, it seems to be the Will of God that you leave us—for a while only," she continued hastily when she saw my speechless horror.

"L-l-leave Nonnberg," I stuttered, and tears welled up in my eyes. I couldn't help it. The motherly woman was very near now, her arms around my shoulders, which were shaking with sobs.

"Your headaches, you know, are growing worse from week to week. The doctor feels that you have made too quick a change from mountain climbing to our cloistered life, and he suggests we send you away, for less than one short year, to some place where you can have normal exercise. Then it will all settle down, and next June you will come back, never to leave again."

Next June—my goodness, now it was only October!

"It just so happened that a certain Baron von Trapp, retired Captain in the Austrian Navy, called on us to-day. He needs a teacher for his little daughter, who is of delicate health. You will go to his house this afternoon. And now kneel down; I want to give you my blessing."

I knelt down. The fine, delicately small hand made the sign of the Cross on my forehead. I kissed the ring and, as through a veil, I had a last glance into those unforgettable eyes, which seemed to know all about sorrow and suffering, but also victory and peace. I couldn't utter a single word.

"Now then, go and do it, and whole-heartedly, too."

That was all.

A few hours later I was seated on one of the green benches under the old chestnut trees at the Residenzplatz in Salzburg, waiting for the bus that was to take me to Aigen. One hand was clasped tightly around a piece of paper which said: "Captain Georg von Trapp, Villa Trapp, Aigen bei Salzburg"; the other one held the handle of an old-fashioned leather satchel, which stood next to me on the bench, and which contained all my earthly possessions, mostly books.

Under my arm was pressed the neck of my guitar. Years back, when I had started to work my way through college, I had bought it with my first self-earned money. It had accompanied me everywhere, on all the many trips and hikes through the Alps, up to the holy hill of Nonnberg. And now it went with me into exile.

I was still bewildered, everything had happened so fast. I tried to review the last few hours, which had passed like a bad dream. After I had come back from Reverend Mother Abbess, my Mistress of Novices, Frau Rafaela, was already waiting for me in the candidates' room, her arms full of clothing. When I had entered the convent a year before, I had exchanged my Austrian costume for the black dress and black mantilla of the candidates. My own clothes had been given away during the year to some needy persons after the Chapter meeting had decided I was to be admitted for reception. I could see that Frau Rafaela felt embarrassed. She looked a little helplessly at the clothes on her arm, which had belonged to another novice who was a little shorter and wider than I. She chose one dress and, obediently, I put on an old-fashioned blue serge gown with funny latticework around the neck and sleeves. I put it on three times, because I could not make out which was front and which was back. Next came a leather hat, which looked exactly like a fireman's helmet. It went right down to my brow, and I had to give it a little push when I wanted to see Frau Rafaela, who just said:

" Now let me look at you."

As she stepped back a little, her eyes wandered from the hat down to the blue dress, on to the black stockings and heavy, black shoes. She nodded approvingly.

" Very nice—very elegant."

Frau Rafaela was a saintly, elderly nun ; the day of her farewell to the world dated back at least thirty years. I feel pretty sure now that I must have reminded her vividly of the young ladies of her own day.

Then came a few instructions: On my day off I should always come back to the convent ; I should remember the doctor's advice to get enough sleep and exercise—but moderate, moderate ; and finally, I should always bear in mind that my home and place was Nonnberg, and although I had to deal with the people of the world, I was *just loaned* to them.

My heart ached when I had to bid farewell to the other

three young candidates with whom I had shared the big, lofty room overlooking the green valley of the Salzach River. While Frau Rafaela bent over a little scrap of paper to write down the name of the place where I was to go, I took in with one last glance the picture of the large, oblong room with the six windows, the white-curtained cells along the wall, where we slept, the large table in the middle, and the huge, old-fashioned *Kachelofen,* the European tile stove which can radiate so much comfort and warmth in the severe Salzburg winters. How happy I had been there, and how long it would be until I should be back; but " Thy Will Be Done " was painted in faded, old-fashioned letters over the door on the whitewashed wall.

A few more words, a final blessing, and for the last time my fingers dipped into the pewter holy water font. For a few moments I knelt at the choir grate, looking down to the main altar, asking Our Lord for strength. Then the old oaken door opened with a cranky squeak, unwilling, it seemed to me, to let the youngest child of Nonnberg go back into a world from which it would much rather have protected her.

When I stepped from the cool archway into the centuries-old graveyard, my eyes, half-blinded by tears and the bright sunshine, fell upon the inscription on a weathered gravestone: " God's Will Hath No Why."

Then I was on the road that led down the hill on which Saint Erentrudis had built her castle of God in the eighth century. And a castle it was, built on solid rock, with its huge walls nine feet thick at the foundation. Where this foundation seemed to grow out of the rock a little terrace had been cut into the stone. Here I paused for a few moments, looking over the railing into the deep valley from which the rock rose steeply for almost three hundred feet, down where the houses of Salzburg nestled to the green mountain-side. I was still higher than the steeples of the churches. I looked over the quaint old Grabendächer (" ditch roofs," a roof construction frequently used on old houses in Salzburg), followed with my eyes the silver ribbon of the Salzach River, way over to the mountains from which it came. Over there must be Aigen, where I was to go.

Where I was to go—for heaven's sake—I had to reach the bus; and down I went the hundred and forty-four steps, two at a time, forgetting already the very recent admonitions. On the Residenzplatz I learned that the next bus was due in half an hour and so, a little breathless from running, there I was now sitting on one of the green benches.

I felt quite uprooted and a little empty in my head. What was to come next? My eyes fell on the crumpled piece of paper in my hand, and I read again, " Captain von Trapp." That made me wonder. I had never been at the seashore, nor had I ever met a sea captain in my life. I knew them only from story books and pictures.

" I guess he is an elderly man with a bushy, grey beard, red cheeks, and sharp, blue eyes," I thought to myself. " Most probably he chews tobacco and spits. If he is a captain, he must have been around the world many times. Surely all his walls must be plastered with trophies, lion and tiger skins, and weapons. It will be awfully interesting."

At the same time I felt a certain awe creeping into my heart, because surely he would shout a lot, as sea captains are supposed to be very gruff. At this very moment I remembered the story of the Mutiny on the Bounty, a silent picture which I had seen just before I entered the convent, and which had haunted my nights for quite a time. . . .

A terrific noise interrupted my anxious thoughts. In a cloud of dust, a big vehicle roared across the Residenzplatz and stopped right in front of me. A man dismounted from the bus. I wanted to see if he was the driver, but my leather helmet fell over my eyes, and I could see only as far as his mouth, from which protruded a toothpick. Pushing the hat back a little, I saw a driver's cap.

" Is this the bus for Aigen?" I asked. The toothpick man nodded.

" When are you leaving?"

" At once."

For a moment he looked searchingly around to see whether there were any more passengers. I stepped in and sat down on the right front seat, my precious belongings close beside me. My satchel looked exactly like the bag of a country doctor. The driver stepped inside, closed the door, and said: " *Zwanzig Groschen* " (tenpence). After a gentle push on the helmet I looked up at him and, while he was getting the change, I watched the toothpick. He could wave it up and down and sideways, move it from one corner of his mouth to the other, even while speaking or spitting, but he never lost it.

The driver sat down at the wheel, pushed a button, and, squeaking and groaning, we started down the Residenzplatz, across the Mozartplatz, down towards the Salzach River, in such sharp and masterful curves that twice I landed on the other side of the bus. After a few minutes we crossed the bridge over the Salzach River, the Karolinenbrücke, and almost immediately we were in the open country, passing by a few estates with large gardens and then meadows and fields. Several times we stopped abruptly to take farm people aboard. They all seemed to know each other, shouted greetings, yelled answers, because with all that roaring and rattling you had to raise your voice quite a bit even to say a word. Mr. Müller, as I heard the people greet our driver, had to answer many questions, give many explanations, laugh at jokes. Between cigarettes he spat artistically through a little hole in the left front window, but he never dropped the toothpick.

After about twenty minutes' drive, the bus stopped suddenly and, pointing the toothpick straight at me, Mr. Müller said, " Aigen."

I got out and was immediately enveloped in a smoke screen. After the bus had disappeared and I had pushed back my helmet, I could see only one house, which said " Inn."

" Do you know the Villa Trapp?" I asked a man who was smoking in the doorway of the inn. He didn't say whether he did or not, but he came out on the dusty country road and, pointing with his pipe across the meadow to a group of large trees, he said.

" There."

On the right side of the railroad tracks across the way the road was lined by a high iron fence, which seemed to encircle the park of an estate. On the other side, wide meadows stretched towards the foot of a pretty high mountain, which I knew was the Gaisberg. The narrow road seemed to lead straight to the foot of it. No, there was a turn. It had already been quite a long walk, and I had changed my things from one hand to the other several times. I tried to peep into the park, but the trees and bushes made a solid green wall. Perhaps these were the trees which I had seen from the bus stop. Then there must be a house, *the* house. And there it was. Suddenly the iron bars opened into a wide driveway, and beyond a large, green, oblong patch of lawn, through the yellow leaves of old horse-chestnut trees I caught glimpses of a building. I stopped for a moment, pushed back the nuisance of a hat impatiently, and looked. Here now was the place! I was torn by conflicting feelings: there was still the sadness of the hurried farewell from the beloved sanctuary, and there was a strong curiosity about the exotic home of a real navy captain, mixed with some awe of the captain himself. . . .

" But you can't stand here for ever," I told myself.

As I stepped from under the trees to the gravel driveway, I had a full view of the big grey mansion with a little tower on the right corner. Ivy covered this side of the house. My attention was immediately attracted by the windows on the first floor. They were exceptionally tall. I could see something red and white hanging from a wall inside. Two steps led up to a heavy, two-winged, arched, oaken door. It opened with a little squeak after I had rung the door-bell.

" Is this the Villa Trapp?" I asked the good-looking man who stood in the doorway, dressed in a grey Austrian costume, only with silver buttons instead of the familiar staghorn.

" Yes, m'm."

" I am the new teacher. Are you the Captain?"

Not a muscle moved in the tanned face.

" No, m'm, I am Hans, the butler."

" How do you do, Hans," and I stretched out my hand to greet him.

He shook it a bit hastily, I thought, and didn't seem quite at ease. He took my satchel and ushered me through a double glass door into a great hall, which extended the full height of the house, bade me sit down, and disappeared quietly before I could say another word. I was somewhat disappointed. In the small mountain village of Tyrol where I came from and where everybody knew everybody else, we were never in such haste. I should have liked to talk a little while to the friendly-looking man and ask a good many questions before I had to face the first sea captain of my life. But perhaps this was the way butlers had to be. I had never met one before in my life. There weren't any in our mountains, nor in the boarding-school in Vienna, nor at Nonnberg, either. They only occurred in novels and movies, like sea captains.

There I sat on a richly-carved, dark chair, which reminded me somewhat of the choir stalls in the Abbey. Curiously I looked around for the lion and tiger skins and the strange weapons, but only a few ancient pieces of furniture stood in the large hall, and two dark oil paintings hung on the wall. Through the large windows I had admired from the outside, the full sun shone on an exquisite staircase, which wound upwards in an elegant curve. The red and white hanging from the wall turned out to be the largest flag I had ever seen in my life. It was at least thirty feet long, red—white—red, with a huge crest in the middle.

Suddenly I heard quick footsteps behind me, and a full, resonant voice exclaimed: " I see you are looking at my flag."

There he was—the Captain!

The tall, well-dressed gentleman standing before me was certainly a far cry from the old sea wolf of my imagination. His air of complete self-assurance and somewhat lordly bearing would have frightened me, had it not been for his warm and hearty handshake.

" I am so glad you have come, Fräulein. . . ."

I filled in, " Maria."

He took me in from top to toe with a quick glance. All of a sudden I became very conscious of my funny dress, and sure enough, there I was diving under my helmet again. But the Captain's eyes rested on my shoes.

We were still standing in the hall when he said: " I want you to meet the children first of all."

Out of his pocket he took an odd-shaped, ornamented brass whistle, on which he piped a series of complicated trills.

I must have looked highly amazed, because he said, a little apologetically: " You see, it takes so long to call so many children by name, that I've given them each a different whistle."

Of course, I now expected to hear a loud banging of doors and a chorus of giggles and shouts, the scampering feet of youngsters jumping down the steps and sliding down the banister. Instead, led by a sober-faced young girl in her early teens, an almost solemn little procession descended step by step in well-mannered silence—four girls and two boys, all dressed in sailor suits. For an instant we stared at each other in utter amazement. I had never seen such perfect little ladies and gentlemen, and they had never seen such a helmet.

" Here is our new teacher, Fräulein Maria."

" *Grüss Gott,* Fräulein Maria," six voices echoed in unison. Six perfect bows followed.

That wasn't real. That couldn't be true. I had to shove back that ridiculous hat again. This push, however, was the last. Down came the ugly brown thing, rolled on the shiny parquet floor, and landed at the tiny feet of a very pretty, plump little girl of about five. A delighted giggle cut through the severe silence. The ice was broken. We all laughed.

"This is Johanna," her father introduced the little giggler, "and here is our baby, Martina."

What a delicate child, I thought. Reservedly she held both hands behind her back and glanced at me silently and critically.

"Hedwig is already a big schoolgirl," and the father pointed to the third of the younger ones. All three had their hair cut in low bangs, whereas the fourth girl, whom the Captain introduced as, "My eldest daughter, Agathe," wore a large white hair ribbon atop her shoulder-length curls. I felt a strong liking for that young child with the unusually grave countenance and the shy little smile. I wished with all my heart we might become good friends.

There was no time, however, at this moment to try, as their father was continuing: "And here are the boys, Rupert, the eldest of them all, and Werner."

Rupert seemed to have his father's somewhat aloof bearing. Werner was a little fellow with eyes like dark velvet, whom I wanted to take into my arms and hug there and then.

"Which one is my pupil?" I asked the Captain.

A shadow came into his smiling eyes when he answered: "You haven't met your pupil. I will take you to her."

With a nod he dismissed the children.

While I followed him up the staircase, he explained.

"This child has been a problem to us for years on account of her poor health. Ever since she had scarlet fever, her heart has remained weak. Now she has had influenza, and doesn't seem able to recover. Poor little one."

At the second-floor landing the Captain opened a door, and we climbed another flight of stairs, this time narrow and winding to the third floor and our destination, a large, sunny room opening out on a balcony. Propped up on a mountain of pillows in an ancient, oversized, carved wood bed, sat a little girl.

"This is Maria, Fräulein," the Captain said, and bending over the yellowish little face with the dark rings under the

large black eyes, continued in a tender undertone, " I am sure
you two will get on really well together, little one. You even
have the same name."

A faint smile lit the small face, and a little voice answered,
" Yes, Father," and, " I am very glad to meet you, Fräulein
Maria."

" Now Fräulein must go to her room," the Captain explained, " but she will be back to see you soon."

As we descended the staircase together, he turned suddenly
and asked: " Well, how do you like the children?"

The question took me unawares

" They have the most beautiful eyes I have ever seen," I
stammered, " but they all look so pale and serious."

I hated myself for saying this, which their father could very
well take for unduly quick criticism, so I hastened to add:
" But they are all very well behaved."

" Not always," said the Captain with a little twinkle.

Then suddenly serious—he had evidently heard more than I
had intended to say—he added in a lower voice while we were
continuing down the stairs:

" You see, you are the twenty-sixth in a long line of nurses,
governesses, and teachers we have had to look after them
since their poor mother died four years ago. That will explain
many things to you. The last teacher stayed with us only two
months, but I have the feeling it will be different this time."

" Yes," I smiled, " nine months."

Then he opened the tall, white door for me, and with the
words, " The bell will ring for dinner soon," and a slight bow,
he took his leave.

It was a large, sunny room with a big bay window. An
oriental rug covered most of the floor. Heavy antique furniture and costly wallpaper gave it a grand air. The white
bed in a niche was covered with pale blue silk ; the table in the
middle, under the carved chandelier, with heavy brocade. In
Nonnberg we had no rugs, no silk, no brocade ; but on the
walls hung old paintings and wood carvings of Our Lord and
Our Lady and all the dear saint. At every door one found a
holy water font made of pewter or silver or pottery. Nothing
of this kind could I find in my new room. At the foot of the
bed stood a simple stool on which lay my shabby, worn
satchel and the unfortunate little hat ; the guitar leaned against
the bed. They felt like strangers here, and so did I. I sat

down on the stool, took them into my lap, and for a moment I was quite forlorn and lonely, when a rich, strange sound made me jump up: the dinner bell.

A little later we all met again in the fine dining-room. At the head of the table was the Captain. The children sat along both sides. The other lower end was taken by a middle-aged lady. I sat at her left, the baby at her right. I learned that she was Baroness Matilda, the *Hausdame,* who presided over the whole household. She had a kind, friendly way about her. Her whole bearing breathed refinement and reminded me of lavender.

This hour in the dining-room added a few more questions to the many that already crowded my mind: Those many different silver and crystal dishes—what were they for? Why did Hans, the butler, wear gloves—indoors—all of a sudden? What was the matter with his left hand that he held it so tightly to his back? (Perhaps there was a hole in the other glove.) Why did the Baroness ring that little bell? Why didn't she call him when he was only standing right behind the door? And so on, and so on.

After dinner I was told that I was free for the evening to do my unpacking and get settled.

Well, the unpacking didn't take more than five minutes. The toothbrush and the few pieces of underwear, the brown velvet dress, looking hopelessly like a sack, and the dozen books were quickly arranged. The satchel and the little hat wandered into the darkest corner of the huge wardrobe. The New Testament and the Rule of Saint Benedict, together with a little cross, were placed on my night table.

Then I went over to the window. In the red light of the setting sun there stretched a large park with meadows and groups of big trees and meadows again. And a little farther I saw, sharply drawn against the pale evening sky, the profile of my beloved mountain, the Untersberg, just as we had seen it every day from Nonnberg. And there were all the others, too: Tennengebirge, Hagengebirge, Staufen, Watzmann.

I felt a little better already. When you are a child of the mountains yourself, you really belong to them. You need them. They become the faithful guardians of your life. If you cannot dwell on their lofty heights all your life, if you are in trouble, you want at least to look at them. The man who wrote three thousand years ago: " I will lift up mine eyes unto the hills, from whence cometh my help," knew this, too. And even Our Lord, when He was weary and tired out and wanted to be alone with His Father, ascended a mountain.

Happily, like a little schoolgirl, I made myself a calendar which showed two hundred and fifty days, the exact number I should have to endure in this house. The first day was crossed out, and the last thought which went through my mind at the end of this important day was: After all—I don't belong here ; I am just loaned.

II. *Glories of the Past*

The next few days I lived in a continual state of bewilderment. Nothing—nothing at all—was familiar to me in this house. First, I had to get used to the different people. There was the Baron and there were his seven children. There was Baroness Matilda, and then came the staff of servants, headed by Hans, the butler. In the kitchen reigned Resi, the round, good-natured chief cook. Once in her early years she had cooked on an English steamer. She had been in Australia and India, and sometimes in the evening she would tell the little kitchenmaid, Maraindl, gruesome stories about pirates and cannibals. It happened usually on such occasions that the two housemaids, Poldi and Lisi, and Pepi, the gardener, gathered in the kitchen, too. And even Hans preferred to clean the silver in the kitchen because " there was better light." Resi's stories were just too good to be missed.

Only Franz never showed up in the kitchen. He didn't need to listen to Resi's wild stories. He had been the Captain's orderly while on active duty in the Navy, and he could have told stories himself about submarines and torpedoes, but he thought his stories too good for the kitchen. He lived with his family in the big house, too. As the Captain did not need an orderly any more, Franz was in charge of the farm. Being a farmer's boy, he had adjusted himself better to the change in his way of living than his master. Every now and then, however, one could see the Captain and his former orderly smoking a pipe together in the evening after their work was done, talking about the glorious times in the Navy.

Besides the large family and the servants, which amounted already to twenty persons, there was the spacious old house to get used to. So many rooms, hallways, corridors, bay windows, balconies—and in the rooms, so many quaint things I had never met before.

On the third day after my arrival the Baron left for a hunting trip in Hungary. The same evening Baroness Matilda said to me during supper: "When all the children are in bed, wouldn't you like to come over to my room?"

I accepted gladly, and started immediately to list in my mind the most important questions about the children, the house, and last, but not least, the Captain himself.

"Come in and make yourself at home," Baroness Matilda's high-pitched, soft voice called in answer to my knock on her door. I went in, but I could not make myself at home right away. There was too much of something in this room; what was it? An instant later I knew it was ruffles. The white lace curtains at the windows fell in wide, ruffled curves. The bed had what seemed to be a petticoat of long muslin ruffles all around. The dressing-table with the large silver mirror and the many tiny bottles and flasks was also clad in white muslin with big ruffles. The chaise-longue, which reached diagonally into the big room, had a rich display of silken ruffles. And even the silken cushion on which the Baroness had been resting displayed a yellowish halo of ruffles around her head. My rather masculine mountain-climber's heart shrank back from so much femininity. I must have stopped involuntarily in the doorway, for, "Won't you sit down, dear?" said the friendly lady with the wide black velvet ribbon about her throat.

Next to the chaise-longue, on the little ebony table, stood a silver tray. Baroness Matilda took from it a crystal carafe, removed the silver stopper, and poured golden wine into two crystal glasses. Then she put an odd-shaped ceramic dish on my lap, filled with the Austrian pastries, *Mozart Kugeln* and *Vanilla Kipferln,* and said: "Help yourself."

Then, raising her glass, she continued with a warm undertone in her voice: "Welcome, welcome, and may you never have a successor!"

It took me a moment to realise that this meant she wished me to stay until the children were grown up and would not need a teacher any more. Now, wasn't that nice, and I started to warm up—ruffles or no ruffles.

I had never been spoiled with sweets or cakes in my life; and those delicacies on my lap simply loosened my tongue, and I poured out questions to my heart's delight. Patiently and smilingly the Baroness answered the hundred-and-one whys and wherefores, until I said, finally: " There is one thing that I understand least of all. Why does the Captain not look happy with those precious children, this wonderful home of his, and everything money can buy?"

The smile vanished from the face of my companion, and she repeated: " Everything money can buy—that is very little. Oh, the poor man has lost so much!"

Baroness Matilda looked forlornly into the golden glow of the lamp. I felt rather embarrassed now; perhaps I should not have asked questions about the master. Perhaps now I should take my leave and go to bed, and I fidgeted uneasily in my chair. Baroness Matilda seemed to awaken from deep thought. She turned to me again and said in a friendly manner:

" No, you don't have to go yet, my dear child. I may just as well tell you the whole story. The Captain is not always easy to understand, and this may prove a key for you in future happenings."

And then I listened to a very odd story. Captain von Trapp had been born and brought up on the seashore, as his father had also been in the Navy. At the age of eighteen he had earned his first decoration fighting in the Boxer Rebellion in China. He was one of the first to realise the importance of the submarine in warfare. He applied for a transfer to Fiume, where the newly invented torpedoes were being built for all Europe. This transfer decided his whole life. He was given command of one of the first submarines the Austrian Navy put into service.

The young lady who christened this submarine was the grand-daughter of the inventor of the torpedo and owner of the torpedo-plant, Robert Whitehead. When the submarine was christened, the heart of its commander was captured. Hers was the fairy-tale combination of rare beauty, charm of character, and fabulous wealth. Before long they were married. In Pola, the Austrian Navy Yard, they built a costly villa overlooking the blue sea, and they were very happy.

The outbreak of World War I brought a sudden end to this fairy-tale. All civilians had to leave Pola. The young wife went with their two little babies to stay at her mother's estate in the Austrian Alps, and the Captain's hobby suddenly turned into a grim profession.

He soon found out that those first submarines had not yet passed the stage of experimentation. Exhaust gases swept through the boat causing the crew to be poisoned. The periscope could not be raised or lowered, but the whole boat had to be moved with the periscope. However, Captain von Trapp truly did miracles with the poor material he had. He haunted the shores of the Adriatic Sea, he crippled convoys and very soon he had cleared the home waters of enemy ships. Soon his breast was covered with medals, headed by the rarest decoration Austria can give, the cross of Empress Maria Theresia ; and I learned that this highest award an Austrian officer could receive in time of war had been founded by the Empress as an award for an act of personal bravery performed on one's own initiative at one's own risk, sometimes even against orders. That meant if the act were successful, one was given the Maria Theresien Cross and automatically raised to the nobility. But if it should happen to fail, one was faced with a court martial.

He became a legendary figure among the gallant heroes of the Army and Navy as the war went on. His family had grown to five children now. His friends prophesied that at the end of the war he would certainly be made an Admiral. His whole nation was proud of him. He was not only popular, but really beloved. And then it all turned out so differently. Austria was defeated and stripped of her entire sea-coast. The proud Imperial Navy was no more. In the prime of life near the peak of his fame the Captain was brushed aside in the whirlwind. Now he was a captain without a ship, which in his special case meant almost a body without a heart.

Only his wife, the queen of his heart and his faithful companion made life still endurable for him. Two more babies arrived after the war. Then an epidemic of scarlet fever took his young wife. Half of his life had died with the Navy. Of the remaining half, most seemed to be buried with her.

" The shining hero of Austria's youth became a silent man with an empty look in his eyes," the Baroness went on. " He moved his seven children from the familiar scenes of his happiness to this newly purchased estate, which is not haunted with memories. He became restless. He tried to go back to sea

again. He started the Vago Shipping Company. After that
he went into the lumber business, which he soon gave up to
try to do something with ships on the Danube. He travelled,
he went on long hunting trips. He again tried different
businesses, but nothing thrives if done with an aching heart."

"But how about the children?" I could not help asking.

"That is really the saddest part of the story," the Baroness
answered in a depressed voice." He loves the childrn more
than anything else in the world. He provides everything for
them that money can buy. He supplied a whole staff of servants, a governess for the older one, another governess for
the little girls, a nursemaid for the baby, a private teacher
for Maria. That is what we had before you came. It was a
pity! The governesses fought each other and had to be
changed frequently. All these people were brought in to take
the place of the one. Somehow, he is a little shy with the
children. They seem to remind him too much of their mother.
He never stays long at home. He drops in unexpectedly,
showers them with presents, becomes restless very soon again,
and leaves for another trip. His relatives have persuaded him
now to think about one person to replace this whole staff—a
new mother for his seven little ones."

And with these words the Baroness rose:

"We expect his engagement to Princess Yvonne to be announced at any time."

From the bottom of my heart which was stirred by pity and
sympathy I added to my night prayers shortly afterward:

"Dear Lord, send him a good wife who will be a good
mother to his dear children, and let him be happy from now
on."

III. "*The Baron Doesn't Like It. . . .*"

As the weeks passed by, I grew more accustomed to my work.
There was a certain routine to be followed every day. The
Baroness liked to rest in the mornings. I was in charge of all
the children, had to wake them up, take care of their break-
fasts, and see the older ones off to school. That was quite a
business because there was so much to think of. The children
had to wear leather hats, leggings and leather gloves. On

rainy days rubbers and umbrellas were added. I had managed
in an incredibly short time to muddle things. One morning I
could find only left gloves and right leggings, and it always
took a long time to get hold of the respective mates.

Desperate, I looked for help.

" Couldn't we get some sturdy hobnailed boots." I approached Baroness Matilda, quite exhausted from hunting for
some rubbers.

" Two left leather gloves got lost," I had to admit.
" Wouldn't woollen mittens be less costly and more practical
for the children? And you know, Baroness, a *Wetterfleck* for
each one would really be a bargain."

" A what?"

" But Baroness, everybody wears a *Wetterfleck* nowadays,"
I laughed at her blank look. " You know, those woollen capes
with a hood. Then we would be rid of those dreadful
umbrellas."

The Baroness listened politely.

" I always thought an umbrella a great comfort," she said
finally. " Maybe it would be handier for the children the
other way—— But you know," and she sighed resignedly,
" the Captain likes it this way."

When the older children had left for school, I began classes
with Maria and Johanna. The latter had started out bravely to
walk the two miles to school with the others. There were no
school buses in Austria. Little Johanna was quite exhausted
from her long walk every day, and so it was decided that I
could teach her at home for the first grade.

It was sheer joy to teach the children, different though they
were. Maria was very delicate. On account of her heart condition she had to be kept completely quiet. She was not
supposed to run or climb, nor play any wild games.

How hard it is for a child always to stand aside when other
children play and have lots of fun! But Maria was an
exception. She never showed any disappointment. She was
always friendly. Only once in a while I saw an expression on
her face which showed extreme longing, almost hunger, in the
beautiful dark eyes, while she watched her sisters and brothers
at noisy play. The first time I saw that look in her eyes I
resolved to do everything in my power to make up somehow
for the many sacrifices which were asked of the child.

First, I tried to make school as fascinating as possible. She was intelligent and grasped everything immediately. There were twelve main subjects of study: religion, grammar, composition, literature, history, geography, physics, botany, French, geometry, algebra and Latin. Besides these we had drawing needlework, and music theory. She was especially gifted in mathematics, science, and music theory, but we simply flew through all the other books as well. In six weeks we had completed all the work for the first regular school term. I was almost troubled about so much enthusiasm and thoroughness. Often I came to her room and wanted to interrupt her in school work, saying: " That is plenty for to-day, Maria. Let's play a game of backgammon."

Then she usually lifted a hot little face up to me, and, with eager eyes, said: " Oh this is so much more fun, Fräulein Maria," pointing to an algebra problem or some intricate design in geometry.

As long as she was happy, I thought, I simply didn't have the heart to add any more " don'ts."

Maria was definitely not a communicative child. She kept everything to herself, but one day she confided: " I don't really mind so much if I cannot run around with the others, but what I *do* mind is that I have had to give up my piano lessons."

I remembered that I had found in the music-room two mahogany violin-cases.

" Oh, how nice! Who plays the violin?" I had exclaimed to the Baroness.

" Nobody now."

I had understood.

But with Maria now in mind I went to the Baroness and asked: " Could I take one of the violins up to Maria? She could have it in her room and practise only a little every day."

I was not refused. I was even allowed to look for a teacher to come twice a week for lessons. The quiet child beamed with happiness, and the frail little fingers proved to be very clever on the violin.

Johanna was different. I never had to stop her in school work. Oh, no, quite the contrary! The little lady had a good mind for studying, but she just loved a comfortable life. After the first half-hour of sitting up straight, she usually tried to climb on my lap, " because I can hear you better." She was incredibly inventive in distracting my attention.

This plump little girl with the white skin, pink cheeks, and black hair was so pretty that people used to turn around in the street and stare. She had the most expressive large, dark eyes, and dimples in both cheeks when she smiled; and she smiled always.

Baby Martina, however, was entirely different from both my pupils. She did not seem affectionate at all. She didn't want to be kissed or hugged. When I wanted to take her on my lap, she stiffened. She rarely smiled. I wondered about that serious little youngster. She was fascinated by the lessons, though. For hours she would stand next to Johanna, with her hands behind her back, watching with her large, dark eyes everything I said or did. The minute I turned to her, however, and addressed her, she dived under the table and stayed there quiet as a mouse for the rest of the lesson. At the same time, she was not shy or bashful, as I had thought at first. If she wanted something, she was outspoken. She seemed to me cool and rather matter-of-fact, until I saw her tenderly hugging a Teddy bear which was her inseparable companion. I knew quite clearly, though, that a child's confidence is like a walled castle for which one must have the key. It wouldn't do any good to try to break the lock and force entrance. As I had not been invited yet, I knew I had to wait patiently outside.

School in town started at eight o'clock and lasted until twelve. Of course, there were no school cafeterias, and the children were sent home for their noonday meal. Four times a week they were expected back at two o'clock for some more lessons until four or five. Wednesday and Saturday afternoons were free.

The manor was surrounded by a large garden, beautifully designed. Close to the house were borders of dahlias, chrysanthemums, asters, and many flowers and shrubs I had never seen before. Gravel paths divided the well-kept lawns into large patches leading to meadows, shaded by small groups of singularly beautiful, large trees—elm, maple, and pine. On one side, the estate was enclosed by a patch of woodland. On the other, hidden behind a tall screen of *arbor vitæ*, were the garage, the cow barn, and the greenhouse with the vegetable garden, from which a path lined with currant and gooseberry bushes led to a large orchard.

Baroness Matilda and all the children showed me over the whole estate on their first free afternoon. When we passed by a large bed of tall yellow flowers, Rupert said proudly. " This is *echte amerikanische Goldrute* (genuine American golden-rod). Papa says it is expensive, and we are not supposed to pick it. Pepi, our gardener, takes special care of it with a special kind of manure mixture."

I admired whole-heartedly this noble guest from America, whose golden blossoms attracted all the bees of the neighbour-hood.

When we came back from our round trip, Werner took my hand and said: " Let me show you my favourite."

We went over to the north side of the house. There stood a group of trees, evergreens, which looked neither like fir nor spruce. The needles were softer and smoother. The branches swayed gracefully in the wind.

" Papa says these are foreigners, too—Canadian hemlock," the proud boy announced. " They are very rare, but I will let you have a little piece." And he presented me with a tiny twig about an inch long.

I was quite overwhelmed by it all, and could not help ex-claiming; " What a paradise for children!"

Agathe, who was walking right in front of me, turned around and asked, quite astonished, " Why?"

" Well," I said, " just think of the many wonderful things one could do in such a wide garden, the many games one could play, and . . ."

" Oh, that's what *you* think," interrupted Agathe, and her young voice sounded very wise. " But you see, if you want to play ball, for instance, the ball always runs off the gravel path into the meadow. If you have to get it out of the damp grass, you get wet feet and catch cold. Or if you try to play in the woods over there, there is so much undergrowth, your hair gets caught, your dress gets torn, and you get scolded. So you really can't play in the garden much. We usually take walks."

Amazed, I stopped right in front of the house, and was just about to explain that I was not of the same opinion, when Baroness Matilda interrupted hastily: " Agathe is quite right," and gently pushed me to the door.

To my distress I learned during the next weeks that it was

true: you can't play in the most beautiful garden if you have always to take care of sailor suits and nice shoes on week-days, silken dresses and white socks on Sundays. You couldn't expect a white sailor blouse to look the same after you had climbed that spruce over there in the corner. But do you *have* to wear a white sailor blouse when you want to climb trees? I thought to myself. And now I had it!

Quite excitedly I rushed to the Baroness's room, not even waiting for the *Herein* after my knocking, to pour out my newest idea.

" Oh, Baroness Matilda, couldn't we buy play suits and sandals for all the girls? They wouldn't have to watch their dresses in the garden and would have a really good time. Before Supper, of course, they would change into sailor suits again. And couldn't we please have a volley ball and net for the girls, and a bat for the boys, and spear and a disc too?" So far, I had looked around the house in vain for these items, which were inseperable from my memories of college years. Baroness Matilda must have attended another school, though, as her face did not light up at the mere sound of these words. She said politely:

' It all sounds very interesting, indeed, Fraulein Maria; but you see, I would not *dare* to order any of those—' play suits,' you said?—without asking the children's father first. You know, that Baron wants the children always to look clean and tidy; and those games you mention—I have never even heard their names. When I was a young girl, we used to amuse our-selves by playing croquet. The children could play that on the big lawn when the weather is dry; otherwise, we stick to our healthful walks through the gardens."

After the last good-night to the children, I went straight to my room. For a long time I sat on my bed in the dark, brooding about the Captain. That man was funny! He had a big house, a wonderful garden, and lots of money. Couldn't he find a way to let his lovely children enjoy all this instead of jamming them into silly clothes which spoiled all their fun!

The great sympathy I had felt for the Captain after having heard his life story faded somewhat, and I changed the end of my night prayer into: "—and let the children be happy from now on."

Now it was November, and the trees had shed their last golden tear; the weather was often rough. Long periods of

rain set in, the famous " Salzburger Schnurlregen," which put
an end to our walks.

It was a rainy Saturday afternoon. Everyone had finished
his homework. The older children came over to us in the big
nursery, hanging around, wondering what to do. Werner's
eyes fell on the guitar, which was hanging on the wall near my
bed.

" Can you play that, Fräulein?" he asked.

" Yes, I can," and I went over to fetch the instrument.
" Let's sing something."

After a few chords I started a well-known folk-tune. The
children listened very attentively, but silently. I stopped.

" Why don't you sing with me?"

" We don't know that song."

" All right, let's sing another one."

But they didn't know that one, either, nor the third, nor the
fourth.

" What songs *do* you know, children?" I finally asked.

" ' Silent Night,' " little Johanna stated truthfully.

The others giggled, but I had started already: " Silent night,
holy night." A little shyly, a little thinly, we sang the first
verse in unison.

" Let's do it again. This time you sing the first voice, and I
shall sing the second."

So we did.

" Who dares to sing the second voice now, so that I can sing
the third?" I asked.

Maria and Werner wanted to try. I was quite astonished
how well it sounded. No one was bashful any more. With
full voice we sang now all three verses of " Silent Night," and
it did sound lovely.

Then I put my guitar down and said: " Now let's think
hard what other songs you remember."

After quite some time we had worked out a small list: a
few Navy songs, some of them in Italian, which they had
learned from their father, one hunting song, two funny songs
in our native dialect, two or three church hymns, the first
verses of the " Linden Tree," " Heiden Roslein," " Die
Lorelei," two more Christmas carols, and the national anthem.
That was a rather meagre collection, indeed. They didn't
know a single one of our wonderful, old folk-songs.

When I said, " Do you know this one?" and started a few

chords of an old ballad, they all cried: " No, but please sing it." And so I sang my favourite songs, one after the other. The little ones were huddled at my knees. The older ones had settled themselves on the table in order to watch me playing the guitar, when suddenly the door opened.

" Did nobody hear the dinner bell ring? Oh, children, how awful, sitting on the table! What would Father say?

The next day was Sunday, and it was still raining. It had been arranged that the Baroness and I should take turns having Sundays off. This was my Sunday on. Baroness Matilda had left to visit some friends. The children were enthusiastic about learning new songs. They all seemed to be quite musical. It didn't take long at all to teach them the old songs in simple settings. After supper the boys begged: " Let's make a fire in the fireplace in the library. That's so *gemütlich*."

That again was something new to me. With interest I watched the boys light the logs, which had been prepared by Hans. Very soon we all sat on the thick, soft carpet, looking into the flames, I in the middle with the guitar—and we sang our whole repertoire; eight old songs and six new ones.

" But girls, *girls*! Ladies never do that. I told you your father does not want you to sit on the floor. Take those low stools."

The Baroness had obviously returned from her visit. There it was again: the restraining hand of their father.

Bang! went the E string.

" We have to stop now," I said, " a string has broken."

IV. *An Austrian Christmas*

Christmas came nearer and nearer. Around the large table in the nursery we had long conferences about what to make for Father and Baroness Matilda, and for Grandmother, who lived in a castle near Vienna. I even suggested it would be nice if every child has a surprise for every sister and brother. That kept us very busy. The big, round table was covered with paper and paints, knitting wool, needles and thread. The boys' room soon looked like a workshop, with the smell of glue fighting the smell of Werner's white mice.

While the hands were busy, the mouths didn't keep still either. We were learning Christmas carols, each evening a new one, out of the treasury I had acquired when, with a group of boys and girls from the Austrian Catholic Youth Movement, I had wandered through the Alps. We had stopped in hidden valleys or at lone mountain farms, listening to the people's songs, which had been handed down for generations. There we had found the most beautiful Christmas songs. I knew dozens of them.

One evening Baroness Matilda had left for home to stay overnight with her sick sister. The children and I decided to have a general rehearsal of all our new songs. Maria, who already played simple tunes on her violin, would try to play with us.

We went down and obediently arranged ourselves on the big sofa which stood opposite the fireplace, and on a few comfortable chairs. But that way we were very far apart from each other and could not hear very well, so somehow or other it happened that we all landed again on the thick carpet. Agathe held my guitar. I had shown her how to accompany simple songs. With cheeks red from excitement, Maria played a descant, while we sang in three parts, "In Dulci Jubilo." Suddenly somebody opened the door.

"Papa, Papa," cried the children and stormed towards the tall figure standing in the doorway. Now there! and we were sitting on the floor. I rose slowly, picked up the guitar from the floor and put it on the sofa. Meanwhile the Baron had kissed all the children and, with Martina on his arm, he came over to me.

"I am sorry, Captain," I said.

"What are you sorry for?" and then, with a knowing undertone, "Oh I understand, this should have been a surprise for Christmas. But don't you worry, a surprise it is—children, I can't believe it. It sounded simply wonderful! Let's have some more. No, don't turn on the light. Let's sit right down here. Come on."

And he settled himself comfortably on the floor, pressing his back against one of the heavy seats, pulling the little girls down to his knee.

"You have learned a new song. What is it? Do it again."

"*A* new song?" the children echoed. "Just one?"

S.M.   B

"What do you mean?" said the father. And then, astonished, "Fräulein, are you looking for something?"

I was still standing. I couldn't believe my eyes.

"N-no," and I sat down on the sofa.

"Oh, no, come over here to us, right down on the carpet. Don't you think this is more *gemütlich*?"

I had never doubted that. So I joined the group and we continued singing, and it turned out to be a very nice evening. Time and again the Captain interrupted: "But children, children, isn't that wonderful!"

His enthusiasm was so genuine it was contagious. He praised Maria and Agathe highly for their playing, and all of a sudden, he reached out for the violin himself, and began to play a soft descant to one of our old ballads. Then we sang all twenty-two verses. The guitar played two more chords after the voices had ended, but the violin kept on playing very softly. Nobody moved. Suddenly the Captain stopped and, as if awakening, put the instrument down.

"I didn't think I would ever play again!" he said with a deep sigh. Then he put new logs on the fire, which had burned low, and asked: "Now children, tell me what is the news? How is school? How are you, little one?" And tenderly he pulled Maria's head towards his shoulder. A noisy chatter started now. After the children had told about school, they wanted to know all about the hunting trip. The little girls discovered that Father's pockets were full of rabbit tails, out of which one could make a fur coat for a Teddy bear! Too, too bad that it was eight o'clock and high time to go to bed!

It was the Saturday before the first Sunday in Advent. During lunch I said to Maria: "Where do you usually put up the Advent wreath?"

"Put up what?"

I was aghast. "Don't you have an Advent wreath every year?"

"No, never. What is it?"

"It is a large wreath made of fir greens, holding four candles, one for each of the four Sundays of Advent. People put it up in their living-rooms. It reminds them of the coming of Christmas. They light the candles and sing Advent songs."

"Oh, how nice! Couldn't we have one this year? Papa please buy a large Advent wreath for us."

"Oh, you don't *buy* Advent wreaths. We could easily make one ourselves," I interrupted, and then explained to the Captain that we would need about two basketsful of fir twigs and perhaps one of those wagon wheels from an old buggy I had seen in the tool shed.

"What else?"

"A spool of thread, four wax candles, and eight yards of silk ribbon." The Captain offered to fetch those from town. Everybody was excited getting the Advent wreath ready in time. The gardener was ordered to bring the fir twigs and the boys ran out to fetch the wagon wheel and clean it before it was brought into the nursery.

Then we went to work. The children picked the fir twigs out of the basket and passed them to me, and I wound them around the wheel, fastening them with thread. It took quite some time because it was to be a large wreath. Four long spikes had to be put through the wheel at equal distances to be used as candle holders. When we had just finished and were starting to clean up the mess we had made on the floor, the Captain came back from town. Now the candles were put on the spikes, the ribbon was cut into four equal parts, which were fastened to the wreath so that it could be suspended from the ceiling. Our first Advent wreath was finished.

"What can I do for you now?" the Captain said. I was a little uncertain.

"It should be hung from the ceiling in the middle of the living-room, but as this house doesn't have a living-room, couldn't we have it here in the nursery right above the big round table?"

Armed with hammer and nails, the Captain climbed up on the table. We all held the wreath as he fastened it to the ceiling. Suddenly he stopped between two hammer strokes and, looking down on me, he frowned.

"What do you mean, this house has no living-room?"

"No," I said, "it hasn't."

"How about the big drawing-room, the little drawing-room, the library, and the music-room?"

"No," I insisted, "that is not the same. Father, Mother,

and children really have to live in the same room—work, read, play, and write in it. Then it is a living-room."

The Captain finished and came down. We all stepped back and admired the beautiful big wreath with the four candles. It gave the whole room a festive look and a festive smell too.

"What are we going to do with it next?" asked Agathe.

"Well, to-night the family will gather under the Advent wreath, your father will read the Gospel of the first Sunday in Advent. Then he will light one candle, and the whole family will sing Advent songs and Christmas carols. Next week he will light two candles, the next three, and then all four."

"How do you know about it?"

"Oh, it is just an old custom—one of many."

"One of many—have you more in store for us?"

I had to laugh. "Maybe a few."

"All right then," and the Captain grasped the remaining nails and the hammer. "Let's meet to-night after supper under the Advent wreath in our new *living-room.*"

That was meant for me, I knew. Whether it was only teasing or whether he took my remark about the living-room for criticism, I could not make out. This very thing had troubled me all these weeks: that the family met only at meal-times. Otherwise, the children were not supposed to be to-gether. The boys had to keep to their room, the older girls to theirs, and they were told by Baroness Matilda time and again that they had no business in the nursery with their little sisters. When the older children had begun to visit us recently, knocking politely on the nursery door and asking a little shyly, "May we come in?" I had been tempted to say, "Now stop that nonsense. Aren't you all one family?"

But that was none of my business. It was just one more of many unwritten laws. I simply didn't understand how it could possibly be good to keep the children of one family divided into three parties which, of course, fought each other. I had tried to find out from Baroness Matilda. She wasn't really able to explain it, either, I only learned that this was the custom in most of the aristocratic houses, to have a governess for the older children, a nursemaid for the younger ones, and maybe a tutor for the boys.

Personally, I was depressed about the whole business. I had been told that my field was the nursery, that I had nothing to do with Rupert, Werner, Agathe, and Maria, except for

Maria's school lessons. If I had behaved correctly, I should
have sent the older children away instead of starting to teach
them to sing together. Now, again, had I *had* to say that
about the living-room? I felt rather ill at ease when I thought
of Baroness Matilda. For nothing in the world did I want to
hurt her. How would she feel about this new living-room idea,
about the children being together? But I consoled myself;
she was the one who always referred to the Captain, saying
that things must be done the way he wished. After all, *he* had
pronounced the nursery our new living-room, not I.

After supper that night we and the Baroness Matilda, who
had returned from her sister's, gathered together in the new
living-room. The Captain read the Gospel and lit the candle.
We were all sitting round the table on which a tall, thick, red
candle was burning. This was a surprise from me to the
children. I had brought it from Nonnberg on my last visit
there.

" It is the Advent candle," I had explained to them. " It is a
symbol of Christ, Whom we call the Light of the World. That
should burn every evening until Christmas—just another folk
custom," I said in the direction of the Captain. When I heard
even Baroness Matilda's soft voice joining our little choir, all
the tension left me, and I started to enjoy fully the beautiful
wreath, the sound of the children's clear voices, and the
Captain's violin playing.

Santa Claus does not come to the children of Austria. Nobody
comes down the chimney to fill your stocking; it isn't so easy
as that. All the small and big children of Austria have to
write a letter addressed to the Christ Child on the first Sunday
in Advent. He is believed to come down from heaven, Himself
personally, on Christmas Eve, accompanied by angels and
bring the Christmas tree and the wonderful things under it.
This letter is a very important one, for in it you make known
all your most secret wishes, and at the end you have to make
a personal promise. Then you put it on the window-sill before
going to bed, and next morning your first look will be to see
whether your letter has gone. Good children's letters always
disappear during the first night. Some children, however, have
to wait two or three days, and if this should be the case with
you, you really get quite anxious. It does help a lot in making
you put your clothes tidily over a chair at night.

After the last carol, still sitting around the table, we started to write our Christmas letters. After a short thought I wrote down:

"Dear Christ Child: It would make my life so much easier if You would bring each child here in the house a pair of nailed boots, a *Wetterfleck,* and a pair of wool mittens. I myself do not need anything, as I shall go back to Nonnberg soon anyway."

The excitement of the first Sunday in Advent had hardly died down when the sixth of December came around, one of the most momentous days for all houses where children lived. On the vigil of this day Saint Nikolaus comes down to earth to visit all the little ones.

Saint Nikolaus was a saintly bishop of the fourth century, and as he was always very kind and helpful to children and young people, so God granted that every year on his feast-day he might come down to the children. He comes dressed in his Bishop's vestments, with a mitre on his head and his Bishop's staff in his hand. He is followed, however, by the Krampus, an ugly, black little devil with a long, red tongue, a pair of horns, and a long tail. When Saint Nikolaus enters a house, he finds the whole family assembled, waiting for him, and the parents greet him devoutly. Then he asks the children questions from their catechism. He makes them repeat a prayer or sing a song. He seems to know everything, all the dark spots of the past year, as you can see from his admonishing words. All the good children are given a sack with apples and nuts, prunes and figs, and the most delicious sweets. Bad children, however, must promise very hard to change their life. Otherwise, the Krampus will take them along, and he is grunting already and rattling his heavy chain. But the Holy Bishop won't ever let him touch a child. He believes the tearful eyes and stammered promises, but it may happen that, instead of a sweet bag, you get a switch. That will be put up in a conspicuous place and will look very symbolic of a child's behaviour.

The excitement was great on the fifth. Soon after dark we assembled in the hall, looking out through the large window into the drive. Martina's hand was clasped tightly in mine, her little figure half hidden behind my skirt. You could almost hear Johanna's heart beating, and Hedwig's air of superiority was very unconvincing.

Suddenly one could see the little flicker of candlelight through the bare bushes. A tall figure bearing a lantern and high staff turned into our drive, followed at some distance by a little black fellow. The heavy double door opened wide, and in came the Holy Bishop, reverently greeted by young and old. The white beard which cascaded down below his waist showed his old age. Nobody could see that half an hour before, it had been plastered on Hans' patient face with the help of the white of a raw egg. Saint Nikolaus wore his glasses, as elderly people sometimes do, far down on his nose. He had to, because his eyesight was so good that Resi's spectacles almost blinded him. After he had sat down, he gave the Captain his lantern to hold, and then he produced from under his white cloak a large package with a big golden cross. Through the white paper cover one could read faintly *Encyclopædia, H. to HZ*. In this magic book were written down all the many crimes, big and little, which had been committed by the children of this house. It was quite incredible how well informed Saint Nikolaus was: how Werner had played truant three times instead of going to his Greek class; Hedwig had pinched Martina; Rupert had smoked in secret; and Maria had practised the violin much longer than the doctor allowed; Resi, the cook, had burned the Sunday cake once and then thrown it into the garbage can without telling; Pepi, the gardener, was sometimes slow in getting up in the morning. And Saint Nikolaus shook his finger and frowned at the sinners as they were called to his feet. They all felt uncomfortable, and promised fervently to reform. The Holy Bishop rose and waved his hand towards the door; a big sack was pushed in, which Saint Nikolaus opened. There was a bag with fruit and candies for everybody except Resi, who got a large switch; and she even had to kiss the Bishop's hand when he gave it to her. With a final admonition and his blessing, the holy man left the house.

"How many days still until Christmas?" was the excited question every morning. One morning, when the answer was "only seven," we came down the stairs as usual, and found the double door leading into the big drawing-room, which was usually wide open, closed. New excitement; that meant that the Holy Child with His angel assistants was working inside, preparing the room for Christmas. From then on, the children only tiptoed in the vicinity of those closed doors, and every conversation downstairs died down to a reverent whisper.

The whispering continued deep into the night, when the children were long asleep and the Captain, Baroness Matilda, and I were busy behind the secret door with the still-empty Christmas tree, opening parcels, writing Christmas cards, adjusting small wax candles to small candle-holders which could be clamped on to the green branches. Slowly but surely, the big room began to look like the toy department of a large store. Out of the many-shaped parcels emerged all the blessings of our modern toy industry: a doll house and doll kitchen, a small perambulator with a beautiful baby and, of course, the whole outfit—diapers, bottle, bath-tub, etc.; picture books and games, an electric railroad, an air-gun, a gramophone with records, more books and more games, a new guitar, skates, skis—never in my life had I seen so many beautiful things in one spot. The trouble was that I could hardly keep my mind on my duty, which was to unpack and distribute, because it was so tempting to try out the new games, and look at the many books.

It was the twenty-third, and the little ones had sung all day long the traditional song, " Morgen, Kinder, Wird's Was Geben." They were unusually helpful, quiet and good, knowing that the house, and especially the nursery, was under constant observation by the angels coming and going to the Christmas room. Only Rupert and Agathe seemed to know a little more ; from Maria down, the belief in the holy doings behind the wide doors was unshaken.

This last evening was devoted to the decoration of the tree. It was at least fifteen feet tall. The Captain, standing on a ladder, took care of the top, while Baroness Matilda and I busied ourselves with the lower branches. There were cakes, *Lebkuchen* and *Spanischer Wind*. Hard candies and chocolates had been wrapped in frilled tissue paper, figures and symbols made of marzipan, gilded nuts and small apples and tangerines, all these were hung on red threads all over the tree. Then came a hundred-and-twenty wax candles, loads of tinsel on the branches, and tinsel chains swinging loosely all around the tree. As a finishing touch the Captain fastened a large silver star to the very top. Then we all stepped back and admired the most beautiful Christmas tree I have ever seen in my life. The tables around the walls were so laden with presents that the white linen covers were completely hidden.

The next day was the big night, Holy Eve, as it is called in Austria. Snow had fallen overnight. We went to church with the older children. The church was filled as on Sunday. Everybody goes to confession on Holy Eve, so one had to wait in line. It was quite early and pitch-dark outside. There were no electric lights in the church, and, of course, it was not heated. The people had brought candles with them, fastened them to the pews, and, holding their hymn-books with heavily-mittened hands close to the little flame, they could read the words of the ancient Advent song, which was softly accompanied by the organ and sung by the whole community: " Tauet Himmel den Gerechten." In the flicker of candlelight one could see a neat little frosty cloud in front of every mouth. From under the choir loft, where the confessional stood, one could hear the shuffling of hobnailed boots and also, eventually, the rubbing of hands, the feeble attempts to keep warm when it was below zero outside with yard-long icicles growing from the church roof. But cold belonged to Christmas as heat to the haymaking days. This was as it should be, and nobody gave it a thought.

When Holy Mass was over, we went with the children to the side altar. There in a little wood of spruce trees, was the whole town of Bethlehem spread out before our eyes. The shepherds were already out in the field with their flock. Mary and Joseph had arrived at the cave. They were kneeling beside the manger, which was still empty. Ox and ass, the sheep in the pasture, and the angels in the air seemed to hold their breath, waiting in holy expectation of the little Child to come. Mankind had waited patiently thousands of years for this moment. It couldn't wait any longer ; and this is the very feeling you bring home from church yourself in your own heart after a glance into the still-empty manger: you feel you can't wait any longer.

As everything comes to an end in life, so also the long hours of the afternoon passed. Holy Eve is a fast day, and so lunch was over quickly with only one dish, a thick soup. The children spent the day putting their rooms, wardrobes, and drawers in perfect order. In the afternoon we all dressed in our best, and for the last time, we all met under the Advent wreath, all four candles lit. The servants were called in, and once again we sang the old Advent hymn. Before the third verse was over, the silvery sound of a little bell was heard. This was it! The Holy Child had come. Led by the father of the house, the two youngest girls clinging to his hands, we all went down the curved stairway. After a few steps through the wide-open door, we all stopped in a semicircle, gazing in speechless wonder at the Christmas tree, whose solemn beauty dominated the room. The Captain started "Silent Night." After we had sung all three verses, there was a moment of complete silence. A fine scent of fir, wax, and *Lebkuchen* lingered in the air. The room was bathed in that mild, golden light which only wax candles can give.

Then the Captain went round wishing everybody a blessed Christmas. The spell was broken. Soon the house resounded with "Blessed Christmas." Then everyone was led to his place by the Captain. For a while one heard only the rustling of wrapping-paper, and little more or less surprised cries and exclamations. I was very busy helping to attend to the baby Martina when the Captain came to show me to my own place. There were several parcels wrapped in white tissue paper, and one very large box with the inscription: " For Fräulein Maria for Distribution." Surrounded by the children, I unpacked it, and out came eight pairs of woollen mittens, eight beautiful, soft, grey *Wetterflecks*, and eight pairs of heavy boots. This was a great surprise, and with a guilty heart, I hardly dared look at Baroness Matilda. But to-night was Christmas, and, shaking a finger at me, she only laughed. That wasn't the end of my surprises, though. When all my parcels were unpacked, there lay on my table two beautiful new dresses and a nice-looking hat. What a grateful sigh of relief went up to the Holy Child for such consideration.

After dinner, which had been very early, the Captain asked for some Christmas music. I had been waiting for that. My Christmas present to the family was a Crêche, put up under the Christmas tree. Now I got the big, red candle, and we all grouped around it on the floor. After we had sung our songs, I took Agatha's new guitar and, for the first time, I sang my own favourite Christmas song, " The Virgin's Lullaby."

A few hours later I knelt in my place in the old church at Nonnberg ; I had come home for Midnight Mass. But it was curiously different from my other home-comings. It was very difficult to keep my thoughts collected. Pictures of huge Christmas trees and happy children's faces continued to busy my mind. There was one picture, especially, which I could not shake off, try as I would:

When I was about to leave the house for Midnight Mass, the Captain had come out of his room and, taking my hand in both of his, had said: " I always feared Christmas more than any other day. But this year you have made it very beautiful for us. Thank you." There was a warm light in the fine dark eyes which, for the first time since I had known him, did not look pained and restless. That had made me very happy, but now the picture kept coming back and disturbing me in my prayer.

Turning to the Holy Child, I said fervently: " I thank You so much for sending me there. Please help me to draw them all closer to You."

At this moment the community rose and, with a jubilant voice, the young priest at the altar intoned the age-old Christmas message: " *Gloria in excelsis Deo et in terra pax hominibus bonæ voluntatis* ".

V. God's Will Hath No Why "

The following weeks were very happy ones. Real winter had set in, and the hobnailed boots, mittens, and ski trousers were in daily use. We didn't understand how we ever could have got along without them.

To the great joy of the children, their father refused a number of invitations and stayed at home with them, taking to skiing again and obviously enjoying it.

Then on a beautiful day in March their father announced during lunch while glancing through his mail: " Well, children, Aunt Yvonne is coming."

A moment of complete silence followed. Then Maria said: " Why, Father, do we still need her?"

Quite astonished, the Captain said: " What do you mean?"

" You said you want to marry her because we have no one to look after us; but that has changed now, hasn't it?"

After a short, warm smile in my direction the child looked

eagerly at her father. At this moment Baroness Matilda, who apparently had felt rather ill at ease during the last minutes, ventured the question: " When exactly can we expect the Princess?"

" To-morrow on the noon train, and let's put her in the big room with the balcony."

Princess Yvonne—how exciting! Now I should see the future mother of my darling children. In my romantic imagination I saw a figure out of Grimm's *Fairy Tales;* young and slender, blue-eyed and blonde-haired—I could picture her gliding into the room with soft, fairy steps, a dreamy look in her deep blue eyes, with love emanating from her towards the poor, motherless little ones and their lonely father—Princess Yvonne. The mere name put me in a festive mood, and in my heart I was worshipping her already.

How slowly the time dragged during the lessons of the next morning! Finally, the gong sounded for lunch, and in solemn expectation I entered the big drawing-room, where the exalted guest must be. Oh, had she missed the train? Because the lady who entered now together with the Captain from the library couldn't possibly—but lo and behold, the girls were curtsying, and saying " How do you do, Aunt Yvonne?"

Then I heard the Captain's voice: " Yvonne, may I introduce——" and I looked into cool, but not unfriendly eyes.

" Well, well—the wonder girl of whom I have heard so much," and we shook hands.

During lunch the children chatted about the happenings of the last weeks. Finally, Hedwig broke out: " And do you know, Auntie, what I like most of all my Christmas presents, that's my ski trousers. Now I can do anything outdoors the boys do," and the little face glowed with pure enthusiasm.

With lifted eyebrows the Princess answered, genuinely surprised: " But, my dear, a respectable young lady doesn't wear trousers."

Seven young heads turned to me, looking for support; but when I realised that what I was about to say might also not fit into the picture of a respectable young lady, I blushed and busied myself with my food.

There were no lessons this afternoon, everybody being busy with the regal guest. Sitting at my desk, I tried to keep my thoughts on to-morrow's school work, telling myself over and over again, " This is none of your business—none of your

business at all," when someone knocked at my door, and—
it was the Princess! A little bewildered, I bade her come in
and sit down. She looked at me for a moment, not at all
unkindly.

" My dear child, I have to talk to you." Expectant silence,
and then the blow fell: " Do you realise that the Captain is
in love with you?"

As if bitten by a rattlesnake, I started up. " But—
Princess——! "

Quietly and quite unemotionally she replied: " But he told
me so himself."

With weak knees I sank down on my chair. So far, no one
had been in love with me, nor had I ever been in love. This
extraordinary happening I had met only in books, in the pages
of Goethe, Schiller, and Shakespeare, where being in love
usually ended in murder and blood; and now that that terrific
thing should happen to me, and—and—but if he himself had
told her so, there was nothing to argue about.

I tried to compose myself and say, as matter-of-factly as
possible, the only thing I could think of: " Then I am leaving
this afternoon for my convent. Will you kindly look for
another teacher for Maria?"

Now it was her turn to look startled.

" But why, for heaven's sake? That's no reason to run
away. It's all been explained. Of course, he isn't really in
love, not much, I mean. He just likes you because you have
been so good with the children—maybe a bit too much on the
wild side, but this I will easily settle later."

But nothing she said impressed me any more. I was scared
stiff.

" But how does everything go on from now on?" I wanted
to know.

" Why—exactly as before. In a few weeks the Captain
and I will be engaged, and you will stay with the children
until after our marriage. On our wedding day you must give
a nice little party for them here."

I swallowed dryly, " Won't they be at the wedding?"

" Oh, certainly not," she laughed lightly. " Just think, what
a commotion!" And she shook her head, amused. Then she
went on. " The wedding will be in the summer, and when we
return from our honeymoon, it will be time for school again.
I have noticed that although the children have improved

physically, their manners have suffered badly. The Baron agrees with me that the best place for the girls will be the Sacré Cœur, and for the boys, the Jesuit College in Kalksburg. There they will be among youth of their own standing, and soon they will stop being little yokels."

" But why in the world do you marry, then, if you send the children away from home?" I asked in utter consternation.

Up went the eyebrows again.

" My goodness, did you think I was marrying the children? What a queer little person you are!"

This decided me. I knew instinctively that I couldn't stay ; I wouldn't fit in any more. So I repeated stiffly: " I have made up my mind. I shall pack and leave immediately."

Now the Princess was really worried, and after another unsuccessful attempt to make me change my mind, left me rather hurriedly. With trembling fingers, I started to empty my drawers.

Late in the afternoon I was called down to the library. From the garden I could hear the happy laughter of the children with their father. It cut my heart, and quite helplessly I thought to myself: " No, I can't say good-bye to any of them. I will simply leave."

Then I opened the door of the library. There was the Princess and a strange priest in a brown habit with a long, grey beard. I hesitated at the door.

" This is Father Gregory," the Princess said, " my confessor. I have turned to him to help us out, and he will tell you now what he thinks you should do."

The elderly Father came over to me and, taking my hand, led me towards the table, and very kindly started to explain.

" You must understand, my dear child, that there is nothing in the kind of affection the Captain feels towards you, because you are so good with his children ; but you must also understand that there is a great danger of kindling this emotion into more than merely a fatherly affection if you should leave now, abruptly. Therefore, I counsel you to do as the Princess wants, and . . ."

" Father, this I cannot do," I interrupted, and looked at him imploringly.

" But my dear child, this is the Will of God," the kind old voice stated.

Now I was cornered. It had become second nature through

my training at the convent to look for and to carry out to the best of my ability—the Will of God. I was silent.

Happily the Princess said: " You see, Father, I told you she is quite a sensible girl."

The old priest took my hand again and said: " Now promise me that you will stay here until the Baron and the Princess have been wed."

Tonelessly I repeated: " I promise I shall stay, but only until the thirtieth of June, on which day I shall be received into the Benedictine Abbey of Nonnberg."

With a kind, " All right, my child, go in peace," I was released.

My hands were shaking still as I put all my things back into the drawers again. I was utterly and thoroughly bewildered. Wasn't it already like Schiller and Shakespeare? But, my God, how could it go on now? What was coming next?

The Princess had left, and we resumed our daily routine again. But life wasn't the same, because I had become self-conscious. The heavy burden of my new knowledge followed me through the day. I avoided the Captain whenever I could, and when he wanted to join our games or singing evenings in the nursery, I felt how I stiffened and, at the first possible moment, broke up whatever was going on. I wasn't supposed to mention anything to him of what had passed between me and the Princess, so he absolutely could not make out why I had suddenly changed. Good-naturedly he blamed the spring at first for what he called " moodiness," but after a while I noticed how hurt he looked when, for instance, I declined politely to have him accompany us on a walk or when he wanted to join in our games. If, however, he jokingly insisted on taking part, it wouldn't be long before with some excuse I would slip out. One day we happened to meet in the house doorway. When he stretched out his hand to open the door for me, I stopped him, saying: " Thank you very much, I can open it myself."

This was just a little too much. He walked away brusquely, leaving me very miserable and bewildered. How I hated myself for acting so, and still, I couldn't help it.

Baroness Matilda had gone to the wedding of her brother when, on a beautiful morning in May, I was asked to see the Captain in the library.

" Think what's happened," he greeted me. " Baroness Matilda has broken her leg, and it is such a bad fracture that she won't be with us any more for the rest of the year. What are we going to do? Could you take over the household affairs until I find someone else?"

I laughed right out: " Oh Captain, I understand nothing at all about housekeeping. You see, in boarding-school and then in the novitiate I learned many other things, but not that."

" But couldn't you learn it out of a book?" he asked after a little hard thinking. " The other day I saw in the window of Hoellriegel's Bookstore a book on housekeeping."

In my heart of hearts I had the greatest doubts as to whether this science could be learned out of books, but he looked so eager and expectant that I said: " Well, there's nothing like trying," earning a sigh of relief and a grateful look from his fine eyes. For a moment it was like old times. There was the air of confidence again between us, and I ventured to speak.

" Captain, now I have done something for you ; may I ask you to do me a favour?"

" Certainly, go ahead."

" Will you please get engaged to the Princess straight away?"

With a sharp swing he turned around and, facing me eye to eye, he asked slowly: " Am I doing you a favour by that?"

I was already retiring towards the door, mumbling something about the approaching end of the school year—motherless children—reception at the convent . . .

The same evening the Captain gathered the eight servants in the library and introduced me as their temporary housekeeper, from whom they would have to expect, for the time being, all orders.

He left the next day.

When he said good-bye, he asked: " Would it be too much for you to send me a daily report on how things are going?"

With these words he handed me a book. Glancing down, I read: *The Golden Book for Housewives: A Guide Through the Year, Together with Five Hundred Recipes and One Thousand Household Hints.*

I had never in my life thought about how a household is run. In the boarding-school where I had spent most of my young years, the food was always ready on the table at meal-

times, the rooms were always tidy and clean, the windows
washed, the laundry taken care of ; but it all happened somehow backstage, quite noiselessly. You never saw anybody
doing it ; you only saw the result and took it for granted. In
the convent there were those lovely, humble, quiet lay sisters
with a white veil, who did the cooking, washing, and cleaning.
But we of the novitiate were not supposed to talk to them, so
again I heard no details of how it was all done.

When the Captain introduced me as temporary housekeeper,
I had noticed an exchange of glances between the cook and
the gardener, the first and second chambermaids ; glances half
amused, half-knowing. There was also some good-natured
mockery in the somewhat super-submissive air with which
mighty Donna Resi asked on my first evening in office: " Is
Fräulein Maria coming downstairs after supper to give orders
for to-morrow?"

" What orders?" I asked, and wanted to bite my tongue
immediately after. Oh, what a neophyte I was! But if she
knew, the cook didn't show it, but continued almost respect-
fully:

" Well, whatever you want us to do to-morrow ; me and the
two girls in the kitchen, the two chambermaids and the gardener, the chauffeur, and the laundress."

I almost said: " Oh, please do what you want, all of you,"
but, fortunately, remembered in time that Baroness Matilda
had spent a considerable time every evening in the servants'
quarters. " Yes, I'll come" ; and with this I ran upstairs and
consulted *The Book.*

But nowhere in the eight hundred pages could I find any
indication of what to say to the servants in the form of
to-day's orders for to-morrow.

When I was confronted later with the eight expectant faces,
I tried to solve the problem diplomatically, and asked: " What
did you intend to do to-morrow?" or " What do you suggest
comes next?" That worked fine, and I almost patted myself
on the back for this good idea ; that gave me time to devour
The Book, and in a few days I would not have to ask anybody
for suggestions any more.

I started on page 1, and spent many hours every day in
serious study on how to become a good housekeeper.

Every evening a little note went out, saying. " Dear

Captain: We are all well, and everything in house, garden, and farm is going all right. Sincerely yours."

Three weeks had passed, and we had heard little from the Captain. The children and I received postcards with greetings; that was all. Time was getting short. Only a little over a month lay between me and the convent. So I ventured in one of my notes to add after the " all well ": " And when will you get engaged?"

By return mail a letter came back which said: ". . . I wish I could see your eyes when you read the announcement of my engagement."

The moment I read that, something flared up within me. I sat down immediately and, without any salutation, I put my one strong feeling down on paper: " My eyes are none of your business. I thought you were a man and kept your word. I am sorry. I was mistaken."

Still hot with anger, I ran out and posted this document, registered.

On a beautiful May morning the Captain and the Princess had seated themselves on an old stone bench in the dense woods which led into the famous and ancient park of Castle G——. In many long talks the Captain had tried to convince the Princess that it was time to forget the various obstacles to the engagement; that very morning he had made up his mind not to come back from the walk unengaged.

" Yvonne . . ." he started, and then they heard footsteps. Charles, the old butler who had faithfully served three generations, came down the path hurriedly. On a silver platter he carried a letter.

He said apologetically: " Baron, I thought it might be important. It's a registered letter."

Looking at the letter, the Captain said: " Excuse me, Yvonne, but this comes from home. I hope none of the children is ill," and broke open the letter. He stared at the three lines with no heading and no greeting; after some time he put the letter into his vest pocket. He got up from the bench and seemed deeply moved.

" Well, what's the matter?" the Princess asked. " Anybody ill?"

" No, nobody is ill," he answered slowly; and then, taking

both her hands, he added: " but I know now I cannot marry you, Yvonne ; I love somebody else. I am sorry, but you made me wait too long. You should have taken me when I asked you three years ago."

In deep silence the couple went back to the castle, and the Captain departed immediately for home.

The very same evening the telephone wires carried the message from one castle or *palais* to another that Maria, the young teacher of the Trapp children, was expecting a baby and the Baron, in his loyalty and knightliness, had resolved to marry her. That was why he had had to break off his near-engagement to Princess Yvonne. Because this *must* have been the content of that letter which had made the Captain change his mind, mustn't it?

Who starts such a story? Nobody. It doesn't start as a story ; it starts as an inflexion of the voice, a question asked in a certain tone and not answered with " no " ; a prolonged little silence, a twinkle in the eye, a long-drawn " we-e-e-ell— I don't know." These are the roots of the tree whose poisonous fruits are gossip and slander.

The Captain had come home and had almost immediately vanished into his private quarters. The family saw very little of him ; even for meals he stayed in his study now. All we knew was that he was writing his memoirs and didn't want to be disturbed. Ever since I had cooled off after posting that poisonous little note, I had had an awful feeling in my stomach. What was worse, I couldn't make out what had happened. He didn't look engaged, to me, at least, not according to my conception of a happily engaged man. But there was something unusual about him in the rare moments when he was visible, and I did not dare ask any questions.

One night I tenderly consulted my private calendar, " time eaters " we had called them at school, and it showed only thirteen more days in exile. The next morning I started spring cleaning. Under my direction the maids were taking down the curtains and proceeding to brush the walls, when I saw the three youngest children knock on the door of the study. It didn't take long and out they came again.

Running over to me as I stood on a ladder washing a big crystal chandelier, they yelled from afar: " Father says he doesn't know whether you like him at all!"

" Why, of course I like him," I answered, somewhat absent-mindedly, because I had never washed a chandelier before. I noticed only vaguely that the children had disappeared behind the study door again.

That same night I was arranging flowers in several big oriental vases. This was the last touch, and then the spring cleaning was over, and it had been really successful. When I had arrived at the last vase, the Captain came in. Stepping over to me, he stood and silently watched what I was doing with the peonies.

Suddenly he said: " That was really very nice of you."

An altogether new tone in his voice, like the deep, rich quality of a low bell, made me look up, and I met his eyes, looking at me with such warmth that I lowered mine immediately, again bewildered. Automatically I asked what was so nice of me, as I only remembered that awful letter.

" Why," he said, astonished, " didn't you send word to me through the children that you accepted the offer, I mean, that you want to marry me?"

Scissors and peonies fell to the floor.

" That I want to—marry—you?"

" Well, yes. The children came to me this morning and said they had had a council among themselves, and the only way to keep you with us would be that I marry you. I said to them that I would love to, but I didn't think you liked me. They ran over to you and came back in a flash, crying that you had said, ' yes, I do.' Aren't we engaged now?"

Now I was completely bewildered. I did not know what to say or what to do. The air was full of an expectant silence, and all I knew was that in a few days I would be received into my convent, and there stood a real, live man who wanted to marry me.

" But, Captain," I started out, " you know that in a very short while I shall go back to my convent; and one cannot enter a convent and marry at the same time."

The beautiful eyes saddened.

" Is this your very last word? Is there absolutely no hope?"

" Well "—I had an idea—" you know," I said eagerly, " I have something that you don't have. I have a Mistress of Novices. Whatever she says I'd consider as coming from God. It *is* the Will of God. Let me go and ask her."

And in my eagerness to leave, I did not wait for an answer,

but started right away, heading for Nonnberg. It was a short hour's walk, and I was happy to have found an excuse to visit this beloved place in the middle of the week.

" Now I know," I mused to myself while speeding along the bank of the Salzach, " that he isn't engaged. What could have happened?" I felt sorry for the poor man, but quite relieved for the children. Whenever I thought of that motherless little flock, a pang went right through my heart. But all I could do was pray even harder now that God might send them a good second mother.

With a sigh of relief I dropped on one of the old oaken chairs in the community room where the postulants lived.

" Oh, it's so good to be home," I sighed, and took a deep breath of that incomparable smell of herbs, incense and antiquity.

At this the door opened, and Frau Rafaela, my Mistress of Novices, entered the room.

" Maria, what are you doing here in the middle of the week?"

That made me remember, and I repeated to her the whole " incident."

" And you see, if you tell me now that I cannot marry him because I shall enter here, then the Will of God is made clear, and that must help him, too." Frau Rafaela's old, motherly eyes rested on me, but she didn't say a word. Suddenly she got up and went out of the room. In an hour she returned to tell me that Reverend Mother was expecting me.

I walked through the open galleries, through the cloisters, and up the stone stairs. The same old oaken door, the same squeak when it opened—oh, here I was surrounded by good old friends, and very soon I should be with them for ever. With these thoughts I was already kneeling at Reverend Mother's feet and kissing her ring. She took both my hands in hers and looked at me lovingly and long without saying a word, until I felt rather uncomfortable. Finally she spoke.

" Frau Rafaela has told me your story. As you came home to find out the Will of God in this most important moment of your life, I assembled the community in the Chapter Room. We prayed to the Holy Ghost, and we held council, and it became clear to us "—here her hands pressed tighter—" that it is the Will of God that you marry the Captain and be a good mother to his children."

Minutes passed, and I was still kneeling, trying to understand. I knew this was final, and no argument was possible.
Yes, it was true, I had wanted to know the Will of God; but
now when I met it, I refused to accept it. All my happiness
was shattered, and my heart, which had so longed to give
itself entirely to God, felt rejected. I stared down at the large
ring on the Abbess's hand, and mechanically I read the en-
graved words around the big amethyst: "God's Will Hath
No Why." In true sincerity of heart I asked:

"What does God want of me now, Reverend Mother?"

"He wants you to serve Him well where He needs you
most, and serve Him whole-heartedly and cheerfully."

Slowly I wound my way home. The children must be in
bed by now, I thought, when I opened the big house door as
quietly as possible to slip in unnoticed. But there stood the
Captain.

"Well, and . . ." was all he said.

Timidly I went over; and all of a sudden there came all the
tears I hadn't found before.

"Th-they s-s-said I have to m-m-m-marry you-u!"

Without a word he opened his arms wide. And, what else
could I do—with a wrenching sob I buried my face on his
shoulder. . . .

The next day after breakfast their father told his children
that they had been right; only if he married me, could I stay
for ever. And for that reason he was going to marry me. It
was touching and heart-warming to feel behind all the kissing
and squeezing that followed, the genuine joy and relief of the
children—my children.

Soon afterward the Captain left on a long journey which
would keep him away until the autumn. He explained to me
that he had to do this; otherwise, people would talk.

"Talk? About what?" I said.

"Well, about us."

"But why don't they talk now?" I wanted to know.

But the Captain was somewhat mysterious, and insisted that
it was for the best. If he and I had only known how terribly
busy many tongues had already been all these days.

"I shall come back two weeks before the wedding. Then
you will go to Nonnberg, where we shall meet again on our
wedding day! and then I shall never leave you again."

And he was right. Through the summer months the children

and I grew closer together every day. And the figure of their father grew more and more distinctly into my life with every letter I received from him. It was a happy and peaceful time.

The leaves turned yellow and red, and the first heavy autumn storms shook them from the trees. The Captain came back, and I learned to call him Georg. Then I went for the last time into my beloved convent for a ten-day retreat to get prepared for matrimony, which is indeed a great sacrament.

It was the Saturday before the first Sunday in Advent, November 26, 1927. When the great day finally dawned, I greeted it with a heart full of happiness and readiness to " serve God where He needed me most—whole-heartedly and cheerfully." I was dressed in my bridal gown in the same vaulted room where I had spent the happiest years of my life so far. My three former room-mates, now in the white veil of the novices, helped me dress. Frau Rafaela put the wreath of Edelweiss on the white bridal veil, and then the wonderful bells on Nonnberg began to call. It was time to go down into the church. The whole community accompanied me, and for the last time I walked down the age-worn stairs, over the cobble-stoned yard, passing by the old statues, through the cloisters where the Sisters were lined up for a last farewell. On Reverend Mother's hand I approached the heavy portal. As it opened, I knelt on the threshold for the last time, for the last blessing. Outside the procession had formed. Through swimming eyes I saw a packed church. Oh, and here were the children. The two oldest girls were leading their father, who was in his Navy uniform. The two boys waited for me, and the three little ones busied themselves with my long train. At this moment the big organ began with a jubilant chord. Slowly and solemnly the procession marched up the aisle and up the many steps into the sanctuary, where Father Abbot stood waiting for us, adorned with his golden Ornate. Then the voice of the organ died out, and in the great silence which hovered over the big church, surrounded by the seven children, we promised each other loudly and solemnly to " take each other for better or for worse . . . till death do us part."

VI. Feasts in a Family

After the Christmas vacation life settled down to its normal routine; that is, for the children. But for me everything was new. It was queer—there was the same house and the same people, and still it wasn't the same. Now they were my children, and I was their mother. There was a world of difference. We all loved each other in a new way, and it was very beautiful. If I had to take the same step now—oh, I am sure I wouldn't dare. I would see all the dangers and difficulties in taking over the place of a second wife and second mother. I would be very doubtful whether all seven children would ever take to me. I wouldn't feel adequate to take over so much responsibility—I simply wouldn't *dare*. But at twenty you are beautifully unconscious of possible complications.

Everybody went to school, even Maria, who was well again —except little Martina, who was too young. Quietly she followed me around the house until I settled down to some letter-writing or mending or embroidering. Then, contentedly, she would nestle at my feet.

Everyone was anxious to have all his homework done before supper, because then came the most beautiful time of the day, the evenings spent together. A fire was lit in the fireplace. The older girls brought their knitting, the younger ones their dolls; the boys and their father usually worked on wood, carving or whittling; and I, settling in a most comfortable chair, started to read aloud. It is most amazing how much literature you can cover during the long winter evenings. We read fairy-tales and legends, historical novels and biographies, and the works of the great masters of prose and poetry.

After having read a couple of hours, I would say: "That's enough for to-day. Let's sing now; all right?"

That was the signal for everyone to drop whatever he was doing. We sat closer together and started out. First we sang rounds. You can do that for hours on end, and it is a wonderful schooling for the ear. It leads quite naturally to polyphonic music. The rounds teach you to "mind your own business"; sing your part, never to mind what your neighbour sings.

After the First World War the Catholic Youth Movement

56

sweeping over Austria and Germany had done wonders for music. These young people wanted genuine music again. They went up and down the countryside, collecting real folk-songs and folk-tunes, delved into archives and libraries and copied unpublished music of the old masters. In mimeographed and hand-copied sheets this music went from town to town and brought about a radical change in musical life within a few years.

I was lucky enough, in my student years, to belong to one such group. Boys and girls met in large groups of thirty or forty and had the most wonderful time. A large portion of our free time was spent with music. Out of the enthusiasm of those hours blossomed beautiful settings of the melodies we brought home from our hikes through the mountains, for two, three, four, and five parts, *a cappella* and with the accompaniment of instruments. There were violins and cellos, French horns, and clarinets, and there was the newest and oldest of them all, the revived recorder, the ancient flute. There we sat together by the hour, singing and playing and enjoying ourselves thoroughly.

How grateful I was now for those experiences! Sitting around the table, we worked on at least one new number every evening. If we had more than three parts, I had to take the tenor part, while my husband took care of the bass. How I wished in the depths of my heart that one of the boys would kindly turn into a tenor later; lo and behold—one of them did!

There came a time when we were hardly able to read or sing together because we were so busy, and that was the birthday season. In a large household there are a number of family holidays which occur yearly; the birthday and feast-days. In our particular family we have two distinct seasons: from the end of January to the begining of May, and then again from the end of September to the first of November. My people had only celebrated the birthdays, whereas we on Nonnberg disregarded those and only celebrated the feast-days. These are celebrated on the feast of the Saint in whose honour you are named. Now we put both customs together and, since there were nine of us, there were eighteen holidays right away. It was a matter of course that the lucky one whose holiday came around could expect a present from everyone in the

house ; and of course, one didn't just go to a store and buy
with cold money something turned out by a factory with no
relationship at all to the young sister or brother. How could
you possibly get for any money that particular dwelling
Martina's dwarfies needed, a cross between a foxhole and a
little cave, interwoven with roots, with a carpet of moss, with
furniture made of spruce twigs !

A loving heart and gifted fingers can produce a wonderland
of little miracles, especially after the room next to the library
has been turned into a workshop with work benches, a band
saw, a lathe, and a circular saw.

All great feasts of the Church have a Vigil ; they start, so
to speak, the evening before. So our family feasts were celebrated on the evening before, too. The birthday cake with the
candles was put in the centre of a table, which was also
covered with all the different presents. While I was going to
fetch the hero of the day, the others lined up in a semicircle,
each one holding a flower. The moment we entered the room
they started singing " *Hoch soll er leben!*" the Austrian equivalent of " Happy Birthday to You."

The Birthday Child went now from one to the other and
was kissed, wished a happy birthday, and presented with a
flower. It may come from the flicker of the candles which
mirror themselves in the eyes of a happy child—but there is
always something like a faint flavour of Christmas around
such a birthday celebration. There is an old belief that if you
think hard of a wish and then blow out all the candles on your
cake with one breath, the wish will come true. Then the
presents were discovered and admired and each giver found
out, which meant renewed kissing and hugging. Then he or
she was made master of ceremonies for the next twenty-four
hours. That meant the menu for three meals and the plans for
" what to do to-morrow after school is over."

The feast-days were a little less elaborate. There was no
cake with candles, the presents were arranged around one's
plate at lunch ; but the kissing and hugging and having a good
time were the same, because the root and source of all happiness, that warm love, was the same.

Weeks passed and turned into months. The time between
Epiphany and Ash Wednesday is celebrated in Austria, as in
all other Catholic countries, as a carnival. Festivities of all

kinds and sorts go on until *Fasching Dienstag* (Mardi Gras), when the last ball is stopped sharp at midnight and the season of Lent begins.

On *Fasching Dienstag,* we had our own party. At lunch it was announced that there would be a costume ball in the big living-room, beginning at six. The festive dinner would be at seven-thirty. Of course, the afternoon was free, and all over the house one could hear the tapping of busy feet, bumping of doors, and, as the afternoon progressed, gales of laughter.

When I came down at seven o'clock, trying to look as Chinese as possible in that beautiful costume which my husband had brought from Hong Kong some years ago, complete with shoes and ornaments for the hair, I was almost run down by an ill-mannered sailor, who should not have been admitted in the first place, I thought sharply. Tattooed all over, hands, arms, neck, chest—and you saw a good portion of it, too, through the net shirt—his hat on one ear, smelling of tobacco, he tried to whisper lovely things into my ear. I was a bit annoyed. Georg should not have invited strangers to this home party. And it took me a long time to discover my dearly loved husband behind the dirty sailor boy.

The party was a huge success. There were the three little bears with paws and snoots and all, uncannily well reproduced with camels'-hair blankets and cleverly worked papier-mâché. They could eat out of your hands, they could dance, they were very cute and very rude if you didn't give them a penny each time they begged.

We danced the Walzer, Polka, Sir Roger, Ländler, and other folk-dances.

When the clock struck twelve, the gramophone was stopped in the middle of a waltz. We said one " Our Father " aloud together and wished each other a blessed season of Lent.

Lent, the six weeks' preparation for Easter, is very rigorously observed among the country people in Catholic countries. On purpose I don't say simply " in Catholic countries," because the big cities have shed all these customs. National costumes have been exchanged for street clothes worn the same in Paris, London, New York, or Shanghai ; folk-dances replaced by international ballroom dances ; and instead of folk-customs—the century-old voice of your own people informing you what your forefathers did at certain times and what you should imitate—they have books giving minute instructions on what to wear if you want to be called "smart," how to behave if you want to be "socially acceptable."

The people living in the country still celebrate Lent as it was understood by the many generations since the beginning of Christianity: by voluntary penance and mortification we should participate in the sufferings of Christ in order to be able to celebrate also the day of Resurrection together with Him. We should die to our old sinful self and rise as a new man. To this end fasting is one of the oldest precepts. In Poland, Italy, some valleys of Austria, and especially the Balkan countries, the fast is most conscientiously observed. One meal a day only, and no animal products: no meat, no fish, no eggs, butter, cheese, or milk.

Of course, when Easter comes and these goods are back on the table again, the stomachs feast and celebrate together with the souls, sometimes so much so that a doctor is needed. The money which is saved by fasting goes to the poor, and the time which is saved invested in prayer. Ancient devotions like the Stations of the Cross are much practised. Pilgrimages are undertaken, and the soul, sobered and helped by the bodily chastisement, finds easier access to heavenly things.

Some time before Ash Wednesday my husband and I were discussing what we should do with the children during the season of Lent.

"You know what I really miss?" he said to me. "Catholics don't read the Bible as much as Protestants do. I wish that my children would get thoroughly acquainted with Holy Scriptures." (My husband had joined the Church only a year before I had come into the family.) "Let's start them with the New Testament and let's read it together every evening until Easter. And I think I'll give up smoking," he continued, and this grave announcement was followed by a sigh which seemed to come up from the depths of the earth, for he was a heavy smoker.

Generosity calls for generosity.

"Then I won't even look at sweets or pastry," said I, and my sigh wasn't a bit different, because I have a sweet tooth.

"We shall leave it to the children to choose their own mortifications," said Georg; and it was interesting to see what followed. One saw character in the making from the way each one reacted.

There was the practical-minded little one: 'I shan't pinch

Johanna and I won't spit at Werner—until Easter," and it was
very hard to convince her that this was by no means a supreme virtue.

One of her older sisters, the warm-hearted, enthusiastic type,
said: " I shall carry the little ones' school bags, I shall eat no
dessert at all, I shall say three rosaries a day, and . . ." It was
hard to convince her that the more resolutions you make, the
less chance there is that you keep any.

It turned out to be a beautiful six weeks. The reading of
the Gospels together was wonderful. It proved to be the Book
of Books, the only one in the world to which a four-year-old
girl would listen with enraptured interest, while all the philoso-
phers are unable to measure its divine wisdom.

Then Holy Week was close at hand, with Palm Sunday
ushering it in ; we made little excursions into the woods and
came home with armfuls of pussy willows. With the help of
small branches of boxwood and fir twigs they were arranged
into nice, round bouquets, fastened to a stick about three feet
long. From the workshop we got curly wood shavings, which
were dyed blue, red and yellow and hung over the bouquets.
They looked lovely and cheerful, and on Palm Sunday the
church was a sight. Hundreds of children, each one with his
Palmbuschn, jealously rivalling his neighbours in beauty.
They were blessed in a special solemn way by the priest in
remembrance of the palm branches which were used to mark
Christ's triumphant entrance into Jerusalem.

In the afternoon of Palm Sunday they were taken out into
the fields. Each meadow or field or thicket got its own ; on
each stick was fastened a small bottle with holy water, and the
family went around distributing them while they said the
rosary together. Thus the blessing of the Church was brought
to the meadows, where the cattle would graze ; to the fields,
where the grain for the daily bread would ripen : to the woods,
where the beams for the house and the boards for table and
bed were growing, to protect them against " the snares of the
Enemy ": flood, hail, and fire.

Most of these ceremonies and customs as old as
Christianity were new to Georg and mostly also to the children.
How wonderful it was to travel into that land of wonder with
them. At no other times does the Church display the whole
splendour of her liturgy as at Easter, and who can appreciate
any pageant like a child?

Every morning we walked to the Cathedral a little ahead of time to get a seat in the front pews.

Then comes Holy Thursday. How happily it starts. The huge organ, the choir and the musicians praise and thank Our Lord for the institution of the Blessed Eucharist because this is its anniversary. But suddenly a shadow falls: the Church remembers that on that same Holy Thursday Our Lord started His bitter Passion. He was betrayed by one of His disciples and abandoned by the rest of them, and when He was sweating blood in Gethsemane there was nobody to wipe His face because even His three best friends had fallen asleep. In remembrance of this the Church becomes sad. She silences the organ and the musicians, and the choir goes on singing alone, bewailing compassionately the fate of the Master. At the end of Holy Mass the Blessed Sacrament is carried in solemn procession to a side altar. There it is locked into a tabernacle as Jesus was locked up in a cold and dirty dungeon for the rest of this terrible night. But now the people want a relief to the horror and lonely suffering. The altar is flooded in candlelight and covered with flowers, and people come day and night to keep Him company in love and compassion.

The Gospel of Holy Thursday having told, after the institution of the Blessed Sacrament, the touching incident of Jesus washing the feet of His disciples, finishes with these words: " If then I, being your Lord and Master, have washed your feet, you also ought to wash one another's feet."

Therefore, the venerable old Archbishop, acting as Christ's representative, takes off his gilded vestments, and dressed only in the alb, kneels down humbly before twelve poor old men, washing their feet, drying and kissing them. " For I have given you an example that as I have done to you, so you do also."

Of course, there is no school. The week of Easter holidays has begun on Wednesday, and in all the homes a feverish activity starts: spring cleaning. Only in one corner the artist of the family refuses to let any broom or duster come near him: he is making Easter eggs. First, they are boiled in their colours: red, blue, yellow, green and purple. After they have dried, magic things happen to them. You can erase patterns from the foundation colour with certain acids. You can paint with oil-paint flowers and birds and words, even little bits of music, on them. The words may even give slight indications as to whom this egg is going to belong. You can fasten little flowers, leaves, or herbs on the egg before you throw it into the hot colour bath. When you take it out and remove the string the shape of the flower or herb is clearly outlined. The master of this craft is an important person in the house during these days.

The evening meal is a solemn one. Before the place of the father stand filled wine-glasses and a plate with small buns. He breaks the bun, makes the sign of the Cross over it, and taking with it a cup of wine, he hands it to each member of his household, and they eat and drink in His memory, standing, while the father reads the Gospel of the day After that the family sits down and eats a roasted lamb, and it is all solemn and a little sad and still festive, like the morning in church.

When you come to church on Good Friday, you feel you are entering a house of mourning. The face and voice of your pastor tell you in a half-hour sermon the tragic happenings of the first Good Friday: how the people killed their Best Friend and Benefactor, their Lord and God ; and why? Some out of jealousy ; others, for hatred, or envy, or for fear of losing their business, or even from mere ignorance and mis-understanding.

And you bow your head and take a deep look into your innermost heart, feeling miserable and guilty and so sorry. When the holy service is over on Good Friday, the Church wants to show outwardly that Christ is dead, buried in the tomb. Thus the altars are stripped of their linen, the candle-sticks are overturned, the doors of the empty tabernacle are wide open, the vigil light is extinguished. No flowers, no candles, no sound, only a large crucifix lying on the altar steps, and the people come in and kneel in silent adoration, and then bend to kiss the wounds of the Lord.

But in Austria and other Catholic countries there is still a side chapel of the church where there is great activity. This is the Holy Tomb. More or less elaborately an oriental tomb has been constructed according to the imagination of the local artist, and there one sees the figure of Christ resting in death. It is the ambition of the whole parish to make this resting-place a thoroughly beautiful one. Hundreds of plants are brought by the people, and hundreds of candles and blue and red vigil lights, showing the faith and love of the donors. A guard of honour is there always ; two soldiers on each side presenting arms, two firemen in their best uniforms with shiny helmets and a stern look, two little boys, two little girls, two men, and two women, representing the civil and military elements of the community, paying a double homage, keeping a watch at the tomb of their most beloved Friend, and adoring, at the same time, the One Who said: " I will be with you till the end of time " ; because high above the tomb on a little throne stands the Blessed Sacrament in a monstrance, covered with a transparent white veil.

Then comes Holy Saturday. Immediately you feel a different atmosphere when you come near the church. In front of it is a pile of wood and people standing around with lanterns in their hands. These are the same peasants who walk for hours during the week of Advent to the frozen little church. The door of the church opens, and the priest comes out with the two altar boys and the sacristan. Under the breathless gaze of the bystanders the sacristan succeeds finally in getting a spark out of a stone and thus lighting the woodpile. This morning it has to be a God-made fire which the priest is going to bless, not an artificial one which people have caught and captured in the form of a match.

From this blessed holy fire, the Easter Fire, the priest lights the three candles on the triangle, the symbol of the Holy Trinity, and carries it into the church, singing jubilantly: *Lumen Christi!"* (" Light of Christ!") while everyone answers: *" Deo Gratias!"* (" Thanks be to God!")

Now the church is not dark any more. She has her light back, Christ the Lord. To-day the church seems to try hard to restrain her joy and happiness, remembering that it is only Saturday. Thee choir starts *a capella* and in minor chords, but finally her anticipation of the great Easter glory is overpowering, and she bursts forth into the cry of triumph which goes back through the millenniums: " Alleluia, Alleluia!" Now there is no restraining the music any longer. There is the organ with all its might and powers, there are the trumpets and horns, and the high voices of the violins, and all the bells in the steeple and all the little bells in the church join the human voices in one big, victorious " Alleluia!"

Little children who still believe in the Easter rabbit and the mystery of the Christmas tree being brought from heaven have been told that on Holy Thursday all the bells fly to Rome, where the Holy Father the Pope blesses them, and on Holy

Saturday they travel back to the places where they belong, freshly blessed.

How can your heart not feel some of the happiness of this victory of light over darkness—life over death? Whatever troubles and sorrows may overshadow your path, they have become lighter to-day—thus you have been a witness to the ultimate victory: Christ is risen—also in your life. " Alleluia, Alleluia, Alleluia!" In solemn procession the Blessed Sacrament is carried from the Holy Tomb out of the church through the streets and adjoining valleys to make known to all mankind the message of the great " Alleluia!"

Christianity nowadays is like a big household where many cousins live under the same roof. They all belong to the same clan, but at times they have very different ideas about how to run their family affairs.

Some of them, for instance, have no use for any outside devotion. God is a spirit, and He wants to be worshipped in spirit *only,* they say. Consequently, they have dispensed with all liturgy. They don't want any distracting ceremonies, no incense, no vestments, no music, no pictures and images, not even sacraments—only the service of the spirit.

The trouble is, however, that as long as we live here on earth, we simply are not pure spirits. We have also a body, and in that body, a very human heart; and this heart needs outward signs of its inward affections. And you can't cheat the heart; it knows what it wants, and it knows how to get it. Therefore, we see how, beside the liturgy of the Church, another liturgy has developed, consisting of the same elements. Vestments have migrated from the Church into Glee Club performances with their wide-sleeved velvet gowns and quaint-looking birettas; processions have developed into costly and gaudy pageants; even the ceremonies around the Pontifical High Mass have found a substitute. On the throne, however, is not a bishop, but a pretty girl, the May Queen, or Corn Queen, Orange Blossom Queen, or Potato Queen, who is crowned and honoured.

Well, times change and so may ideas; but the human heart and human nature remain the same. It is very wise for us to remember that we are made of flesh and blood, and to know just *when* our bodies should fast and *when* our hearts should feast. And Easter is such a time!

S.M. c

When Sunday arrives, the greatest of all Sundays in the year, hearts and homes are ready for the Easter joy; both have been cleansed from all dirt and dust in a spring cleaning, inward and outward. Long lines have filed before the confessionals in the church, and contrite hearts have sought forgiveness of their sins. Even the ones who are too busy during the year to come to confession, or so pleased with themselves that they can't find anything to confess, even these obey that old call of the Church: " All the faithful ones shall confess their sins at least once a year, receiving reverently at Easter the sacrament of the Eucharist."

We, too, had stood in line in front of the confessional, waiting our turn. Many times during the year had we been there under the choir loft in the dark, waiting to hear the consoling words: " Thy sins are forgiven thee." But this was a different night. While we stood in the dark, we could see how loving hands were busy transforming the House of God into a beautiful garden with shrubs and young trees, and flowers— flowers—flowers—wherein He could worthily celebrate the anniversary of His Resurrection this coming morning. It filled your heart with happy anticipation of the great Easter message: " My peace be with you."

This morning, when the families walk to church, you see them carrying bundles large and small. On the Sunday of Sundays even the food which will be on the table for a sumptuous Easter breakfast is blessed. The father carried the big ham, the mother, the artistically baked Easter bread with raisins popping out all over, and the children are entrusted with the basketful of Easter eggs and little dishes of salt. Before the solemn service of Easter Sunday begins, the priest pronounces a special benediction over the food. Thus provided with blessings for soul and body, the family returns from the Solemn High Mass. The grown-ups, who have observed the fasting, are full of anticipation of a good feast-day meal, and the little ones want to know when the Easter rabbit is going to come.

" In the afternoon," says the mother, and smiles. And sure enough, in the afternoon when they go out with little baskets through the garden, behind the barn, under the trees, hidden by a bush, there are the most beautifully adorned Easter eggs: painted ones, chocolate ones, some made of sugar or dough. Father and Mother have to come along on the Easter egg hunt. The mother, torn this way and that by impatient little hands, has to admire, and finally help out with her big apron when the baskets are already full. The father strolls leisurely behind them in his white shirt-sleeves, the Sunday coat around his shoulders, while he listens to the outbursts of joy of his little ones.

His sharp eye catches sight of a little red spot at the edge of the wood over there. Oh, yes, that's the blessed palm he put there himself a week ago ; his glance goes slowly all over his little kingdom: the woodland, the meadows, the pastures, the fields, the barns, and the house, his wife, and his children— blessings wherever his eye reaches. And although he couldn't put it into words like city people, deep down in his soul he feels " *that* peace which the world cannot give."

VI. *A Festival Summer and a Baby*

Soon we started talking about the summer, what to do and where to go.

" I should love to take the older children to some of these exquisite concerts and operas," I said. " After all, the whole world assembles here in Salzburg for the Festivals. Why don't we take advantage of it, too?"

Georg was a little doubtful as to the pleasure this plan would provide, but when he saw that I *really* wanted to attend the Festivals, he gave in with a somewhat mysterious smile, as if to say: " You'll see. . . ."

Salzburg was at that time a city of about thirty-five thousand people, built along the river between mountains on all sides. The origin of this ancient place—Iuvavum—goes back to Roman times. It was Christianised as early as the fifth century. It had its catacombs and its martyrs. Later Saint Rupertus built the Benedictine Abbey of Saint Peter, and bade the monks do the same good work they had done all over France and parts of Germany in clearing the woods into tillable land, and likewise in clearing the hearts of the natives into fertile soil for the seed of the Gospel of Christ. Soon afterwards he called his niece, Saint Erentrudis, a Benedictine nun, and built an abbey for her on the hill above Saint Peter: Nonnberg. Around these two venerable places the city of Salzburg began to grow. The old part of the town has not changed much as century after century left its mark, and one sees Romanesque and Gothic churches, Renaissance palaces and Baroque chapels standing in harmony side by side. For most of the year it was a rather quiet town, but during the summer it changed all of a sudden into a metropolis of music. Elegant cars with licence plates from all parts of the world passed slowly through narrow streets, and you could hear as much English spoken when crossing the Straatsbrücke as Salzburg dialect. All the big people of the world of music assembled here: Toscanini and Richard Strauss, Lotte Lehmann and Bruno Walter, and the whole place buzzed with activity. If you didn't make reservations months ahead, it was next to impossible to get a room anywhere. The town put on its best dress: flags could be seen from all the official buildings, standards all along the bridges and all around the Festspielhaus, the festival auditorium.

One morning at breakfast my husband said, looking through his letters: " A distant cousin of mine writes to ask whether we can put him and his family up for the Festivals. He hasn't seen me for a long time, and he says he is longing to renew the old relationship. I didn't know that he was so attached to me. That's how easily you misjudge people," he added regretfully.

The next day again, at breakfast, he whistled through his teeth.

" Now—not for your life could I tell you who he is, but he writes that he is the son of my college room-mate's eldest sister, and I never heard of him. Isn't it funny! He would like to come for the Festivals, too. Well, we have room all right."

When, a couple of days later, an old uncle telegraphed that he also wanted to attend the Salzburg Festivals, and a week after that a cousin from Germany with wife and seven children was wondering whether . . . my husband looked at me and said: " See what I mean?"

They all arrived, aunts and uncles, cousins and friends, who hadn't seen *dear* Georg, of whom they had *always* been so very fond, for *such* a long time . . . and who were *so* happy to meet his lovely wife, and oh, *how* the children had grown . . .! The big house became almost small, so crowded it was.

Cousin Hermann wanted to see the town.

"Rupert, will you go with him and show him . . .?"

"I know," Rupert replied, "The Fortress, Mozart's birth-place, the house of *The Magic Flute*, the Mönchsberg, the Kapuzinerberg, the Cathedral, the Franciscan Church, Saint Peter, Nonnberg, and the Festspielhaus."

Cousin Elvira, who had seen the town yesterday under Rupert's able guidance, was entrusted to Agathe, who would show her the lovely little castle Hellbrunn and the water works. Uncle Edmund, who didn't care, as he said, for old stones and old iron, wanted to visit some of the famous beer gardens around Salzburg with Werner as his guide. Maria conducted a small flock of children to the world-famous puppet theatre, while Georg drove some transient Navy friends up the beautiful mountain road to the summit of the Gaisberg.

And so it went now for the next thirty days. In the even-ings, tired from sightseeing we would go to one of the wonderful operas or to one of those unforgettable concerts; but we were never enough at ease to enjoy it really, because just before one stepped into the car to leave for the opera, another telegram had announced a new-comer "who hadn't seen dear Georg . . . who was wondering whether . . ." And while Leporello surpassed himself in the "Register Aria," I was counting beds in my mind and blaming myself bitterly for not having changed the order at the butcher's.

As the weeks passed, I avoided my husband's eyes. There was a certain glitter, a certain twinkle which annoyed me.

Finally everything comes to an end. When the last guest had been waved good-bye, we sat around the dining-room table alone once more. It was so quiet. Rupert seemed to mumble something to himself, and Maria was deeply con-centrated, counting on her fingers.

Finally they burst forth: "I visited Mozart's birthplace nineteen times. I went all over the fortress twenty-one times, the churches fifteen times, Hellbrunn and the water works eighteen times, and . . ."

Georg put down fork and knife. His whole being seemed to sizzle with glee.

But before he could even open his mouth, I put my hand upon his and said, and every word was underlined: "Yes, I know what you mean. If we want to enjoy music, we shall go and visit a festival somewhere else. But the summer months we shall not spend in Salzburg again."

One day after the guests had left, and the children were playing on the lawn, Hedwig said quite indignantly: " Now, Mother, this is the third time that you haven't played volley ball with us. That's no fun. Come on: here's the ball."

I took them all along with me, and sitting in front of the log cabin in the park, I told them that some time afer Christmas God would send them a little sister or brother.

" Oh, Mother, let it be a boy," sighed Werner. " We have five girls already!"

And Martina said: " If it is only coming after Christmas, how do you know now?"

So I told them.

This was one of those rare hours where heaven seems to touch earth, where a firm bond is woven between hearts.

Advent had come again, the most beautiful Advent of all; that life of real expectation. When the long evenings set in and we met around the fireplace, there was the same atmosphere, which can only be characterised by that untranslatable word, *gemütlich*. There was something new, which one could feel but not put into words. That mood of cheerful anticipation had taken hold of the whole family. The knitting needles in busy young hands did not bring forth lengthy men's socks any more, but the sweetest little sweaters and caps and play-suits and panties, all in blue, of course, because " we already had five girls." Georg and the boys were working noisily on a beautiful cradle; and when I read aloud the passage of a fairy-tale where it says: " And after a year the young queen gave birth to a little son, and they lived happily ever after," Martina looked at her toy dwarfs and nodded gravely.

The Christmas story about the Holy Mother with her Holy Child blooms all anew in your heart when you are living through the great mystery of becoming a mother yourself, a bearer of life.

After Christmas I called on Frau Vogl to make arrangements. She was the youngish widow of a doctor, and had been recommended to me as the best midwife in town. Together we did some figuring, and then it was decided that the baby was due by the middle of February.

"Have you everything ready for the baby?" Frau Vogl asked me.

"I don't know," I said, rather nervously. "I'll tell you what I have: ten dozen diapers; three dozen shirts, size one; and three dozen, size two; six dozen diaper-panties, sixteen jackets, a cradle, a crib, a basket, and a carriage."

"For heaven's sake, stop!" cried Frau Vogl. "You don't expect triplets, do you?"

Very few of these things had been newly acquired. Most of them were still there from the older children. I only had to get them down from the attic, have them washed, ironed and pleated.

By the middle of February Frau Vogl came to stay, and two days later it was obvious: this was the day.

As it hadn't occurred to anyone to bring a doctor into the picture during those past nine months, so it also didn't occur to anybody that I should take even so much as an aspirin. Frau Vogl's presence radiated confidence. Everything was fine, the pain simply belonged to it; thus it was ordained by God Almighty ever since Eve ate the apple.

Georg was sitting at my bedside, and that was very necessary. He knew so much more about it all than I; he had gone through it seven times. He assured me that I was not going to die, and the less I moaned now, the more strength I would have later, and this was only the beginning. He said it so casually that it took the edge off my anxiety. I went through the entirely new sensation that this was not a pain like a toothache; at times it seemed to screw itself into your very bones. These pains seemed to come in regular intervals like breakers at the seashore. The moment they stopped, you felt perfectly wonderful and ready to dance, only to change your mind rather quickly when the next breaker came.

"Will it take longer than half an hour?" I whispered to Frau Vogl, who didn't seem to understand, because she only said: "Breathe deeply."

That was early in the afternoon. When Frau Vogl came back after supper, the uninterested expression on her face changed suddenly. She became all concentration.

Through the open door I could hear the children. They were saying the rosary now. After every decade they sang a song softly and only in two parts, as the tenor and the bass were missing. It sounded to me like angels. What a wonderful prayer the rosary is! For eight hundred years it has carried the sorrows and troubles, the joys and happiness through the hands of the Heavenly Mother to the Throne of God. When we repeat over and over: "Holy Mary, Mother of God, pray for us . . ." it is like the begging of little children who want something with all their heart: "Please, Mother, please! Oh, Mother, please, please!"

With all my heart I joined the chorus silently. Georg hadn't left the room during those long hours. His strong hand was like an anchor to which I clung when the hurricane of pain tossed about the little boat of a frail human body.

During the first weeks of the nine months, we had been rather choosy. It should be a boy—blond-haired, blue-eyed, tall and thin. Georg wanted him to look like his mother, whereas I definitely wanted him to be the image of my husband. The closer the time came, the less fussy we were. If he is only healthy with straight arms and legs, even the colour of eyes and hair wouldn't matter any more. And now it was just the same whether it was a boy or a girl. All the strength of the whole being was concentrated on the one thing necessary:

"Oh God help, help that this Thy child be born healthy in body and soul."

When a piercing little shriek cut through the solemn silence, I heard the children downstairs jump from their seats and jubilantly break into the hymn of thanksgiving by the old master Bach: "Now Thank We All Our God," while Georg was bending over me, kissing me on the forehead.

Then Georg stepped over to Frau Vogl and looked at his sixth daughter.

"Looks like every other newborn baby," he said in the tone of one who knows what he is talking about—"like a little monkey." The spell was broken. Under my feeble protest he left the room "to tell the children."

Had he seen a tear welling up in the young mother's eye? He came back and whispered earnestly:

"But little monkeys are the loveliest, sweetest creatures, and I wouldn't want her to look like anything else!"

What could I do but laugh through my tears? Then he left me to Frau Vogl's professional hands. Later, after the children had tiptoed in to admire the baby and to kiss me good night, I suddenly felt very tired. Right in the beginning of my

evening prayer: " I thank Thee, oh God, for these and all Thy
gifts," I fell asleep. My last thought was:
   " It—was—wonderful ! "

That was in the winter of 1929, when Europe had a cold
spell such as the oldest people couldn't remember. The temperature went down to forty-five and fifty degrees below zero.
Since our churches didn't have heating systems, we asked the
good friend of my Nonnberg days, Father Bruno, to come out
to the house and baptise the baby there. Rupert and Agathe
were godfather and godmother, as they had wished so fervently to be, and the child was given the name: Rosmarie
Erentrudis.

VIII. Uncle Peter and His Handbook

A distant cousin of my husband's, Peter, had also visited the
Festivals in Salzburg the previous summer. With his wife and
six children he had stayed in the friendly little inn half-way up
the Gaisberg, and it was only towards the end of the season
that we had made his acquaintance. The two families liked
each other right away. Their children were the same ages as
ours, and we discovered many common interests in music and
art.

Peter had been a Major in the Imperial German Army. He
was a lovely person with a heart as big as himself, which made
it easy to get on with him. When it came to duty, however,
Peter was made of iron and steel, and as everything in his
daily life was classified as a duty either towards God, or his
fellow men, or himself, there was a lot of duty around.

Peter also loved handbooks.

When Peter was newly married and they were expecting
their first baby, he immediately got the proper handbook,
which would guide him safely through the next nine months.
In the seventh month the handbook said: " Carpets and
curtains should be removed from the bedroom, and the walls
and floor washed with antiseptic." Peter who, as a Major,
had two orderlies at his command, was standing in the middle
of the bedroom, book in hand, supervising these activities. At
the same time Laura, his wife, slipped on the kitchen floor and,

feeling a strange pain, went upstairs, heading for bed, saying to Peter:

"Please, dear, call Mrs. X."—her Frau Vogl—"at once."

Peter merely glanced at her, amazed. Then looking over the rim of his spectacles, he uttered in a helpless tone of voice:

"Laura—impossible! I am only in the seventh month!"

In order to escape another Festival summer, we had made plans with Peter and his family to go down south and camp on an island in the Adriatic Sea during July and August.

We hadn't given it another thought when, at the end of February, Georg received a letter from Peter, saying:

My dear Georg,

I am very sorry to inform you that your idea of camping out-of-doors is not a good one, as I can prove now by experience. I have spent several nights by an open window on the floor of my bedroom, wrapped in a blanket, and I am sorry to say that thereby I have contracted the worst cold of my life. My duty to my family obliges me to cancel our previous summer plans.

                    Your loving cousin,
                              Peter

Georg answered:

Dear Peter,

Sorry about your cold. Stay in bed, drink plenty of hot grog and sweat it out; that's the best way. As far as the summer goes, don't worry. The difference between the temperature of your home in northern Germany at the end of February and the island in July is at least eighty degrees. We'll have a wonderful time.

                    Love,
                        Georg

And a wonderful time we had. First, many more pleats had to be ironed out of Peter's troubled conscience, but finally they arrived at our house about the beginning of July. Looking contentedly over his eighteen pieces of luggage, Peter assured us that the big luggage had been sent by freight to Pola. Pola, situated on the southernmost point of the Istrian peninsula, was the former Austrian Naval Base, which is now Italian, and the island was a few miles offshore.

The main feature of last Christmas had been a bicycle for everyone except little Martina, who got a scooter. Since Peter's older children had brought their bicycles, too, the plan was

this: they should join our older ones and me to start ahead
and tour over the Alps on our bikes. Georg, with Laura and
all the smaller ones, were to follow in a few days by car ; and
Peter wanted to go ahead by train to take care of the luggage.
There were not many cars on the highways at that time, and
the country through which we cycled was so unearthly beautiful—we had a wonderful, wonderful time. In five days we
were in Pola, where we met the rest of our families and, eating
the most delicious fried fish and drinking the dark native
wine, we sat together until deep into the night, telling of our
adventures.

The children were all excited, and surpassed one another
in happy reminiscences—topped by Hedwig who, almost
choked with giggling, said:

" And you know, Papa, what happened? Every day when
we had our big rest at noon, Rupert disappeared. On the
fourth day we followed him, wanting to know what he did.
And do you know where we found him? Sitting in the middle
of a clearing in the woods with a mirror on his knees—
sha-a-a-a-aving ! "

Poor Rupert ! He blushed to the roots of his hair, and you
could easily see how he would have loved to strangle his dear
little sister.

And then it was really time to go to bed. The next day we
hired a big boat to take us over to Veruda, our destination.
When we came to the pier, several men were already loading
huge boxes.

" Heavens ! The big luggage ! " escaped my lips.

That's what it was. Peter, in the thorough fulfilment of his
duty towards his family and himself, had followed the guidance of the *Handbook of Camping* word by word, which tells
you what is the minimum you need per person (*a*) for eight
people, (*b*) for six weeks, (*c*) for sunshine, (*d*) for rain, etc. It
was all in the boxes. Georg and I exchanged a glance. We
knew we would have a good time.

The island had no pier ; one had to wade ashore. Our
luggage consisted of six tents ; and a hammock, plus sleeping-
bag, plus two blankets, and a rucksack with personal belongings, per person. We had camped before.

It had been very, very hot in the morning, and now black
clouds were gathering. A critical look at the sky and Georg
said to us:

" Make camp—hurry!"

In no time the six tents were put up in a circle, and the rest of the luggage stored in the big tent, which would serve as living- and dining-room on rainy days. We had been silently busy, everyone knowing exactly what to do next. Only now I remembered Peter. Where was he?

" Peter, Peter!" I called and followed hurriedly the muffled " Here!" of his answer.

Behind a bushy pine I found what is left to be seen if the whole upper part of a man is plunged head first into a deep box. At this moment he emerged, purple of face, triumph in his look.

" Here it is!" he shouted victoriously.

And what was it? The *Handbook of Camping,* which by mistake had been buried in the very bottom of the biggest box. Nervously he searched for his glasses, which he never, never found, for they were usually pushed up on his forehead. Then opening the book on page one, he said: " Now, cousin, let us commence." And then he read to my unbelieving ears:

" 'The first step to be taken upon reaching the prospective site of the camp is to investigate whether the site is: (*a*) sandy, (*b*) rocky, (*c*) swampy, (*d*) hilly, (*e*) flat.' "

Up went the glasses, and with the voice and air of Julius Caesar, Peter shouted:

" Children, 'ten-*shun*! Let's investigate."

Georg, appearing on the scene and not having witnessed what I had, interrupted the strategic manoeuvre with a suggestion:

" Peter, I think you'd better get your boxes into one of the tents. It will pour within the next five minutes."

I felt sorry for " Caesar," so I said: " The site is flat and sandy—come on!" The first drops, big as cherries, began to fall.

The highlight, when the storm was over, was the unpacking of the big boxes. Looking back on it, I can only compare it with the Boy Scout Department at a big store. Brand-new tents with a rubber floor attached to them; acetylene lamps for each tent; two folding boats with three sails each; and the most elaborate sleeping-bags and fluffy pyjamas; shiny kitchen equipment; a gramophone and records; one box full of books, and one box full of wine, another one filled with silk-hemmed blankets in lavender and pea-green, and dainty cushions; still another filled with canned *delicatessen foods*; and in the middle of this *"Handbook-of-Camping-Come-Alive"* stood Peter, beaming, opening his arms wide and saying: "Help yourselves, help yourselves! We have much more than we need!"

Veruda is one of the many islands off the shore of Istria and Dalmatia. On one side it emerges gently out of the sea, rises gradually to about 150 or 200 feet, and ends abruptly on the other side in a steep cliff. In an hour one could walk around it. The sea had eaten deep into its shoreline, forming many little bays as big as a large room. One part of the island, about fifty acres, was covered with dense pine groves. The rest was fields and pastures. Franciscan Fathers had once owned this beautiful spot. On the highest point of the island the ruins of the church and the convent were still standing. The monks had planted a garden with medicinal herbs. Long after the Fathers had been driven away by Napoleon, the herbs had spread all over the land, and during the hot summer days and nights they exhaled the most wonderful fragrance which one could smell for miles and miles out at sea, thyme and lavender, dill and sage, mint and sweet geranium and rosemary, and many more which we couldn't name. The old walls were overgrown with honeysuckle, wild roses, oleander, and laurel. A walk through this little paradise in the full moonlight was heavenly.

Georg had known Veruda since his boyhood days. He had been born in Zara, half-way down the Dalmatian coast, into the family of an Austrian Navy officer. They had lived a while in Trieste and until 1918, in Pola. He also knew Signor Pauletta, who had owned a large hardware store in Pola before the war and afterwards acquired Veruda and retired there. He had a couple of rooms in the old monastery, and there he lived now, as his island's only inhabitant, very contentedly on fish he caught and vegetables and fruit he planted, needing next to no money. Very rarely he went "to town," which meant Pola. He had invited us to come and camp on Veruda, and now—here we were.

At this moment our host came down from his stony hermitage to greet his guests. His eyes grew bigger and bigger when he saw that fancy display of what modern people, according to the book, need when they want to go "back to nature" and lead a "simple life" in the country. Signor Pauletta, who owned a couple of pots and pans, a Sunday suit, and fishing tackle, was deeply impressed.

" *Varra, varra!*" he repeated many times clucking his tongue. (This means " What do you know about that!")

Our little tent city was erected on the east side of the island, where it slopes gently down to the water, but every day we went up to the cliffs, watching the surf or the big ships out at sea, heading for the Mediterranean, or watching Signor Pauletta fishing. We slept in naval hammocks under the pine trees, and after the first couple of unquiet nights, when you had to pick yourself up from under your hammock several times, it became a most restful way of sleeping. The strong scent of the pines, the quiet murmur of the waves, the moon-light coming down through the branches, the gentle swinging of the hammocks—oh, it was heavenly!

At first, everybody was radiantly happy. Georg, who was the supreme commander, assigned the duties, such as cooking, getting the fresh water from the cistern up yonder, watching the baby, washing dishes. There was a bi-weekly exchange, the two families taking turns. The first thing every morning was a quick swim. Then we met for morning prayer and breakfast. After that little groups formed for fishing or swimming, paddling, sailing, or just strolling around. After a few days we noticed that our children were scattered all over the place, having a wonderful time with the boats, while Peter's children were mostly ashore. Upon investigation I learned that the *Handbook* advised not leaving land if: (*a*) the wind comes from the land, (*b*) cumulo-nimbus clouds are forming on the horizon, (*c*) during the past three days there has been a storm, (*d*) sure signs indicate a storm to come within the next twenty-four hours, (*e*) the temperature is higher than eighty degrees, (*f*) you feel the slightest indigestion, (*g*) or headache, (*h*) or general tiredness. Cousin Peter, therefore, could be seen every morning after breakfast, licking his right forefinger, according to the book, holding it up, and finding sadly that the wind was coming from the land, which it did every morning, changing every night to wind from the sea, all during the summer on this coast, book or no book. To the passionate pleading of his children he only shook his head sadly.

Georg and I had a council of war. It was finally agreed that I was to take care of Peter every morning after breakfast until Georg had successfully sent off all the children. When

the last one was cleared off the island, I would be informed
by a signal on his boatswain's whistle.

The next morning I watched Peter to see what he was going
to do after breakfast, and soon discovered that he was going
to have his morning shave in peace and quiet. Laden with
two sizeable leather cases, several towels and smaller boxes,
he descended into one of those little bays, of which there were
eight or ten next to each other. I changed into my bathing-
suit and made myself at home in the cove next to him,
watching him from behind a stone. It was awful, but what
could I do? It was my order of the day to prevent Peter
from licking his finger before the whistle had blown. I didn't
even know yet, myself, how I would do it. For the time
being, I was perfectly enraptured by what I saw: Lovingly
Peter spread the different towels over flat stones. Then he
opened the first leather case and took out a brush, a piece of
soap, several little flasks, a razor strop, and many other little
items. Then he opened the second leather case, which obviously contained washing and bathing utensils, soap for salt
water, talcum powder, etc. All this was arranged in rectangular
lines, like soldiers on a drill field. Then Peter stepped back
and, after an approving glance, nodded. It was good. But
it became more breath-taking than that. Sitting down on a
low stone, Peter took that leather strop and a razor and,
sticking his big toe through the middle ring of the strop,
holding the other end in his left hand, sharpened the razor,
counting aloud: ". . . twelve, thirteen, fourteen . . ." Merely
by listening I was informed that the book suggested, at least
on Wednesday, twenty strokes. I was spellbound and almost
forgot *my* duty. When he started to produce lather in a lovely
pink bowl, my conscience awoke.

For heaven's sake, I must not let him shave, and, "Peter!"
I wailed, rising behind my stone, "Peter!" not knowing yet
what else to say.

He gave me the clue. "What's the matter, Cousin Maria?"

"You know, I don't like this cove. Would you mind,
Peter, changing with me?"

And now, to my shame, I sat down on a stone, watching
him completely pack and unpack for the next ten minutes,
going through all the procedure patiently once more, con-
sidering cold-heartedly that I *would* have to chase him into
still another cove if I didn't hear . . . But there it was, the

" all clear " signal, and Peter had his uninterrupted shave and I, a good swim.

This had to be repeated for the next few days until Peter was convinced that none of Cousin Georg's arrangements for the children had proved fatal.

It was a wonderful summer, full of adventure and the healthiest out-of-door living. The two families were closely knit together and friendships formed among the children which were to last a lifetime.

The last evening came. We had extended the vacation, and it was high time to go home if the children were to be in time for school. That was now definitely the last evening. With the kind of tender sadness that always comes before a farewell, we sat around the camp-fire. A waning moon shed a greenish light, which only stressed the doleful atmosphere. In the evening the children had asked me to tell ghost stories—" true ones." So I had invented " true ghost stories " of monks wandering around the island not finding rest for their souls because . . . Of a hollow voice which could be heard on moonless nights, moaning and groaning, which belonged to the Emperor Napoleon, who had persecuted this monastery, and would have to groan until somebody rebuilt it and gave it back to the Franciscans . . . Of . . . and soon I had to accompany my young audience to their respective hammocks. Now we grown-ups were sitting around the fire alone.

After we had talked about the rich beauty of these summer months, Peter, once more filling the glasses from the last bottle, said all of a sudden:

" You know, it just occurs to me that after the first few days I haven't even opened a book. By the way, Laura, have you seen that old *Handbook of Camping* anywhere? I mislaid it right at the beginning."

And this was perhaps the greatest tribute that was ever paid to Veruda, that hidden pearl of the sea.

IX.　*An Operation, a Turtle and a Long Distance Call*

It was a beautiful day in May, Rosmarie was two years old. It was Ascension Day, a holiday, and the whole family was in church. Rosmarie had stayed at home with me, and I had told Frau Vogl that it was time for her to come again, perhaps in the next few days. And then it happened, and it happened so fast that I hardly had time to tell Frau Vogl she had better hurry. While the church bells were ringing, little Eleonore hastened into this world. That somehow stuck with her. She still seems to be in a hurry.

On the evening of her baptism—she was named after her godmother, Tante Lorlein—Georg said to me thoughtfully:

" I don't know whether this has anything to do with our having girls all the time, but ever since the first child, I wanted to name one Barbara. You know, for some mysterious reason Saint Barbara is the patron Saint of the Navy. The first child, however, was a boy, Rupert. The next one had to be named after her mother, the third one after her godmother, and so on ; and Saint Barbara seems to send girl after girl until I keep my promise."

" And why didn't you tell me that in the first place?" I asked reproachfully.

When Eleonore was a little over a year old, we were making summer plans again, and went back to Veruda. That joyous life in bathing-suits came this time to a sudden end for me.

On one of our hikes, when I was newly married, we had stayed overnight with a farmer whose children were sick in bed with scarlet fever. Unfortunately, he told us this only the next morning, when it was too late. Sure enough, a few weeks later, Martina and Johanna woke up one morning with high fever and sore throats. I withdrew with the little ones into the guest wing, and there we lived in seclusion. When they were out of danger and up for the first time, it got me. It wasn't a bad case, but weeks after I had returned to human society I still couldn't get rid of a rather annoying backache. I asked a doctor about it, and he discovered that the scarlet fever had infected my kidneys. " But don't worry ; just keep on a strict diet: no meat, no salt, no eggs, no milk, no fat."

Little did I know that this was to be my programme for the next twenty years. Off and on I tried " not to worry ; just keep on a strict diet: no meat, etc." But generally a diet simply disintegrates into eating exactly what you want, but with a bad conscience.

During our weeks in Veruda I felt the pain most disagreeably on our boat rides, especially in rough weather when we got drenching wet. So one day I again went to a doctor. He grew quite serious and talked about kidney stones and a necessary operation. Upon my return home I went to Vienna.

Maria came with me. Since the very earliest times when she had been convalescent and I her teacher, we had grown especially fond of each other.

That first week in Vienna was lots of fun. During the day I was in a private clinic for the necessary tests to be made, and in the evening we went to the opera or the theatre. We enjoyed ourselves thoroughly, and I almost forgot what I was in Vienna for, until the doctor informed me that the tests showed it *was* kidney stones, and an operation was unavoidable. That put an end to our gay visits to the Staatsoper and the Burgtheater. Maria sent a telegram to her father, and he flew up on the day of the operation. The operation proved worth while: nineteen stones were removed, and so much gravel and sand that the wound had to be kept open to drain for several weeks.

I had never had much talent for being sick or keeping quiet, and after the first few miserable days, I found it extremely difficult to lie on my back motionless.

"Could you think of some kind of animal which I could have here in bed with me?" I asked Georg.

He rushed off and came back with three tiny little baby chicks. I was simply thrilled, called them Caspar, Melchior, and Balthazar in honour of the Three Holy Kings, and during the long hours when no visitors were allowed, I had the nicest company. Contentedly they rested on my chest and were perfectly tame. Unfortunately, they did not remain little yellow cotton balls, but grew, and after a week the diaper situation of my baby chicks became extremely difficult. I could see it by the expression on the face of Sister Agrosia, my nurse. Sister Agrosia was a saintly nun with only one fault: In her childlike innocence she believed every word I said, however silly my stories might be. She had stirred in me the urge to make my stories sillier each day, and still I hadn't reached the limit of her credulity.

When it was evident that Caspar, Melchior, and Balthazar had to be removed, Georg went to a pet shop and came back radiant.

"Look what I got you!" and he put a little turtle on my

bed. At this very moment Sister Agrosia came into the room.

"Oh," she said, "what is that?" looking curiously at something she had probably never seen before in her life.

Truthfully I answered: "That is a turtle, Sister."

"A turtle, what is a turtle?" she wanted to know.

That was bad. All my evil instincts were at work.

"A turtle is an animal which feeds on the toes of new-born babies," I said, looking straight into her eyes.

This she *can't* believe, I thought to myself. But I was mistaken. "Oh, oh!" Sister said, and looked with horror at that little brown lump on my blanket. "But we'll have to be very careful and keep the door shut."

I had been given the only vacant room in the whole house, which happened to be next to the maternity ward.

Sadly I must confess that I was not a bit ashamed of myself at that moment, nor was I next morning when I heard from eye-witnesses that Sister Agrosia had been seen sitting on a chair outside my door with a stick in her hand while the little turtle slept peacefully on my chest.

At Pentecost I was still in bed.

"Sister, I would like to go to confession to-morrow," I said.

Kind Sister Agrosia went out to find a priest at the next parish church. Soon she was back, excited and triumphant:

"They have a new priest in the parish, and the pastor said he will send him. I haven't talked to him, but I know you will like him very much. Oh, he is beautiful! He has a face like an angel!"

I must admit that the next morning my thoughts were divided between the receiving of the sacraments and the curiosity to see "Father Angel-Face."

At seven o'clock the door opened, and at one glance I saw that Sister had been right. Father looked like the statue of Saint Aloysius come to life. But now it was time for me to concentrate on my sins. Father got a chair and sat down at my bedside; and after he had pronounced the Latin blessing, I confessed my sins, including all the mischief with poor Sister Agrosia. When I was all through, Father looked up and said only two words:

"*Nem ertem,*" which means, "I don't understand."

Father was Hungarian.

For a split second we looked at each other in desperation,

and then we had a hard time not to laugh. Father commenced questioning me in Latin: "*Have* you done this or *have* you done that?" and I, wanting to answer, "I *have*," or "I *have* not," just said: "*Habeo—Non habeo*"; which was definitely not correct Latin, but accepted by God in His representative.

Soon afterwards my husband came to fetch me from this expensive private clinic. The summer months we again spent in Veruda, and in September we came back to Salzburg, glad to be home once more.

We had hardly walked into the house when my husband was called to the telephone, a long distance call from Zell am See. The distance is only about sixty miles, but it was "long distance", and we were in Austria, where a long distance call or a telegram are used only in extreme emergencies.

And now the voice on the other end announced:

"The banking house of Lammer and Company has suspended payment."

It was our bank.

X. Aren't We Lucky!

It has happened many times that rich people have, in one moment, lost a fortune. When you read about such losses in novels or see them acted on the stage, they always seem dramatic. It is interesting to experience it oneself. That voice announcing the failure of our bank had put a definite period to the end of a very comfortable chapter in our life: the chapter "Rich."

The bank where our money was deposited was owned by a lady, Mrs. Lammer. About this time Hitler and his Nazis across the border began to make things difficult for little Austria. In order to force Austria to her knees, all tourist trade with Austria had been forbidden, thus cutting her lifeline. This caused serious repercussions in the world of finance and Mrs. Lammer was not the only banker who looked with concern into the future. My husband knew and esteemed her as a brave and clever woman. When he heard that she was in serious difficulties with her bank, he took all his funds, safely deposited in a big bank in England, and came to her rescue.

My poor husband tortured himself with reproaches.

"I should never have taken the money out of England," he moaned. "Never! Oh, the poor, poor children!"

"Now, listen," I said finally, "you didn't do that to give yourself a good time. You wanted to help somebody in a desperate situation, didn't you? What do we read the Gospel for? Don't you remember that it says, whatever we do for love of Him, He will reward us a hundredfold in this life, and in addition we get life everlasting?"

After all, we were not exactly starving. But we had to face realities. Most of the money was gone, but there was just enough left to pay the most necessary bills if one lived quite simply. Also there was a great deal of real estate, representing a nice sum. This, however, would not be touched; it was set aside to secure the future of the children. We had to reduce our standard of living, give up the car, send away six of the eight servants, keeping *only* the butler and the cook, close the big rooms downstairs and on the second floor, and live cosily together on the third floor, where it would be easy to get along without a maid. My poor husband felt like a beggar. He was so depressed, and I felt terribly sorry for him as I watched him walking up and down, back and forth through the room by the hour, chewing the edge of his moustache and looking hopelessly sad.

On top of all his worries, I was getting on his nerves too. Somehow or other, I just couldn't share his utter despair. Ever since the moment when we learned the money was lost, I had experienced a strange expectancy. I felt elated, and not for my life could I look discouraged, try as I would. Did I perhaps feel faintly—remotely—that we were just at the beginning of the great crescendo in the song of our life, which would from now on continue uninterruptedly?

The "hundredfold reward" set in almost immediately with the reaction of the children: in their complete unconcern as to whether we had a car or not, their willingness to take over new duties and new responsibilities, and this not in an attitude of suffering and resignation, but with rolled-up shirt-sleeves.

Rupert, the eldest, was the only one not at home. He was in Innsbruck in a pre-medical school, and I went to see him to break the bad news that not only his liberal allowance had to be stopped right away, but he would have to work his way through the university. I came home, glowing with enthusiasm.

" Aren't we lucky, Georg, that we lost that money! How would we ever have found out otherwise how fine the children are?"

And I told him how Rupert had taken it with a smile. And that cheerful smile of the boy went a long way—it lit up the troubled face of his father. When I saw Georg's reaction after so many worried days and nights, my joy was complete. Too much joy can't be taken alone ; it hurts. And so I hugged and squeezed my poor husband until he freed himself laughingly, catching his breath.

" What's the matter with you? You act as if you had made a million dollars "

" Oh, much more," I said. " I have just found out that we were not really rich, we just happened to have a lot of money. That's why we can never be poor. I am so happy to know that we don't belong to those for whom it is so hard to enter the Kingdom of God."

But in spite of all my enthusiasm, something had to be done. We had to earn our living. But how?

In those days we reaped the first harvest of that blessed custom we had started long ago of reading the Gospel together with the children. At every crossroad, in every tribulation, one word or other would pop up that seemed made for the occasion. " Whatsoever you shall ask," said Our Lord, " you shall receive."

" Whatsoever." So we started asking together for the right light, for the right guidance, and the answer was just around the corner in Nonnberg. I went there to ask them to help us pray in this difficult situation.

" Why don't you ask the Archbishop for permission to have a chapel, as so many other castles and estates do?" said Frau Rafaela. " I am sure he would send a priest to stay with you, and you could rent the extra rooms of your house to students of the Catholic University."

As simple as that! The good old Archbishop Ignatius gave his permission most readily. One of the big rooms downstairs, not in use now, seemed just made for a chapel, with a bay window in the corner for the altar ; the pews were on the side facing each other as in a quaint old convent chapel. And the pastor from the parish church most kindly helped us with the most necessary vestments and vessels. One of the professors of the Theological Faculty was looking for a quite place where he could write a scholarly book. He was our first boarder, and he said Mass in the morning and gave Benediction in the evening. Whenever my husband met me alone these days, he said hastily: " Yes, we are lucky, and I wouldn't want it any other way."

But really—weren't we lucky? Never before had we been so close to each other in the family as now, or had seen, with such gratitude to God, the qualities in the children's characters; not a murmur, not a reproach. And never before had we had a priest in our midst, a chapel and the Holy Eucharist in the house. This was not just being lucky; this was a blessing!

I don't know which word to use now; was it funny, comical, or pathetic to watch the reaction of our rich neighbours? One of the worst things that can happen to a rich man seems to be the suspicion that you might want to borrow some of his money. Anticipating this grave danger, he has to prevent it by all means. So whenever our old friends met my husband, they started talking about the bad times and how they didn't know how to make ends meet. Once Georg came home really angry.

" Just think what happened?"

" Here we go!" I thought as he walked to and fro in big striding steps, chewing his moustache.

" First I met Maxi." (One of the richest men in the countryside.) " Out of a blue sky he started to explain to me that even if his own brother were to ask him for a loan, he would have to refuse. ' In these times, you know,' " and he imitated Maxi's mournful tone of voice. " And a few minutes later," he continued, " I met Baroness K., and she said, almost disappointedly: ' I met your children the other day and I was astonished how well they look and how cheerful, and still so neatly dressed." *Still*—— I love that! Say——" And he stopped short in front of me. " Are those people crazy? And don't tell me again I'm lucky!"

" Yes I do," and I kissed him in the middle of his angry mouth, " because you are. Very lucky indeed. For all the money in the world you couldn't have found out who your real friends are, and now you know."

At this he had to laugh, and after you have once laughed, you aren't really angry any more.

A year later the house was full of people, young professors and students from the Faculty. Never before had we had so much fun and such interesting evenings. We didn't make much money from the boarders, but enough to meet the bills and keep the big house going.

Seldom before had there been so much laughter, so many spirited discussions, so many interesting people to meet. Professor D., our first boarder, had quickly become a very dear and wonderful friend. When his book was nearly finished, his publisher came to visit him, and stayed afterwards for a cup of tea in the library, where the fire in the fireplace was roaring. It was a miserably cold day in November. This was only the first visit of many, many to come. Otto Müller, the young publisher, was counted among our closest friends, and shortly all the writers, scientists, and professors who came to visit him landed in our house. What richness that brought into our lives, especially to the growing children. On such evenings I couldn't quite suppress a triumphant look at my husband who, to avoid hearing the dreaded word "lucky," put his hand soothingly on mine, saying "I see what you mean."

During all that time we had never stopped singing and making music together, much to the enjoyment of our house guests. The new chapel was a strong incentive to sing more seriously than ever before.

At Easter, 1935, Professor D. had to make a journey, and asked a priest friend to come and say Holy Mass in his stead. Afterwards at breakfast the young priest, whose name was Father Wasner, said: "You really sang quite well this morning, but . . ." and he explained in a few words several important things to us, and then and there at the breakfast table, made us repeat a motet, conducting it from where he was sitting. None of us knew then just how lucky we were:

This was the birth of the

TRAPP FAMILY SINGERS

XI. " Never Again "

It will be very interesting one day to follow the pattern of our life as it is spread out like a tapestry. As long as we live here we see only the reverse side of the weaving, and very often the pattern, with its threads running wildly, doesn't seem to make sense. Some day, however, we shall understand.

In looking back over the years we can discover how a red thread runs through the pattern of our life: the Will of God.

After the first Lent when my family had started to read the Gospel together and had since kept up this practice until it had turned into a habit, it became clearer all the time that this was the message Christ came upon earth to teach us. It is the heart of our religion—of all religion—to do the Will of God.

And here we had found our guiding star which should lead us faithfully through all tempests into the final haven.

When Father Wasner found that we were seriously interested in our home music, he came more and more often to join us. He proved to be an outstanding musician. A master on the organ, he also played the piano beautifully. But his greatest charm was his way of making music simple and uncomplicated. What a joy it was to listen to his mellow voice when he sang the Leider of Schubert, Brahms, and Hugo Dolf. And to this day we have never ceased admiring his vast knowledge of musical history and theory. He has never behaved like one of the great, who dwell in unapproachable light. He simply was full of music, and wherever you touched him, it came out.

What a wonderful summer! Father Wasner came every day, and singing now became serious. With enthusiasm we plunged into deep waters. Motets and Masses by Palestrina, Lasso, Vittoria for the chapel, which we could never have tackled alone, we studied now under the guidance of a true musician. How that old music came alive, how we revelled in those ancient tunes!

These months still belong to our most precious memories. It was a time of first love. The music welled up from our hearts simply for pure love of music. At that time we sang because we had to, and nobody and nothing could stop us. We

89

didn't need an audience. We didn't even want one. It would only have disturbed us. In the morning we sang for God alone, for His greater honour and glory during the divine service. In the evening we worked on madrigals, ballads, and wonderful ancient folk-songs in settings by old masters, and we sang them to our hearts' delight outside in our park or in one of those mountain meadows overlooking the valley. Six hours spent like this was nothing at that time. We were intoxicated with music, drunk with the wonder of song.

On a memorable day in August, 1936, we were sitting together once more behind a screen of pines in our park. It was late in the afternoon, a Saturday. Everybody had stopped working and changed into Sunday clothes. Together we had said the rosary, a ritual which began our Sunday. During the week we had been working on the motet, "Jesu Meine Freude," by Bach. Now we sang the movements already memorised, the different verses of the chorale and that wonderful fugue. And then we sang over and over again our newest favourite of which we were especially proud because it was in English: "The Silver Swan" by Orlando Gibbons.

All of a sudden we were interrupted by a strange clapping of hands. A little bewildered, a little embarrassed, we went around the pine screen and met—who could describe our amazement?—the one whom we had so far admired from afar as Marschallin in *Der Rosenkavalier,* or as Fidelio—none other than the great Lotte Lehmann.

She had heard that we had let our house in previous summers and wanted to inquire about renting it; and now, just by chance, she had heard us sing, hidden behind the pines. Right there and then she proved how really great she was; for only the great ones can appreciate the achievements of others. With what enthusiasm, her beautiful eyes glowing with warmth, she talked about our "art," which made us blush and want to kiss her.

"Oh, children, children," she exclaimed over and over again; "You must not keep that for yourselves, that precious gift. You must give concerts. You must share this with the people. You must go out into the world; you must go to America!"

Her genuine enthusiasm swept us off our feet. Not that we believed it. Even the poor boy in the fairy-tale can hardly believe it when he is suddenly told he is a prince.

" Don't forget," our illustrious guest continued, " you simply have gold in your throats!"

But the mere thought of having to step on a stage was so frightening that the gold—hidden in the depths of our throats anyhow—was no temptation at all.

" To-morrow is the festival for group singing. You must take part in that contest. You simply must!" She coaxed earnestly and fervently.

Pale with anticipated stage fright, we insisted:

" N-n-n-n-no . . . n-n-n-n-never!"

My husband was aghast. He loved our music, he adored our singing; but to see his family on a stage—that was simply beyond the comprehension of an Imperial Austrian Navy officer and Baron.

" Madam, that is absolutely out of the question," he said, and meant it.

" Oh, not at all," Lotte Lehmann said with a twinkle in her eyes. Finally, believe it or not, she had us all convinced. She herself made a telephone call which, at this late hour, entered us in the contest.

After Lotte Lehmann had left with renewed expressions of her enthusiasm and best wishes for good luck for to-morrow, we woke up. What *had* we done?

When our name was called the next afternoon, we stumbled on to the stage, stepping on our own and everybody else's feet, alternately blushing and growing pale, with a lump in our throats and a wild fear in our hearts. Why had we ever said " Yes "? In a daze we sang our three numbers, and none of us can remember to-day which ones they were. A gentleman down in the audience tried hard to look mildly interested but perfectly detached. Poor Georg! Our only wish, when we were offstage again, was to evaporate immediately, but we had to stick it out and wait for the awarding of prizes. As if in a fog, we saw the judges return from their conference. Silence settled over the vast crowd, and from afar we could hear the announcement:

" The first prize is awarded to the Trapp Family from Salzburg."

I remember that I didn't understand the meaning of these words, because I applauded wildly with the other people. We had then to go on the stage once more and receive our prize, a diploma signed by the Governor of Salzburg. More applause, more shaking of hands, smiles all around—but when my eyes searched around for my husband, his seat was empty. He had left in despair. Success or no success—the whole thing was a nightmare to him. It pained him bitterly to see his family on a stage, and only the solemn family resolution never, never to do such a thing again put his troubled mind at ease.

XII. From Hobby to Profession

The summer with all its excitements had passed, and the family had settled down again into routine life.

It was a great day when I walked up the hill to Nonnberg with my little daughter Rosmarie holding on to my hand, entrusting the child to those sacred walls for schooling. Years before, I had torn myself away from this beloved spot with so much heartache, but in a way I had never altogether left. Carrying out the doctrine of the Will of God, I and my family with me, while living in the world, never became wholly a part of the world; and here I came back now with my dear little child. It was with tears and laughter that I stood in the parlour and handed the little one over to Frau Gertrudis, who had shared the times of waiting for the novitiate with me.

A few days later a telephone call came from the Salzburg radio station. It was like a stone thrown into a quiet lake. The manager had heard us at the festival, and ever since he had wanted us on the air.

" Please be up at the Mönchsberg next Saturday at four o'clock. Thank you." And he hung up. It didn't even occur to him that somebody might perhaps decline such an offer. Of course, we wouldn't go. We had said we'd never sing in public. During lunch I casually mentioned the call at our table.

" You said no, didn't you?" asked Georg rather anxiously.

" He didn't give me any time. He just told me and hung up. But I'll telephone after lunch."

" But, Mother, perhaps it is the Will of God that we sing on the radio," said Hedwig. She meant to tease her father. But was it a joke? How did we know? The fact that we resented it so fiercely ourselves, that we didn't *want* to appear in public, that we loved our privacy more than anything—did that mean that we could act accordingly? We had to admit that there was absolutely nothing wrong about singing over the air; the opportunity had been brought to us from the outside; our music might bring joy to many people all over Austria—and what could be said against it?—simply that we didn't want to do it. That didn't seem enough reason, even Georg said with a deep sigh; and to our own astonishment, we found ourselves on Saturday at four o'clock at the studio on the Mönchsberg.

Kurt von Schuschnigg, Chancellor of the Austrian Republic, was a very busy man. He rarely had time to spend with his radio. Once in a great while he turned it on. This time, I am told, he listened, fascinated: a small choir sang from Salzburg. He had never heard any of their selections before, but ardent music lover that he was, he was entranced by this beautiful music. A thought flashed through his mind. There was a great reception to be given by the Chancellor for national and foreign dignitaries, the diplomatic corps and military authorities—his first public appearance since the recent death of his wife. For the entertainment he had engaged the Vienna Philharmonic Orchestra, and ever since, had looked for another artist, something out of the ordinary. Now here it was, and the Chancellor pushed a button and wanted to know the whereabouts of that singing group, whose voices were still coming to him over the air in Bach's "Hymn of Thanksgiving." And out of the enthusiasm of the moment, he sat down and wrote to that Trapp Family in Salzburg.

One doesn't get a letter from a Chancellor every day. A deep silence followed, after Georg had read the letter aloud. A pained expression came over his face.

"That doesn't mean that we have to accept, does it?" and he looked pleadingly at me.

"Of course not," I wanted to say. But I said, "I don't know."

And again we went through the same agonising procedure to find out what was the Will of God in a situation where our own wishes and likings pointed sharply in one way. What could we possibly say against it? There was nothing wrong, not even undignified. With the Vienna Philharmonic Orchestra, we would be in the best company. This invitation from the Chancellor should be regarded as an honour instead

of a bother. Again, the only thing against it was that we didn't
want to. That settled it. On the appointed day we stood in
front of a great audience, having been introduced by the
Chancellor himself, and sang. The applause was very warm.
" That was something entirely different," we heard all
through the evening.

I noticed a gentleman talking enthusiastically with my husband and Father Wasner, champagne glass in hand. Was it
the champagne? Never shall I know, but I learned that we
were going to give a public concert in the Kleinen Musik-
vereinssaal two months hence.

Now our singing evenings at home turned into rehearsals,
our hobby a profession.

On the appointed day we arrived at the ancient building
which housed the large, the medium, and the small auditoriums. Rows and rows of cars were parked outside. All those
people couldn't possibly have come for us! No, they hadn't.
There was a sensational attraction, a guest from far-away
America, a world-famous Negro contralto, Marian Anderson,
giving a concert in the big hall. The whole Press had turned
out ; and during intermission, as they were there already, they
casually looked into the small hall to see what was going on.
The next morning we read in the newspapers that they had
all enjoyed immensely the first concert given by the Trapp
Family. And so had the audience. A little bit in a daze, a
little embarrased, a little bashful, and already a little proud,
we received congratulations afterwards in the artists' room.
Slowly, slowly, Georg lost that feeling that he was sliding in
a dentist's chair while he listened to his family ; and when
somebody said, " You really should sing during the Festivals
in Salzburg," he even smiled.

It was the dream of every artist in the world to be allowed
to give a concert during the Salzburg Festivals. But there
were so many sopranos and basses, tenors, violinists and
pianists that they had to wait their turn patiently. But there
was only one singing family, and this was not a concert ; it was
a festival. In the first row sat Lotte Lehmann with her husband! During the intermission people stormed backstage, and
at the end of the concert managers came from nearly every
European country with contracts and invitations. Lotte
Lehmann kissed us and was proud of us, and we were truly
happy. We bought a scrapbook and pasted in the criticisms

from Vienna and Salzburg and the picture of Lotte Lehmann and us. Then we put the contracts, to which one from an American manager had been added, into a drawer and retired into private life. We thought this was the end of our concert activities.

Little did we know that it was only the beginning.

Those ladies and gentlemen from France, Holland, Belgium, England, Italy, Denmark, Sweden, and Norway had not been joking. Early in September we heard from them that their respective countries were eagerly expecting us.

Now it became clear that what had started in a playful way, was growing into a serious activity. There seemed to be a definite plan behind it all, leading to some distant goal, which we could not perceive as yet.

A European concert tour, the possibility of showing our children the beauty of God's world and the wonders man has made: cathedrals and palaces, art galleries and museums—it was exciting and breath-taking. At first it all seemed impossible with the children at school and Father Wasner teaching at the Seminary and editing a newspaper. In such moments this is a most consoling thought: only one thing at a time can be the Will of God. If he wants us to act in a certain way, He has to help us with the obstacles. He always does.

The difficulties melted away like snow in the April sun. Rupert, who had started his medical studies at Innsbruck, and Werner, who was in practical training for agriculture, could arrange a few weeks' absence; Father Wasner, with permission readily given by the Bishop, found a substitute for all his activities; friends of ours, a married couple, would take care of house, little children, and guests. Even the order of the invitations worked out ideally, except for the Scandinavian countries. These had to be postponed for another year.

In preparing the programmes for this first concert tour Father Wasner went to archives and libraries to copy unpublished works. There he discovered that the ancient masters had written great music to be played on the instruments of their time, the recorder, viola da gamba, and spinet, the forerunners of our flute, string quartet, and piano. Instrument-makers in Munich and Kassel made for us a set of violas in different sizes, a spinet, and also a set of recorders: soprano, alto, tenor and bass recorders. Very serious practising started now.

In December we started out. We sang in Paris, London, Brussels, and The Hague. Everywhere an enthusiastic audience greeted us. Newspapers talked about the musical miracle of a singing family. People said how different it was from any other concert, and managers talked about return engagements ; we saw the cathedrals and castles, the galleries and museums and the wonderful countryside of France, England, and Belgium. The second part of the trip took us to Italy. We sang in Milan and Turin, in Assisi and Rome. If sightseeing had been interesting before, now it became really breath-taking. Besides those unique treasures of art stored in the churches, palaces and galleries of Italy, there were also many holy places to be visited. It was a combination of concert tour, sightseeing trip, and pilgrimage.

We sang for kings and queens ; we had an audience with the Holy Father, Pope Pius XI, and sang for him the " Ave Verum " by Mozart ; we spent ten happy days in Assisi in the steps of Saint Francis. We walked on the Via Appia, whose cobblestones had been trodden by the feet of the Apostles, into Rome, and knelt in the Colosseum and the Catacombs. These weeks were filled to the brim with happy and holy excitement, and success—success everywhere. We were " a rising star on the musical horizon."

A great thing we had learned on this trip: that music is an international language which speaks from heart to heart and doesn't need the medium of a human tongue. Whether our audience was French, English, Dutch, or Italian—in our music we could talk to them across the barrier of a foreign language. We sang to them what our hearts were so full of: " God is so good ! And He is so good to us all ! Let us forget all quarrelling in the world and be happy together. Let us love one another as He loves us ! "

Music—what a powerful instrument, what a mighty weapon !

" And the Lord said to Abram. Leave thy country and thy people, go out of thy father's house and come into the land which I shall show thee." (Gen. 12, 1.)

It was March 11, 1938. After supper we went over to the library to celebrate Agathe's birthday. Someone turned on the radio, and we heard the voice of Chancellor Schuschnigg say:

" I am yielding to force. My Austria God bless you! " followed by the national anthem.

We didn't understand, and looked at each other blankly.

The door opened and in came Hans, our butler. He went straight to my husband and, strangely pale, said:

" Herr Korvettenkapitän, Austria is invaded by Germany, and I want to inform you that I am a member of the Party. I have been a Nazi for some time."

Austria invaded! But that was impossible. Schuschnigg had said it wouldn't happen. He had said in public that Hitler had promised not to invade Austria. It must be a mistake, a misunderstanding. But the voice of this same Chancellor had just announced: " I am yielding to force."

At this moment the silence on the radio was broken by a hard, Prussian-sounding voice, saying: " Austria is dead: Long live the Third Reich! " Then it went on to announce the title of a Prussian military march.

We all went into the chapel silently. And there in the dark you could hear only sobbing and deep sighs. It was as if we had heard, without warning, of the death of a dearly beloved one.

Still in a daze, we gathered together. The birthday was forgotten. We followed Georg's eyes. He was looking at the flag from his submarine, which was hanging above the mantelpiece, surrounded by pictures and trophies from old Austria.

" Austria," he said, and tears choked his voice, " you are not dead. You will live on in our hearts."

We all wept. The little girls, huddled in my arms, cried

loud and bitterly. They didn't understand what it was all about, but their young hearts felt the sorrow of the hour.

"I want to send a telegram. The address is: Dr. Kurt Schuschnigg, Bundeskanzleramt, Wien. The message: May God bless and protect you always."

I doubted very much whether by this time any telegram would reach our Chancellor, but still I was glad and proud of Georg.

"Listen," said Werner, opening a window, and in came, in rich, heavy waves, the sound of numerous bells. We could distinguish the Cathedral, Nonnberg, Saint Peter's, the Franciscans, but there must have been many more. Father Wasner called a priest friend of his, inquiring about the bell-ringing. The Nazis were marching into Salzburg. A Gestapo man with a gun was supervising the ringing of the bells in every church.

"Close the window, it's cold," said Georg. But I knew it wasn't because of the cold; he didn't want to hear the bells. But what was that? The window was closed and the bells seemed to grow louder—really—they came out of the radio now, and before we could catch our breath, the sharp voice announced:

"Now we want the whole world to hear how the people in Austria greet their liberators. They rush to their church steeples, and all the bells in the whole town of Salzburg are ringing out their grateful joy."

Such a mean lie! Werner jumped up, his eyes flashing, his fists clenched. But what could one do? Nothing.

This was only the first lie in an endless chain. From now on we led a double life. Whatever we had lived through during the day, we listened to in an altogether different description in the evening over the air—until you wanted to take an axe and smash the radio.

"Will you do me a favour and promise me something?" asked Georg next morning. "Please don't go into town for the time being."

"All right," I answered.

He was worried enough as it was, and I didn't want to increase his anxiety.

The very next morning the children coming back from school told me that the whole town was like a lake of red, huge flags with the Swastika practically covering the fronts of the houses all over the place. The next thing we learned from friends in the town was that every house owner had been told how many flags to put out, what size, and where. Over the radio the world was informed that not even during the Festival time had Salzburg looked like that. " The happiness of its inhabitants in unsuppressible."

Lunch. Supper. Nothing had changed outwardly. Everybody was sitting at his usual place, Hans coming and going with plates and dishes, serving noiselessly. Hans was much more than a good butler. After the loss of our money, he had stayed on at a much smaller salary. He seemed to be as genuinely attached to us as we were to him. All the children were very fond of him. He was their confidant. He always seemed to have a solution to their problems. Now there was a strained expression on his face as he walked around the table.

He knew why Georg had said so pointedly at the beginning of the meal: " I think we are going to have a late spring this year. Have you seen any bulbs coming out in the garden?" and then continued to talk about flowers and the weather. He knew that we didn't trust him any more, that we were afraid of him. He didn't belong to us any longer; he belonged to the Party.

And this was only the beginning. Soon you didn't know whom you could trust. You might rush in to see a friend and blurt out your indignation, only to discover by his raised eyebrows and strange silence that he didn't share your opinion. That was bad, because at the same time he might feel it his duty to inform the authorities about your " lack of understanding."

The town looked like a military camp, German soldiers on every street corner and, so the radio told us, the German Army advancing on Vienna, wildly greeted by the people of every village or town through which they came, Austria in an ecstasy of jubilation. To this we didn't pay much attention. We knew by now how that worked. It only hurt to know the whole world was listening to these broadcasts, and the people in foreign countries did not yet know . . .

Weeks passed, and it was as if you were living by an open grave where they had buried your dearest one. We hadn't known until then how strong the love for your homeland could be. When we learned that it was forbidden by penalty of death to sing the Austrian anthem, which had to be replaced by the Nazi song; that it was a "must" order from now on to use, as the sole and only greeting, "Heil Hitler," and nothing else; that Austria was wiped off the map, incorporated into the Third Reich, that its very name had disappeared, even in its compound forms, and been replaced by "Ostmark," "Niederdonau," "Oberdonau"—each time a dagger seemed to go through our hearts.

We learned that the love for your homeland comes even before the love for your family. Automatically we went through our days. No one was concerned about anyone, but all of us were deeply concerned about Austria and her fate. Our cheerful house of song had become a house of mourning.

For days there had been a great anxiety in the air; would there be war? The last plea of the Chancellor had been: no shooting. After all, when the big brother, eighty million strong, falls upon the little, with only six million, what good does it do to fire a few guns?

Easter passed, but no "Alleluia" resounded in our hearts this year.

May came. The ban had been lifted from me. I could go into town. But after the first time I had had enough. I was on my bicycle and wanted to go shopping. At least five times I got caught. The new government had made every other road a one-way street, and one wasn't allowed any more to go this way or that. The places and streets had new names, too, and with all that superabundance of red material hanging down from the houses—you simply didn't recognise your own home town any more.

One day in May a tall gentleman came in a Gsetapo uniform and informed us that the Führer would visit Salzburg, and every single house or dwelling must be hung with flags.

"I have been told that you do not even own a Swastika flag. Is that true, sir?"

"That's correct," answered Georg.

"May I ask why?"

With a dangerous twinkle in his eye, Georg replied:

"Because it's too expensive. I can't afford it."

Shortly the gentleman returned with a big package, a brand-new, huge red flag with a black spider in the middle.

"Oh, thank you," said Georg.

"Won't you put it up right away?" inquired the zealous one.

" I don't think so."

" And why not?"

" You know, I don't like the colour. It's too loud. But if you want me to decorate my house, I have beautiful oriental rugs. I can hang one from every window."

I didn't have a quiet minute for days after this interlude, trembling whenever the telephone or the door-bell rang. Amazingly enough, nothing happened.

How long would this go on? The children came home from school saying that this or that old teacher wasn't there any more, new teachers, even a new principal, taking their places.

" This morning we were told that our parents are nice, old-fashioned people who don't understand the new Party. We should leave them alone and not bother. We are the hope of the nation, the hope of the whole world. We should never mention at home what we learn at school now."

" Mother, listen what I learned in school to-day," and little Rosmarie's eyes looked frightened. " The teacher said Jesus was only a naughty Jewish boy Who ran away from His parents. That's all. That isn't true, is it, Mother?"

" Mother, the teacher wants you to see her in school," announced Lorli, the proud first-former. I went the next day. The teacher, a strange lady, was quite friendly.

" You must do something about your little girl, or you will get into serious trouble soon," she warned me. " When we learned our new anthem yesterday " (how hard it was not to wince visibly at the word " our ") " she just didn't open her mouth. When I asked her why she didn't sing with us, she announced in front of the whole class that her father had said he'd shoot himself before he would ever sing that song. Next time I will have to report this "—and her eyes all of a sudden, didn't look friendly any more. I thanked her and went home with a heavy heart.

That same evening I took Lorli on my lap and tried to explain:

" Look, Lorli. You must never, never, do you undersand, never tell anything at school that you hear at home. If you do, Father will be put in a concentration camp, and Mother will be put in a concentration camp, and so will Rupert and Agathe and all your sisters and brothers. We'll all be put in a concentration camp if you don't keep silent. Do you understand me?"

Wide-eyed, she listened and nodded.

A few days later: "Mother, the teacher wants to talk to you again."

"What is it now?" I thought, and went with heavy misgivings. "Madam, this is the last warning. When we practised our new greeting, 'Heil Hitler,' your little girl wouldn't raise her hand, and pressed her lips together. I had to ask her repeatedly what that meant, and then she only answered, 'Mother said if I tell in school what is going on at home, Father will be put in a concentration camp, and Mother, and all my sisters and brothers!' Madam, you will understand that this is going too far."

Yes, I understand. I went home and told Georg.

"Well," he said, "only a few more weeks to go until the end of the school year. Don't forget, we are right in the middle of a revolution. Things like this are expected to happen. They will calm down. By next autumn everything may look different."

So said his lips, but his eyes betrayed him.

We went to visit some friends. First we parents were alone together and carried on a whispered conversation, emptying our burdened hearts. All of a sudden our host beamed and exclaimed, somewhat unnaturally, it seemed to me:

"What a lovely performance that was last night. I have never heard 'Fidelio' so well sung."

I didn't know what to make of it and felt a little stunned, when I heard a young voice behind me say:

"Yes, Father, I think so, too."

Oh, I hadn't noticed, the youngsters had come into the room. From now on the topic of conversation was "Fidelio," but even that got painful very soon.

"Bruno Walter will never be allowed to conduct Aryan music again because he is a Jew."

How strange these words sounded from the lips of an eleven-year-old!

"It's better to stay at home," said Georg that night, and for the first time I noticed that he looked old and worn.

School was over, and Rupert came home from the university. The stories he had to tell didn't cheer us up either.

The "thousand-mark barrier" had been lifted with the invasion, of course. Since little Barbara had announced her coming, I was not feeling so well. My old ache flared up worse than before. There was a good specialist in Munich, and Georg wanted me to see him. So we set out one day for Munich. Had I known what the doctor was going to say, I most certainly would never have gone.

"Your wife cannot have another child," he informed my husband; "at least, not until the kidneys are back to normal. They are both badly infected."

"But what can we do now?" and Georg sat down on a chair as if his knees had grown weak. He looked frightened, and I was getting angry with the doctor. I tried to motion to him behind Georg's back.

But he didn't even look at me, and simply said in a very insistent tone of voice:

"The child has to be removed, of course, immediately."

This made me indignant.

"What do you mean, ' of course '? That is not ' of course ' at all. On the contrary, it is absolutely out of the question—we are Catholics, you know."

Now the doctor seemed seriously worried.

"The child won't be born alive; this much I can tell you. I just hope," and he turned to Georg, " I shall be able to save the life of the mother. She has to go to bed and stay there and keep a very strict diet," and he started scribbling things down. "Keep her absolutely quiet—no excitement—the blood pressure is very high."

Outside in the street, I said: "I don't believe a word of what he said; but if it makes you feel better, I'll keep to the diet until Barbara is here."

"But think of the other two times," and Georg looked so worried. Yes, it was true. Since Lorli's birth in 1931, I had lost two children for the same reason, the bad kidneys.

"All right; I'll do everything the doctor said: keep quiet, diet, and all. That's all *we* can do at the moment—besides pray. Oh, Georg, let's pray especially hard that God may let us keep this little one, our Barbara."

In the midst of all his worries Georg had to smile when he heard me talk with such assurance of " Barbara." From the first moment we had known about it, we had decided that this child would not have five or six more names like the others, but only one single one: Barbara. Saint Barbara in heaven would have to recognise the fulfilment of Georg's old promise, and from then on she could send boys into this family.

" And now I would like to do something," I said. " Let's go and see the ' House of German Art.' "

That was a new picture gallery only recently opened in Munich at the edge of the English Garden, and there was a lot of talk about it. The Führer, who surprised his people so often with new talents, had taken care personally of the selections for this exhibition. He had also chosen the colour of the geraniums around the building, and in the opening speech which, of course, had been broadcast, he had stated that in the past the German people hadn't produced any art—until he had inspired them; but from now on they would soon be leading all nations.

We went and saw for ourselves. This exhibition proved all kinds of things, but not what the Führer had indicated. There wasn't a single masterpiece among the selections, but there were many pictures of such crude reality that my heart ached when I saw one school class after the other, girls and boys, walking through. (We learned that it was obligatory for all schools to visit this exhibit.) Then we came to the most famous picture in the House, for which a whole wall was reserved: the Führer in medieval armour on horseback, sword in hand. In passing by this picture, one was obliged to salute it with raised arm, pronouncing enthusiastically: " Heil Hitler." Georg didn't want to pass by; he didn't want to see any more. He had had enough. Seeing me linger behind, he said impatiently and dangerously loud:

" What are you hanging around here for—come, let's go."

I certainly wasn't hanging around for the pictures, but I had discovered something.

" Georg," I said, " I smell something: frankfurters and beer," and I sniffed, looking searchingly around.

And beyond, there was a sign. " Restaurant." Never before in any of the great galleries of renown in Vienna, Paris, London, or Rome, had we seen this combination; but when you thought a little bit, you could understand the point. In the Louvre or the art museum in Vienna, or the Palazzo Pitti in Florence, a restaurant wouldn't have made any money at all, since the works of Raphael, Rembrandt, Michelangelo and Fra Angelico made you forget hunger and thirst. It was altogether different in the " House of German Art."

Frankfurters and beer or a cup of coffee and cake were a most necessary antidote to what you had just gone through.

Gratefully we followed the smell and found ourselves in a very elegant, rather crowded restaurant. We were shown to a table, and very soon we noticed two things. Although the big room was full, there was only a distant murmur to be heard, everybody was talking low, and—no one smoked.

When the waiter came to take our order, he whispered: "Have you seen him?"

"No," I said, and then, "whom?"

"But look! The Führer! At the next table!"

And so it was. At the very next table sat the Führer of the German people, surrounded by six or eight S.S. men. The latter were drinking beer, and Hitler raspberry juice, because one of his innumerable virtues was that he didn't touch alcohol, nor did he eat meat. For the next forty-five minutes we had a first-class opportunity to look at the Messiah of the Third Reich. Among his bodyguard there must have been a good joker, because every few minutes they all roared with laughter in a way that is not considered as good manners among educated people. The gayest of all was "he." He slapped his thigh and roared so heartily that twice he started to choke. He rose from his chair, only to fall backwards in helpless merriment. His thin hair fell over his forehead, his arms waved in the air, his world-famous moustachelet quivered—he was an embarrassing sight. If one hadn't been so deeply interested by the fact that this man held the fate of many millions in his hand, one wouldn't have looked a second time at him . . .

Outside again, we walked in the English Garden, a very large and beautiful park. After a long silence Georg remembered some letters in his pocket and started to open them. Suddenly he stopped, and very excitedly handed me a letter.

"Read this!" In very polite words the Navy Department inquired whether Commander Trapp would be interested in taking over one of the brand-new submarines and establishing a submarine base " eventually " in the Adriatic Sea, and later in the Mediterranean. Georg was speechless. His own submarine had been forty feet long, had leaked, and could hold only five men. These new ones—it was like comparing Noah's Ark with the *Normandie*. He started walking fast. I could hardly keep up with him. We were on the main avenue of the park lined with red-flowering chestnut trees in full bloom.

As Georg stormed full speed towards the other end, he said: "Listen. This is the chance of a lifetime, this really is.

Just think what can be done with such a submarine. It is perfectly incredible. I am sure you could even cross the Atlantic without refuelling!" And, chewing his moustache, he reached the other side of the park, firmly convinced. " Of course one has to accept such an amazing offer."

We turned back, and suddenly he said: " But what do they mean, ' eventually in the Adriatic Sea and later in the Mediterranean '? They must be pretty sure of going there some day. That means war. I can't run a submarine for the Nazis, can I? Of course not. It's absolutely out of the question."

We were on the other side and turned again. On the way back: " But perhaps it's wrong not to do it. After all, he is the head of the State now. I am a Navy man. This is really the only thing I know and can do well. Perhaps this is the Will of God!" and he waved the letter. " Everybody is warning me to think of the future of my children, which is gravely endangered, the way we live now. . . .

Once more we turned. I knew there was nothing I could say. This is one of the times when a man is all alone—just he and his God. It is one of those dangerously precious moments when he has to say yes or no, and only he can make the decision. I prayed silently and fervently: " Thy Will be done."

Our speed slowed down remarkably. We were heading for the exit of the park. Before we reached it, Georg came out of deep, deep thinking and, a little woefully, he said: " No, I can't do it. When I took my oath on our proud old flag, I swore: ' With the Emperor for God and my country.' This would be against God and against my country. I'd break my old oath." With this we went to the station and home.

Rupert was waiting for us at the train. Our brand-new doctor! Two days before the invasion Rupert had graduated from medical school.

" Look what I've got here!" he said, and handed a letter to his father.

" Another letter!" I thought, and closed my eyes. I could hear my doctor: " Absolutely no excitement." Barbara had chosen the wrong moment, of this I was sure. This letter was also an inquiry. Would Rupert be interested in coming to Vienna and taking a responsible position in one of the big hospitals? They needed doctors.

Of course they needed doctors. All during the last months they had in a most shameful manner persecuted, killed, and imprisoned thousands of Jews in all parts of the country, and now they were short of doctors, lawyers, dentists ; no wonder the young fledgeling doctors were advanced in a hurry.

" Of course, I can't accept," Rupert said. " The only question is how to word it politely enough. They'll be quite offended. I'd have to consent to all kinds of treatments and manipulations which I am not allowed to as a Catholic—and as a man. So far, I haven't used the Hitler greeting once, and I'd like to keep out of it."

" How do you intend to earn your living?" asked his father dryly, but also proudly.

A stubborn expression came into the young face.

" There must be a way somehow. It's worth trying."

And that matter was settled.

The week was not yet over when a long distance call from Munich stirred us from our quietude for good. The Trapp Family had been chosen as representatives from the Ostmark (formerly Austria) to sing for Adolf Hitler's (" our beloved Führer ") birthday.

That meant we were made. From then on we could sing morning, noon and night, and make a fortune.

Hans had his day off. After Rosmarie and Lorli had been put to bed, Georg called the family together. He told them about the offers he and Rupert had received and about the great temptations of both, and also the very glamorous possibilties opening up before our eyes through this flattering invitation to us as singers: and what did the family think about it?

After the first minutes of stunned silence, voices were heard.

" Will we have to say ' Heil Hitler ' then?"

" Will we have to sing the new anthem on the stage?"

" How about Father Wasner? The Nazis don't like priests?"

" In school we are not permitted to sing any religious songs with the name of Christ or Christmas. We can hardly sing any Bach for that reason."

" I am sure we'd have a tremendous success in Germany with our programme, but will it be possible to keep up our ideas and remain anti-Nazi when we take their money and their praise?"

Silence.

" We just can't do it."

" This will be the third time we say no to a flattering offer

from the Nazis. Children," and their father's voice didn't
sound like his everyday one, " children, we have the choice
now: do we want to keep the material goods we still have:
this our home with the ancient furniture, our friends, and all
the things we are fond of?—then we shall have to give up the
spiritual goods: our faith and our honour. We can't have
both any more. We could all make a lot of money now, but
I doubt very much whether it would make us happy. I'd
rather see you poor but honest. If we choose this, then we
have to leave. Do you agree?"

As one voice came the answer: " Yes, Father."

" Then, let's get out of here soon. You can't say no three
times to Hitler—it's getting dangerous."

The next morning saw my husband and myself at the Archbishop's palace.

" Your Excellency," he said, " this is a secret, and I ask you
to treat it as such. My family and I have decided to leave
the country secretly very soon. Father Wasner has become
like one of us. He is in the same dangerous position we are,
since we declined the offer to sing for Hitler and he is our
conductor. Furthermore, as editor he runs many risks. It
might be wise for him to leave, too. We have nothing to offer
him. He would have to share whatever will be our part. We
go—for better, for worse—but we want to ask you to send
Father Wasner along with us if you see fit, for we have asked
him and he is willing."

The Archbishop had become very, very serious. After a
long while he got up and said:

" Will you please come again to-morrow for the answer?"

Next morning when we were ushered into the large audience
hall at the Archbishop's palace, the door opened and in came
His Excellency in his red cassock.

" I haven't talked to anyone, nor asked anybody's advice.
I only prayed for light; and now I tell you this *as your
Bishop*: It is the Will of God that you leave now and take
Father Wasner with you." Then he raised his eyes and looked
out through the window at the dome of the cathedral, and
slowly he added: " It may be that some day this will prove
of great value to this diocese."

He gave us his blessing and left.

Once more their father assembled the whole family, little

ones and all, Father Wasner included, and related what the Archbishop had said " as our Bishop." We all felt that now we were beginning a new chapter of our life, to which their father seemed to give the outline when he said:

" We have now the precious opportunity to find out for ourselves whether the words we have heard and read so often can be taken literally: ' Seek ye first the Kingdom of God and His justice: and all these things shall be added unto you.' "

PART TWO: AMERICA

I. On the "American Farmer"

It was September, 1938.

"There's the *American Farmer*," said the friendly bus driver who had taken us to the docks in London, pointing to a rather small white ship.

"How many passengers will be on board?" Georg asked the steward who showed the Trapp Family to their cabins.

"Seventy, sir. It's a nice number. I've been on big boats but I prefer this one. You get to know all your passengers. It's almost like a big family."

"How long will it take to reach New York?"

"Eleven days, sir. We are a small boat, only seven thousand tons. But you'll enjoy your trip, I'm sure."

And we did, very much so. From the first day we felt that friendly spirit on board. The passengers were mostly Americans going home. Our cabins were close together, and in the dining-room a large round table had been reserved for the Trapp Family.

"Children, I can't believe it," said Georg when we all met for supper; and with this he spoke for all of us; we couldn't believe that we were really on our way to America.

"I feel almost dizzy, so much has happened in so short a time," I said. "It all seems like a dream, Just imagine: six weeks ago to-day . . ."

"We left home for . . ."

"Mountain climbing in South Tyrol, Italy," said Werner.

"Yes, and in order not to make anyone suspicious, we had to leave in our usual clothes; and now when people on the boat see our Austrian costumes, they want to know whether we are Dutch or Norwegian," said Hedwig laughing.

"Then came the anxious weeks of waiting," continued Rupert.

"What waiting?" Lorli wanted to know. The little one had followed our conversation, wide-eyed.

"Don't you remember, Lorli," Agathe explained to her little sister, "when we were in the mountains in St. Georgen,

110

how we prayed every morning: ' Dear Lord, let us get safely
to America." You see, such a trip is very expensive, and we
had no money. There is a man in America who wants us to
give concerts there, so Father wrote to him and asked him to
lend us the money for the trip and send us the tickets for the
boat. That's what we were waiting for in St. Georgen."

" It's only a week since the tickets arrived," said Father
Wasner. " It seems incredible to me that I got the permission
to go to Italy. Do you remember how we felt when we read
in the newspaper that the very day after we all left, the
frontier was closed, and nobody could leave the country any
more?"

" Yes," said Rupert. " And how lucky we were, Father,
that the Italian Government had not allowed your Navy pen-
sion to be paid outside Italy. In that way enough back pay
had accumulated to pay for our stay in St. Georgen and our
tickets to London."

" I can't get over it," I said, " how nice it was of Mr.
Wagner to send us the tickets."

After we left the English coast, we came into rough
weather. The population in the dining-room diminished overnight. Where were all those gay people chatting happily in
many different languages, who had been enjoying last night's
supper? At breakfast the next morning the waiters in the
dining-room had hardly any work to do. I had come down
with Georg, but the rest of the large round table which had
been reserved for the Trapp Family remained empty. After
breakfast I went from cabin to cabin, and I found my poor
children in all stages of wanting to be dead, the truest sign of
seasickness.

" And you'll be next. You'd better lie down," said Georg,
and looked at me worriedly. " By the way, how is Barbara?"

" Oh, just fine," I replied, withdrawing obediently to my
cabin, which I shared with the little girls. Lemon-coloured,
they had been tucked away by their father in deck-chairs. In
spite of all prophecies of the doctor, Barbara didn't seem to
have minded the excitement of the last months, nor my in-
ability to keep to the diet and bed rest. She was supposed to
come some time after Christmas, and she seemed to have
decided to keep her date.

Back in my cabin, I went to bed as I had been told, and
waited to get seasick. For a long time I sat there, but nothing

happened. The boat was thrown around like a ball. It moaned and cracked, it bent over from one side to the other, but my stomach seemed to be undisturbable. Nobody came, and I was getting bored. And hungry. When the gong sounded for lunch, I got up and placed myself as the lone representative of the Trapp Family at the large table. Georg, the other survivor, went from one cabin to the other, holding heads.

After three days the storm was over, and the deck became populated with greenish, hollow-eyed figures, who recovered speedily in the warm sun. The sea was now like a mirror.

It had become clear to me that we had to learn English, as in America all the people talked that language.

" All right. If I have to learn English, let's go ! "

When my husband noticed my eagerness, he said teasingly :

" Do you know how you can learn English in twenty-four hours ? You learn every hour one-twenty-fourth ! "

This was about what I had in mind when, on the first clear, sunny day with people on deck, I came along, fortified with a pencil and pad, listening a little while to the people talking. When I had discovered a group of English-speaking ladies and gentlemen. I approached them and said, with the politest inflexion of my voice, the only phrase I knew :

" Please, vat is fat ? " pointing to my watch.

" A watch, " a gentleman answered, looking very friendly.

" E Votsch, " I wrote down seriously. " And fat ? " pointing to my ring.

" Ring, " he answered.

" In English, please ? " I asked.

" Ring, " he repeated and smiled.

And this was the beginning of a unique English course. These people saw my serious desire to master their language in as short a time as possible ; they also understood the necessity, and they turned out to be perfectly wonderful about it. After we had pointed all over me, them, and the immediate surroundings, I filled my little note-book with such precious words as :

E Neiff	Dschuhss
E Spuhn	Refjudschie
Dschentlmän	bjutifull
Tscheild	ei
Manni	juh

Soon we proceeded from mere words to little phrases, like:

Haudujudu	Haumatsch
Denkswerrimatsch	Hooatsdeteim

One day dear Miss Powell, an English actress and a very lovely lady, started to work on my pronunciation.

"You must not say 'vat,' darling," she told me. "Say 'Hoo-wat,'" and she brought forth a little mirror— "'Hoo-wen, hoo-were.'"

Most eagerly I "Hoo-wat-ed" into the little mirror a mile a minute, feeling very English.

One of the group, an American doctor, was a wag. He also took me alone for private lessons and, without warning, taught me a lot of slang. With a serious face I wrote down: "If someone is very excited and you want to calm him down, just say ... If you want someone to leave the room quickly, just say ..." I was deeply grateful to Dr. Johnson, but especially so some weeks later when situations arose in which his advice came in most handy.

Our Americanisation process took on speed. Our friends gave us some real American drinks: ginger ale, Coca-Cola, and root beer. Ginger ale was fine, but Coca-Cola and root beer I declined decidedly, after the first taste.

"That's too American," I protested.

We learned from Dr. Johnson the American currency: pennies, nickels, dimes, quarters, and bucks.

We learned our first American songs: " My Old Kentucky Home," and "Old Black Joe," in new settings by Father Wasner, and we liked them very much. On the last evening there was a great party, and already I could understand a good deal of what people were talking about, thanks to our new friends: Victoria Powell; Dr. Johnson; Mary Hugo, a teacher from Duluth; and the nice American consul who was going home to Cincinnati from the South Seas. They say that the first impression of a person is the real one, and you will come back to it time and again. This was our first meeting with the American people, and our impression was that they are kind, generous, and helpful.

When we woke up on the last morning, we were passing Nantucket, and soon we would be in New York. Everybody was at the railing and there, like a mirage, the tremendous towers of Manhattan emerged out of the fog.

This—was—America!

II. The First Ten Years are the Hardest

Bewildered—completely bewildered—that's what we all were when three taxis spilled us out on Seventh Avenue at 55th Street in front of the Hotel Wellington, us and our fifty-six pieces of luggage: all the instruments in their cases, the spinet, four gambas, eight recorders, the big trunks with the concert costumes, and our private belongings, one of the bags marked "Barbara von Trapp," containing all the dainty little things our babies had worn.

While I was standing on the sidewalk waiting for the unloading, I spelled slowly what the huge lighted letters said; D-R-U-G-S-T-O-R-E." It was the first time that I had met the word. In Europe we didn't have drug stores. How relieved I felt!

"That's good," I thought. "I am living in the hotel with the drug store. I can never get lost in New York!"

The tallest houses in Vienna have five or six stories. When the elevator took us to the nineteenth floor, we simply couldn't believe it, but rushed immediately to the windows and shudderingly looked down into the deep gorge, at the bottom of which crawled little cars and tiny men. That was the first thing we reported home: "and we live on the nineteenth floor!"

The friendly gentleman from our concert manager's office who had helped us through the Immigration and installed us at the hotel left us now with a friendly, "See you to-morrow."

Our last meal had been lunch on board. It was around eight o'clock and we were all hungry. But we were not on the boat any more, where we had just sat down to a full table three times a day. The cruel question had to be raised now: How much money had we? After all the pockets had been emptied and every nickel and dime from all twelve of us had been collected, it showed the fabulous sum of four dollars. That had to do for supper and breakfast, and to-morrow we would ask Mr. Wagner, our manager, for some money in advance. The boys were sent downstairs with two dollars to buy bread, butter and fruit. Fresh fruit had been scarce on board, but on land the autumn is a good time to buy fruit

114

cheaply, and so we feasted on quantities of apples, plums, pears, and grapes.

As we were all very tired from so much standing around and waiting, we soon went to bed. After putting our shoes outside the doors of our rooms, as was done in all European hotels, we retired, only to be awakened one by one by the night watchman, who informed us that our shoes most certainly would not be shined next morning, but they might not be there any more, and we'd better take them in. Funny.

Next morning I wanted my husband's hat ironed before he appeared at the manager's office in it. To my great astonishment I learned in the lobby that for this I had to go to a shoemaker's.

Georg and the boys brought back the startling news that their shoes had been shined at the barber shop!

What a strange country!

Now I went to look for that shoemaker to straighten the hat. I went around the block and around another block, and around a third block, not paying any attention to the numbers of the streets. I didn't have to. Just in case I should get lost, I knew where I belonged. It hadn't occurred to me to remember the name of the hotel. After quite some searching I found my shoemaker. The hat was ironed, but I discovered that I was completely lost. Never mind. I stepped up to the next policeman and said very politely:

"Dear Mr. Cop, where is hotel with drug store?"

To this very day I have a tender affection for those tall New York policemen, because this one got me back safely to the Wellington.

Then we went to see Mr. Wagner. The nice gentleman had come again to guide us. First we walked over to Sixth Avenue, which at that time had an elevated, also the first of its kind in our experience. I was deathly afraid, and clung tightly to Georg's arm when I had to cross the street with trains roaring over my head.

"The quickest way is the subway," and our friendly guide dived at once into a staircase, which obviously led under the street. This was really frightening. What a noise! On one side of the platform express trains thundered by, while on the other, locals came and went. The very air was in vibration, and I, simply rooted to the ground, decided not to take one single step in any direction. I was sure I would die there.

Neither I nor Barbara could stand a second more of this. Then I found myself in the inside of a howling train, from which we were spat out a few stations further along. When we reached daylight again, I was near tears.

"Georg," I pleaded, "promise me that we will never do that again."

But before he could do so, our guide had another good idea.

"This is Macy's, one of our largest department stores," he announced beamingly. "On the eighth floor they have a wonderful toy department. Let's take a quick look. The kids will like that."

And in the store we were, and for the first time in my life I was confronted with a staircase which moved by itself. First I stared at it, thinking this in itself was an exhibition piece; but when I saw people step on it and be moved upwards in front of my very eyes, I got an uncomfortable feeling, as though I were witnessing witchcraft. When invited, however, to take the fatal step myself, I most vigorously declined. Meanwhile, a number of people had gathered behind us. We were obviously blocking traffic.

"Go ahead, don't be silly," whispered Georg encouragingly. With a lump in my throat, I put out one foot hesitatingly, but when it touched that moving thing, I quickly drew it back as if I had been bitten by a snake. Now good-natured, kind-hearted Americans gathered around me, and good advice from all sides made the situation even more embarrassing.

Behind me my little girls giggled: "Look, Mother is afraid," and I wished I had never landed on this continent.

"Close your eyes, lady, and take a step."

This was the best advice given so far. Now I was on it. How would I get off? That is easier. The staircase just slides you off, whether you want to or not. And this repeated itself seven times: "Close your eyes and take a step." Seven times? Oh, no! Up to this day whenever I have to use an escalator, I close my eyes and take a deep breath.

Finally we left Macy's, and were seated in Mr. Wagner's office, and the elderly gentleman with the round, rosy-cheeked apple face looked like a very nice grandpa. We thanked him again for sending us the tickets for the *American Farmer*. He most willingly let us have money in advance. The concert tour would start in a week. So far, he had eighteen dates from the forty promised. His diction was not so clear as Victoria Powell's, so I had difficulty in understanding him. But this I did understand when he said in parting in a very comforting tone and with a twinkle: "The first ten years are the hardest!"

My greatest worry had been: how to keep Barbara's presence concealed from the world. At home I had had Mimi, a seamstress in a near-by village, a smart little woman. To her I had confided my secret problem.

"Oh, that's very easy, Madame," she had said right away. "All you have to do is see to it that you are always a little fuller above than below. Then you will just look stout, that's all."

"But Mimi, how can I possibly arrange that?" I had asked a little helplessly.

"Let me do that for you," she had answered somewhat cryptically, and told me to come back again in a week.

On the appointed day she had presented me with three sizes of supplements to my upper width. Number 3 was perfectly enormous. Unbelieving, I glanced from the pinkish things on the table to Mimi, who nodded approvingly.

"Yes," she said, "I mean it. You put them on in due time. Number 3 will even take care of twins, and no one will ever get an inkling."

It was now September, and I was wearing Number 2. With a sigh of great relief, I noticed that the contraption seemed to work. Mr. Wagner didn't give the slightest sign of astonishment at finding me so portly.

Very happy, with money in our pockets, we took our leave. No, thank you, we would not need a guide any more. We had learned how simple it was to get around in New York. After Fifth Avenue comes Sixth and Seventh; and the streets are not named after flowers, birds, trees, or famous people as they are in Europe, but they are numbered.

Now we were out for a really good meal. Months ago we had learned to read a menu from right to left; and whatever it said on the menu of the hotel dining-room, which was fastened inside the elevator, it was too much. We discovered an eating place opposite the hotel called "Cafeteria." The prices were very reasonable, and the people who owned it were Chinese and very friendly. There we assembled three times a day. The limit we could each spend for lunch was

thirty-five cents; breakfast fifteen cents; and supper, fifty
cents. But at that time, in choosing wisely, one could get
plenty—except me. I was always hungry. I tried so hard to
restrain my appetite because a glance in the mirrors and the
show windows had shown me that I was slowly taking on the
dimensions of a chest of drawers. But on that first afternoon
I soon felt ravenously hungry again, and went out to look for
some inexpensive food. In the window of a delicatessen it said:
" Sandwiches five cents." The size of a sandwich in Europe is
decided by the degree of elegance. The more elegantly you
want to serve it the smaller it will be, until it reaches the size
of a silver dollar. Thinking of the size of an elegant European
sandwich, I ordered ten. I had to wait a little while, and then
a friendly girl came with a big tray holding ten American
sandwiches! To my shame I must confess, I ate six.

Next morning we couldn't find Rosmarie and Lorli. They
were in none of our rooms, they were not in the lobby—
where could they be? After half an hour's frantic search, when
we had almost reached the point of announcing to the police
that they had been kidnapped, one of the bellboys came and
notified us that they were riding up and down in the elevator.

" Yes, Mother," and Lorli's eyes sparkled, " up to the
twenty-seventh floor. Now I can write to Susi, this is nine
times as high as she lives!"

None of the people we had met on the boat lived in New
York. We had no acquaintances and no friends, no letters of
introduction to anybody. We discovered the New World by
ourselves. We learned the difference between uptown and
downtown. We found out that museums and galleries could be
visited free of charge. We discovered the vast possibilities in
a drug store, where on a Sunday when everything else was
closed, you could buy anything from pencils and stationery to
hot-water bottles, alarm clocks and jewellery of any kind and
description. We learned to sit at the counter with poise and
order in the tone of an old-timer: " Ham on rye," or " Two
soft-boiled medium."

Wherever we met fellow-countrymen, we heard true adventure stories. There was, for instance, the lady who wanted to
buy cauliflower.

" How much?" she asked the grocer.

" Ninety cents," was the answer.

"What?" She was outraged. "Behold your cauliflower. I can become cauliflower myself for forty cents around the corner!"

(Such things happen when you take words from your own language and translate them into similar-sounding words in English, thinking they mean the same thing. The word for "keep" in German is *behalten* and "get" is *bekommen*.)

Another incident happened to a priest friend of ours. When he first arrived in this country, he went to a religious house.

The lay brother who showed him to his quarters asked:

"Is there anything else you would need, Father?"

"Well," said Father thoughtfully, "a set of new bowels every Saturday. Just hang them on the door-knob."

The lay brother seemed so startled by this request, that Father had to point to a towel in his room to illustrate his wish.

Every morning we walked through the ravine of 55th Street out into Fifth Avenue and over to Saint Patrick's Cathedral. It is as large as one of the largest cathedrals of Europe ; but there on the corner of 50th Street, it was overshadowed by skyscrapers. After Father Wasner's Mass there, we walked back to the Chinese Cafeteria.

We needed a laundry. As with everything else, it was a question of money. One morning the boys, who had walked back from Mass a different way, told us triumphantly they had discovered the cheapest laundry in town, a Chinese man who asked six cents for a pound. We collected all our dirty laundry. The Chinaman came and smiled and nodded. Two days later he came back, and we couldn't believe our eyes. He must have boiled everything at once in one tub, and since one of our blue aprons was not colour-fast, everything, every blouse, every white shirt, every handkerchief, was of the same deep blue.

We didn't want to take the little girls on the concert tour. We looked for an inexpensive boarding-school. Mr. Wagner's office helped us. We found the Ursuline Academy in the Bronx for thirty-five dollars a month apiece. When we left Rosmarie and Lorli in their new school, we felt sorry for them. They had grown up in the country surrounded by meadows and trees, and there in the Bronx there was only asphalt; not a single blade of grass was to be seen. But the Sisters were very nice and kind, and the children would learn English faster than we.

We really didn't need any organised sightseeing trip through New York. Every time we stepped out of the hotel it become a sightseeing tour. There were, for instance, the fire-escapes, those enchanting, winding stairs outside of the houses. The trolley cars and the buses were different from the ones at home. There were news stands with so terrifically many different papers and magazines, and the newspapers themselves of the size of sheets for a baby's bed. Enchanted, we watched men climbing on something like a throne and cute little coloured boys falling over their shoes in a holy fury until they were as shiny as mirrors—and this right on the street! Why didn't the people all stop and watch? Well, and then the people! There were Negroes, men, women, and children. Oh, and what cute children! There were Chinese people—maybe they were Japanese, one didn't know. Most of them talked English, but we also heard Italian and German, Yiddish and Greek. And there was the climate. Although it was now October, it was hot and damp, quite different from Salzburg. Then there was the speed. What an experience to go down Broadway for the first time when the movies were over. What a noise, what light, what a rush; or to cross Fifth Avenue around noon, or Wall Street at five o'clock. All this first and most overwhelming sight in New York didn't cost much. It was thrilling and frightening—it was wonderful and terrible— these first steps into a new continent: *our* discovery of America!

While the others explored the city, finding places like the Public Library, Central Park, Radio City—Barbara and I preferred to stay at home in the hotel. My mind was stubbornly set on learning English. I read every advertisement in subways, on buses, on street corners, and in elevators. I memorised the menus, and with the help of a small dictionary started to read a copy of the *Reader's Digest*. I was envious of Father Wasner, who already read without a dictionary. Rupert was outrageously good. He had been presented by one of the ladies on the boat with a fat book, called *Gone With the Wind,* and he was already half through it. I wanted so badly to catch up with them.

I invented a method all my own, in which I wanted to apply what I learned about one word to as many like-sounding words as I could find. This proved later to be fatally wrong, and it still haunts my English of to-day. For instance, I had learned: freeze—frozen. I wrote underneath in my precious little notebook : " squeeze—squozen," and " sneeze—snozen." When I admired the tall " hice ' in New York, I got quite offended because they seemed to overlook the logical similarity between " mouse—mice " and " house—hice." I talked about the " reet " of my teeth, feeling perfectly correct in doing so. Wasn't it " foot—feet " after all?

Especially it is bad if you translate the Bible literally. The effect was tremendous when I informed a group of people with whom I had come to talk in the lobby, that: " The ghost was willing, but the meat was soft."

But what a triumph you have after so much trouble and work, after so many unexpected fits of laughter, after hours of spelling and learning by heart, when one day the nice coloured man in the elevator says to you:

" Ma'm, yo' English is getting better every day."

From then on you can hardly discover any trace of an accent in your speech. You feel rewarded for all the blood, sweat, and tears of the last week's English battle.

Then comes the great day when you feel like graduating. The man at the desks asks you sincerely and confidently:

" How many years did you study English before you came to this country, madam?"

Mr. Wagner must have made a mistake when he said, " The first ten years are the hardest." He must have meant the first ten *days!*

III. Getting Settled

The day arrived when a big blue bus with the inscriptions " Special Coach " and " Trapp Family Choir " quivered in front of the Hotel Wellington, swallowing the fifty-six bags and the ten members of the Trapp Family Choir. As we had no home in America, we had to take all our luggage with us. A friendly, broad-shouldered driver greeted us. Very soon he grasped the idea that his was the noble task of introducing us into American ways of thinking and living, as we were the greenest greenhorns he had ever driven over American soil.

He did a perfect job. From time to time he used to holler: "Let me explain something to you!"

That was a warning which made everyone stop doing whatever he was doing whether it was eating, sleeping, reading, or merely looking out of the window, and listen enraptured to an explanation such as, for instance: "This is the largest airplane factory in the world"; or, "Now we are coming into Kentucky—hillbillies and moonshine." Remarks like this were somewhat mysterious to us. In my little dictionary I could find neither "hillbillies" nor "moonshine," but somehow it was an impression of the State of Kentucky which stuck with me for years.

But all that came later. First the blue bus drove to Easton, Pennsylvania, up the steep hill of Lafayette College for our first concert. Mr. Wagner and all his office staff had come. All of a sudden we became conscious of the fact that this was not just another country—this time we had crossed an ocean; this was now a new continent, and to-night was the first concert. Would it be a success or a failure? These reflections made us more and more solemn, and when finally the great moment came and we had to step out into the footlights, we felt again as miserable and self-conscious as we had been in Salzburg. But there was no Lotte Lehmann sitting in the first row. A thinnish applause greeted the bashful new-comers.

Applause! A whole book could be written about it. The innocent reader might think that applause is applause. How wrong he is! If he only knew how many shades of applause exist, and how finely the ear of the artist is tuned to it. There is the thunderous applause of the later years, when you come back to a hall which is packed with people who are looking forward to your return. How heart-warming and inspiring! There is the polite, thin, applause lasting not long enough to let you get to the middle of the stage to make your bow—the mild applause for the new-comer or beginner—not very helpful. There is the hardly audible applause delivered by society ladies in gloves at morning musicales, and sustained by politely covered yawns. You don't care much because if you have advanced to morning musicales, you don't mind any more. There is the warm, lengthy, enthusiastic applause after a good concert from a sincere audience, demanding encores. That makes your forget your tiredness and makes your encores the best numbers of your programme. There is the routine applause of well-educated people, the concert public, whose ancestors had always attended concerts; who, while they applaud, mildly and steadily, gaze with raised eyebrows into their programmes, questioning: "Who was that fellow Palestrina, or Vittoria, or Thomas Morley? We have never heard of them before, but it was quite nice." These are the staunch supporters of musical life, the ones who give a new-comer a chance.

Later you learn to accept applause as a challenge, and to work up a concert from the "thinnish" to the "enthusiastic" response.

But that is later, and this was our first performance in the New World. In looking over the programme now, we know: first, it was much too long; secondly, too serious. What helped us to perform the miracle, to reap at the end some really enthusiastic applause, must have been our whole-hearted sincerity. The people in the auditorium simply couldn't help feeling that it was all entirely genuine. It came from the heart, and that's why *they* took it to heart. After each number when we came backstage, Mr. Wagner's face looked a little less tortured, and Georg finally even whispered:

"He said it's going fine."

But at the end of this evening we were perfectly exhausted. After a whole concert tour nowadays we are not so "out" as we were in Easton, Pennsylvania, on that memorable October day.

But you get *that* excitement only once. Slowly it becomes a routine, the bowing and smiling, coming and going.

Very soon we found out that the concerts were not the hardest part of the evenings. That started with the receptions. The very word we learned to dread. We were lined up in a row, and people started to file by, murmuring their names and insisting that they were very glad to meet us, or that they had enjoyed every minute of the concert. You try very hard to meet each remark with a genuine smile and say something intelligent. After a few dozen times you have exhausted your meagre vocabulary, and even the smile on your face freezes into a permanent wave. You forget to change the rings from your right hand to your left, and you don't dare do it now, but regret bitterly this grave mistake. You wonder how many inhabitants Roanoke, or Springfield, or Lexington has. You start wondering whether these are all new-comers, or whether the first ones have lined up again and are coming for a second round of handshaking.

Georg especially hated that kind of torture with all his heart. I hardly dared look at him when, after a concert, the chairman of the Ladies' Committee would announce cheerfully:

"And now we have a little reception."

Who could describe my astonishment, however, when one evening as we were lined up as usual, I noticed a mischievous light in my husband's eyes after we had already greeted at least a couple of hundred ladies. He simply beamed and said something to each one. I had to find out, and moved closer and closer, until I had, all of a sudden, to use my handkerchief to suppress a severe attack of coughing. I had heard him say in our native tongue:

"376, 377, 378 . . ."

And each lady answered, quite flattered:

"Oh, thank you!"

He was counting them! When we finally met, coffee in hand, all he said, with a twinkle in his eye, was:

"611!"

Once we gave a concert in a small college conducted by Sisters in the south. It was their first concert, and Reverend Mother, a tiny, elderly nun, was nervous. She was bustling around backstage with eyes like a frightened bird. I felt sorry for her, and wanted to console her. Then it flashed through my mind: "If somebody is very nervous and you want to calm him down, simply say . . ."—and I said it as friendly and reassuringly as I could.

"Oh, Reverend Mother, please keep your shirt on."

She did.

Another time—this was in the Middle West—we were invited to a Bishop's house. By that time we had learned that there are Bishops and Bishops. Some are informal and paternal, so that you can almost forget who they are and say, full of confidence, "Father." Some, however, can never quite take off the mitre, so to speak. They are Bishops every inch of them. There you meet all the dignity and authority of the

Church. It is quite breath-taking. Such a one had invited us to dinner, and, of course, it was a formal dinner with speeches and so on. There were also his Chancellor, a few Monsignori, and other dignitaries, and, sitting next to the Bishop, I was exhausting my best English a mile a minute. After grace was said, on the way from the dining-room into the library, the Bishop and I met in the doorway. Politely he motioned me to go first, but, of course, I knew better, and wanted His Excellency by all means to precede me. Motioning to each other, we caused a traffic jam. Then again the teaching of Dr. Johnson came to my mind. "If you want someone to leave the room quickly, just say . . ." And so, looking up into the Bishop's eyes, I said confidently and with my best enunciation:

"P-lease, Bishop—scram."

It was now December, and I was wearing Number 3. The newspapers mentioned the "stately" mother, the "majestic" figure, but that was all. I avoided looking into mirrors or show windows, and was wondering whether it wasn't perhaps twins, and whether the other one would be a boy. It didn't occur to me, however, to ask a doctor. After all, I wasn't sick; not really, at least, because very swollen feet and a severe ache in the back I had learned to get used to.

Barbara and I found it harder each day of this tour. It was not exactly fun to be jostled for hours and hours in a bus, to change clothes several times each day before, during and after concerts, to rehearse every morning and sing every evening, to climb in and out of the bus, to sleep each night in a different bed, and to eat those strange new kinds of food, such as mayonnaise on a pear (pooh!), or ham cured with sugar, or melons with pepper and salt. On the other hand, it was absolutely impossible to procure for love or money a single bite of one of the special dishes for which I longed with my whole being. It seemed so silly, but often for hours and hours I would dream of Schinkensemmel, or Apfelstrudel. But Barbara and I didn't have time to pay too much attention to these little hardships.

Everything went along smoothly until a certain evening, the last one before reaching New York. We had given a concert in a very small town in Delaware. We had stopped at the one tiny hotel in the place, which was built alongside the railroad

tracks. With no presentiment of what was to come, I said
" good night " to my family and went to my room, which was
the only one on the fourth and top floor.

I had hardly fallen asleep, when I dreamt I heard a lion
roaring. I tried desperately to run away, and it seemed as if I
couldn't. In the moment of utter desperation I woke up. But
what was that? Wide awake, I could still hear the lion, and
his roar came nearer and nearer. I was scared to death. Now
something terrific was right beside my bed, roaring and thun-
dering. The whole house was shaking. My bed was shaking,
Barbara and I were shaking, too. Then the noise faded away,
and with a heart pounding loudly, I listened until everything
was quiet. Just as I was about to settle down to sleep, the
whole thing started all over again, coming now from the
opposite direction. Now I was really quite frightened. I
wanted to call for someone, but there was no telephone in the
room, and besides, just that night I had forgotten to inquire
the room numbers of my family.

And so the night crept on with a crescendo and decrescendo
of the lion's roaring, and with Barbara and me becoming more
and more frightened all the time. Toward four o'clock in the
morning I felt an unusual pain. Now I became really alarmed.
What if something should happen here and now in this lonely
little hotel room.

In moments of extreme danger you become supersensitive.
Out of the grey past pictures arise going way back to your
childhood days perhaps, and you are able to understand
voices which, in everyday life, you are too busy to hear:
" Maria has helped—Maria will always help." Have you ever
been in one of the famous pilgrimage churches in Austria,
Italy, or France—in Lourdes, for instance? Have you seen
there the hundreds of little votive pictures, crutches, silver
hearts, waxen hands and feet—the words repeating themselves
all over the place, scribbled on the wall, embroidered in old-
fashioned style, painted simply or artistically: " Maria has
helped—Maria will always help." Such places do not grow
overnight. They are the result of the tears and prayers of the
centuries. If you have knelt in such a house of prayer, if you
have ever taken your troubles and worries there—when you
are thousands of miles away, a grown-up person, all of a
sudden the image of all this will come back to you in a
moment of severe fright.

I sat up in bed straight, folded my hands, and said aloud:

"Dear Blessed Mother, help me. Let nothing happen to this child. I promise to bring her in my own arms to your chapel in St Georgen, and a large candle, too."

How I wish that no one were too "grown up" to understand what inexpressible peace can settle down on a troubled heart. It is the peace which is promised to them who "become as little children." I lay back and fell asleep almost immediately, sleeping calmly and long into the next morning.

When I awoke, my entire family was assembled around my bed, looking weary after a sleepless night, and highly astonished to find me sleeping so soundly. They, too, had been disturbed by the roaring lion which, on investigation, proved to be nothing more than the trains between New York and Washington.

While passing through New York, we wanted to report to "Grandpa Wagner" how nicely everything had gone with the concerts. This was Barbara's eighth month, and by now I was convinced that anyone had to be blind, deaf and dumb *not* to notice "it." In the course of the conversation I remarked casually:

"Of course, I shall be happy when the baby is finally here."

The old bachelor jumped up as if stung.

"Whose baby?" he asked.

"Why—mine——" I said innocently.

The effect was tragic. He cancelled immediately all our remaining concerts, and our tour came to a sudden end then and there. He really had had no idea—wasn't that too bad! What a blow! Fewer concerts meant less money, and we needed every cent.

What next?

A little depressed, we went to the Hotel Wellington.

There we met Mrs. Pessl, the mother of Yella Pessl, the harpsichordist, and a former acquaintance from Vienna. She and Professor Alexander Wunderer, the first oboist of the Vienna Philharmonic, had already encouraged us greatly during the first stages of our musical life back in Austria. It was good to see her again.

"Well, children," she said, and came directly to the point, "there is only one thing to do if you want to have a success in America. You have to give a Town Hall concert. Every artist who wants to make his way has to do that. And for that you need a publicity agent."

" A what?"

" Why—don't you have someone to do publicity for you?" she asked, quite astonished.

" To do what for us?" we asked lamely.

That was too much for that kind-hearted lady.

" But children, children, this is terrible!" And there and then she called the girl who did all the publicity for Yella, and had her come over to the Wellington. We shouldn't lose a day, Mrs. Pessl insisted.

Edith Behrens came, and she and Mrs. Pessl explained to us the meaning and importance of a concert in Town Hall, New York. It would cost us $700, and at this thought we shuddered, but it might be worth millions, and this made us hopeful again. It should be soon, as soon as possible, and Mrs. Pessl's eyes wandered over me. No Number 3 could cheat her, I could see that. The first date available at Town Hall would be in two weeks, Edith learned on the telephone. Father Wasner approved the idea most heartily, and with a deep gulp we accepted.

" That gives us time for publicity," Mrs. Pessl said, very satisfiedly; and so it did. Our peace and our privacy were gone. Edith followed us with one or more photographers wherever we went, whatever we did, and pictures appeared in the newspapers: The Trapp Family Eating at the Chinese Restaurant; The Trapp Family Sightseeing; Craning Their necks at Rockefeller Centre; Window Shopping on Fifth Avenue; Looking Out of the Bus; Getting into a Trolley car; Crossing the Street; Coming Down Steps. We got used to the idea of jamming up steps in stores, hotels, movie houses —everywhere—to be photographed while doing so; Father Wasner (oh, how he hated it!) Directing, Reading a Score, Eating English Muffins (his favourite breakfast dish); Getting a Shoe Shine.

Then came the interviews by *Time* and the *Times, Life,* the *Herald Tribune,* the *Sun,* the *Daily News, P.M.*: " When did you arrive in this country?" " How do you like America?" " Why did you leave Europe?" " What is the difference in the food?" " Why do you wear those funny dresses?" We tried desperately to talk about music and our programme, but

Edith assured us that the public was much more interested in the other questions.

One single consolation there was to this awful Town Hall project; we could make our very own programme; and we did. For the first part we chose the three hardest madrigals we knew (after all, we wanted to show what we could do!), and the second part was devoted to the whole motet: " Jesu, Meine Freude," all forty-five minutes of it. That was a programme to our heart's delight.

As we were completely unknown, Mrs. Pessl had suggested that her daughter, then already quite well known as a harpsichordist, should join us in this recital, taking turns with us, in rendering pieces on the harpsichord.

The great day came, and with it our great chance. Earnestly and solemnly we stood on the stage in Town Hall; no make-up, no unnecessary smiles, all worthy of the occasion of performing Bach's great motet. The hall was three-quarters filled. Much of it was " paper," much of it was curious managers from all over the place, listening to this new attraction, a singing family. How good were they? Would they appeal to the broad public all over the country? Was there any money in them? Many of them left before the last chorale sounded solemnly through the air: " Jesu—meine—Freude!"

Some people, however, were seriously touched, and some even came to tell us so. A tall, young-looking man rushed backstage and with moist eyes, taking my hand in both of his, said in a very moved tone of voice:

" This I am sure was exactly as Johann Sebastian would have wanted it to be. You must come and see me at the Public Library. I am Carleton Smith."

Now came a sleepless night of waiting for next morning's newspapers, which would decide our fate in print. Either we were made now, or . . .

But next morning Edith, Yella, Mrs. Pessl came excitedly, each waving newspapers, exclaiming: " Wonderful! Excellent! Grand!" They read to our buzzing ears that we were " like no other family alive "; that " when eight members of one family sing and play as did the Trapp Family ensemble at Town Hall on Saturday afternoon, music would seem to have achieved one of its miracles "; " as a choral group the Trapps proved admirable. They evidently possess either perfect pitch or an extraordinary memory for tonality. The

E

effects achieved in Praetorius, Lechner, Isaac numbers were already those of musicians of discriminating taste. Their work in the difficult Bach motet was accurate and veracious in the conveyance of the composer's intentions. It was all-round musicianship "; crowned by an important daily which gave two long columns and said, among other things: " There was something unusually loveable and appealing about the modest, serious singers as they formed a close semi-circle about their self-effacing director for their initial offering ; the handsome, portly [!] Madame von Trapp in simple black, the others in black and white. It was only natural to expect work of exceeding refinement from them, and one was not disappointed in this "; and so on, a long column. By now, most of us were hopping around in joy and jubilation. Finally someone intoned: " Nun Danket Alle Gott," Bach's great hymn of thanksgiving. We were so terribly happy that we were " made," although we didn't know yet what that meant.

On Monday morning we paid the promised visit to the Public Library to see Carleton Smith. He was talking to a gentleman whom he introduced to us as Professor Otto Albrecht from the University of Pennsylvania in Philadelphia.

" Otto is a music lover, and I told him all about you," Carleton beamed. " By the way, what are your plans?"

" We are looking now for a place where we can stay for the next weeks. This hotel is so expensive," said Georg.

Professor Albrecht's face lighted up.

" I know a furnished house which is for rent, not far from where I live."

And, in a genuinely American way, he made a couple of telephone calls and everything was fixed. The rent was one hundred dollars a month, and we could come right away.

Georg and the older girls went ahead with Otto Albrecht to fix up the house. It was very close to Christmas now, and Barbara and I simply loved the idea of settling down and having nothing moving under us for a while. The house was in Germantown, Philadelphia. When we got out at the North Philadelphia Station, there were Georg and Otto Albrecht and several cars waiting. On the way from the station to Germantown Georg said:

" It is perfectly incredible. Absolute strangers, friends of Otto Albrecht, stop with their cars, come in, find out what we don't have enough of. Then they return with spoons, forks and knives, glasses, blankets, one brought a bed, another one pots and pans, and one even came with a carload of records. There is a victrola in the house. Now they have come with their cars to help me to install my family. They are Quakers, from the Society of Friends, as we used to call them in Europe."

The Society of Friends. They were not new to me. After World War I when I was in my teens, a student in Vienna, the famine became so terrible that it was impossible to study or do any work. For a bite to eat one would have sacrificed everything. In that most crucial moment the Society of Friends came to Vienna with food, and every student and every school child got one hot meal a day. If it had not been for that one hot meal a day, I might not be alive now. Such a thing one never forgets ; and there they were again crossing our path—the " Friends."

When we entered " our " living-room, the fire was burning in the fireplace, and from the victrola sounded the great " Hallelujah Chorus " from *The Messiah.*

Georg, noticing how tired I was, took my hand and said reassuringly: " And all these things shall be added unto you."

Yes—even friends—one of the rarest gifts in the world.

IV. Barbara

The next day was Sunday, and in the evening two cars stopped before our house. Out came Otto Albrecht and Rex Crawford, a friend of his.

" We want you to meet Henry Drinker," said Otto, and told us to get into the cars. " He is a great music lover, and once a month he has a big party in his house, singing *a cappella* music just the way you do. I am sure you'll like each other." And off we went.

In a very large music-room there were about a hundred and twenty people gathered around a tall, boyish-looking man. We were too far at the back and couldn't hear what he was saying, but that wasn't necessary. He was simply radiating enthusiasm. Then he raised his hand—silence fell upon the hall, and he conducted his guests in the *Requiem* by Johannes

Brahms. We had been given the music, and we sang with
them. Mr. Drinker was neither a great conductor, nor had
he an outstanding voice, but never mind that. He was as
sincere a lover of music as we had ever seen. When an
especially beautiful passage had just finished, he interrupted
the music, dropped his hands, and said with contagious fer-
vour:

"How marvellous! How simply wonderful! Oh, let's do
it again?"

And we did it again. After an hour of such intensive
music-making everyone seemed to be ready for the buffet
supper. During this intermission we were introduced to Mr.
and Mrs. Drinker. Otto told them about us. At the end of
the evening, when most of the people had gone home, Otto
asked us whether we would sing one number for our host. We
gladly did, and chose our favourite Bach chorale: "Wie
schön leuchtet der Morgenstern." With this one number we
sang our way directly into the hearts of the Drinkers.

Christmas passed quietly and peacefully. Dorothy and Rex
Crawford, Miriam and Otto Albrecht, our neighbour, Mrs.
Hurlburt, and some more of their friends, the Drinkers included, dropped baskets and packages at our door, and the
poor refugees from Austria saw themselves confronted with
six turkeys and baskets with pies, fruit, and other edibles,
books and toys for the little ones, and books and records for
the grown-ups. When Georg had seen my tears at the mere
prospect of having electric lights on the trees, he went all over
Philadelphia, and finally found real candles and candle-
holders. Now the last cloud had vanished, and it was the most
beautiful Christmas we could remember. With Peter and
John we had to say to our friends: "Money we have not,
but what we have, we give you," This was our music and our
prayers. We invited them on Christmas Day for a party to
help us with our many cakes and pies, and sang for them two
and a half hours—the best we had to give.

The day after Christmas I saw it was time for Barbara and
me to get ready. I asked Rupert to bring me Barbara's suitcase, and emptied its contents on my large bed—all the
precious little things: baby clothes of fine muslin with tiny
pleatings; costly embroidered coverlets; delicate little silken
gowns; fancy show dresses; every item with a tiny embroidered monogram and coronet. I had just laid them out all

over the room when Mrs. Drinker appeared on the scene. Not without pride I showed her these little treasures.

Quietly her eyes wandered over my exhibition, and perfectly unmoved, she asked dryly:

" And who is going to wash and iron all this every day?"

I hadn't thought that far ahead yet. When Mrs. Drinker noticed this, she took over immediately. With the eyes and mind of a general she surveyed my almost desperate situation: a battle to come, with no ammunition to fight it.

" Pack that silly stuff away and come with me. We'll go shopping for some sensible things," I tried hard to swallow my hurt feelings, while she tried just as hard to drive home the point. While driving over to Germantown she said: " A baby doesn't need all that. Three shirts, a couple of dozen diapers, and a pair of rubber pants is enough. You have to become practical now—practical, don't you see? You are poor, don't forget." The words sounded hard, but her eyes showed a kind heart. How lucky I was to have such a sturdy friend to put things straight for me in those bewildering days.

Of course, I had expected that we would go to a baby shop, as I would have done in Europe. But, oh no! It was one of those big department stores, in which I always felt so absolutely lost.

But Mrs. Drinker headed straight for the baby counter. There we bought a few sober-looking knitted things, which I didn't even recognise as shirts at first. Mrs. Drinker took no notice at all of my reserved, almost hostile silence towards American baby clothes. She did all the shopping necessary, and in no time we were sitting in the car again and driving home. She was very pleased. It was a " White Week," and everything was marked down.

" Aren't you glad?" she said. " You have saved more than three dollars on the whole deal!"

" Yes, Mrs. Drinker," I answered meekly, but unconvinced.

There wasn't much time to lose now, and I went out to find what, with the help of my dictionary, I learnt was a " midwife," like the indispensable Frau Vogl. I learned that in the whole neighbourhood there were only three midwives to be found, all of them Negresses. At that time I was a little afraid of coloured people, whom we had never seen in our country, and who still seemed to us a little legendary.

Oh, time and again, Mrs. Drinker told me that one *had to*

have a doctor and one *had to go* to a hospital to have a baby. I was finally persuaded to make one concession: the doctor. But go to a hospital—that was ridiculous. Why? What for? I wasn't ill. In Europe you only went to a hospital when you were dangerously ill, and many people died there, but babies were born at home. Would they in the hospital allow my husband to sit at my bedside? Could my family be in the next room, singing and praying?

I tried to explain that a baby had to be born *into* a home, received by loving hands, not into a hospital, surrounded by ghostly-looking doctors and masked nurses, into the atmosphere of sterilisers and antiseptics. That's why I would ask the doctor to come to our house.

But I had to find the doctor first. I tried many, but each time I mentioned the word "at home," they didn't want to take the case.

When I was very tired and discouraged, I found a young doctor in our neighbourhood, young and a little nervous about the whole idea, but he said he would come.

I consoled him.

"Don't you worry. There is nothing wrong. I know all about it. It is the most natural thing in the world. You just have to sit in the next room, and I'll call you when I need you."

His eyes widened, and he opened his mouth to speak, but closed it again in utter amazement.

And so it happened. The evening came when I knew it was time. Everything went the old way. The family gathered in the living-room, reciting the rosary aloud. Then they sang hymns. Then they prayed again. The doors were open, and I could hear them. Georg was there next to me, and his good, firm hands patted me once in a while, as he repeated: "Soon she will be here, our Barbara," and then we both smiled. The doctor had not come yet.

Then it had to be: "Call him now and tell him to be quick!"

When he arrived, he looked troubled. He had a nurse with him—a sweet-looking young girl. They were washing their hands when all of a sudden I had to squeeze Georg's hand very hard, and time seemed to stand still. Then I heard a funny little squeak. The doctor turned to me and said—I couldn't understand what—and then carried something in his

right hand through the room. It was all over. At that minute
a full chorale downstairs started: " Now thank we, all our
God!"

The doctor, in the middle of the room, turned around.

"What's that?" he gasped.

And then I saw what he was holding: my precious baby—
head down!

My heart almost stopped. I was sure he would drop her.
"Watch out—don't break her!" I cried.

"Her! Why—it's a boy!" he said reproachfully.

What? I must have misunderstood. Georg bent over me.
"Barbara is a boy," he smiled.

My heart started singing: " Now thank we all our God!"

V. What Next?

The little baby boy weighed ten pounds two ounces when he
was born.

When he was three days old, he was carried into the parish
church, where Father Wasner received him into the fold of
Christ in the Sacrament of Baptism. He was given the names
Johannes Georg. That was our first great family feast in
America.

From his tenth day on, he cried bitterly almost day and
night, until I desperately called the doctor. He discovered
that there was nothing wrong with the precious boy; he was
only hungry. I felt guilty and ashamed. But how horrified I
was when I learned that I should give him orange juice—raw
orange juice! and squeezed bananas—raw bananas! With my
European upbringing that meant almost murder. But
Johannes was an American boy, and throve very soon on
carrots, spinach, and juices, and there was no more crying to
be heard.

The next weeks were a wonderful change. For months we
had been living in our suitcase, every day another hotel.
Now we were all together again. The little girls were back
from the boarding school in New York, and we had our own
household. The older girls took turns in the kitchen and
household duties, and Martina helped me with the baby. The
lovely young nurse, Anne, showed us how to do things in

America. There were, for instance, the diapers. In Europe they are square. You fold them so that they are three-cornered and knot them around the baby's legs. In America the diapers are oblong, and you pin them with safety-pins. That and the raw orange juice took me a long time to get used to.

Almost every day we had company: the Albrechts, the Crawfords, the Drinkers. They took the family to the symphony concerts on Friday afternoons; to the Franklin Institute; to the Art Museum; for rides through beautiful Fairmount Park; to parties at this or that friend's house.

Through Mrs. Drinker we got acquainted with Ravenhill Academy, where the little girls went to school from then on. Unlike the school in the Bronx, it was situated on the very outskirts of town, surrounded by big gardens. Very soon Rosmarie and Lorli felt very much at home with the Sisters and the new schoolmates.

The question arose now: what to do next? Much of the money we had earned with the concerts had gone into the boat tickets which Mr. Wagner had advanced, and the daily living expenses, and the Town Hall concert. Our first contract had been for forty concerts, of which we gave only eighteen, but Mr. Wagner said he could easily have fixed the other dates after Christmas if it hadn't been for the baby. There was nothing we could do about that. The contract had expired anyway.

We had arrived in America on a visitor's visa, which expired in March. Our friends advised us to apply for an extension, which we did after Christmas. Everybody assured us that these extensions were a mere formality: they were always granted. But our visitor's visa only allowed us to earn money by giving concerts. The money which was left would carry us, if we were very thrifty, perhaps into the summer.

What next?

These were the things we talked about, Georg, Father Wasner, and I, in these days, but as we couldn't find any solution, all we could do was go on with *our* part: to seek the Kingdom of God.

Every morning we walked to the parish church, where Father Wasner said Holy Mass.

The weather can be disagreeable between December and March. The house was small for our large family, and it was very poorly furnished. There wasn't enough of anything, in spite of the Friends' help. We simply were too large a family. Most of all, there was never enough food; and if you are hungry you easily get irritated, especially when the immediate future looks insecure. So for the moment, to seek the Kingdom of God was, for us, to take it all with a smile and in genuine gratitude, because weren't there many others much poorer than we?

One day in February Mr. Wagner arrived unexpectedly at our house. He brought with him an agreement, again for forty dates. Since the baby was here, there would be no trouble, he promised, and happily we signed our second American contract. The tour would start in September. One great worry was lifted off our shoulders. From September on, we would be secure again—and until then? Oh, there would be a little concert here and there, our friends assured us, and if there was only one a month, we could keep alive on it.

Then one morning came the fatal letter. The U.S. Immigration and Naturalisation Service informed us that our application for extension of temporary stay was not granted, and we had to leave the United States at the latest by March 4. This was a cruel blow. We had burned all our bridges behind us, and would never dare go back home again, and now America wouldn't allow us to stay here.

Now—what next?

It was such a shock that for the moment no one could say or think anything. Each one swallowed his private disappointment and fear.

One thing was certain: we had to leave. There wasn't much time to secure tickets for so many people on one boat. In the newspaper we saw that the *Normandie* would leave New York on March 4. Georg went to the French Line and was able to secure twelve tickets third class to Southampton. After these tickets were bought, there wasn't much money left, and what would we do in Southampton?

Then it came to us: A year ago we had had an offer from a Danish impresario for an introductory tour of Scandinavia; two concerts in Copenhagen, two in Oslo, and two in Stockholm.

" Let's get in touch with this manager to see if he can take us now."

It had to be done by cable, although that again was expensive. Then came fearful days of waiting. And what if he did not accept us?

We started to dissolve our household, giving back the borrowed blankets, beds, spoons and forks. The Crawfords had kindly offered to store in their attic things which we didn't want to carry with us twice across the ocean; so we started dividing our goods into "takables" and "leavables," as Hedwig said. But the usual cheerfulness was missing. Everybody went about his duties rather silently.

About two thousand years ago something similar had happened to a group who left their homelands, merely following an idea represented by a star: the three Holy Kings. When each one of them notified his people that he was about to set out on a long journey to go and find somewhere a new born King, their friends must have shaken their heads in disapproval: "I hope you won't regret it." Then for weeks and months they followed the star, which guided them into the land of the Jews, into the very capital, Jerusalem, and then—it disappeared; and when they thought they had reached the goal, they found themselves in complete darkness. Nobody knew anything about a new-born King, and the words were ringing in their ears: "I hope you won't regret it."

What a temptation to wish never to have left. But after God had tried their faith and their patience, He came to their rescue. They were shown the way, and the star appeared again. "And seeing the star, they rejoiced with exceeding great joy."

That was the story we talked about on March 1. Only three more days to go, and still no answer from Europe. It was a dark moment, and no star to be seen. Then we chose the three Holy Kings for our special patron Saints. We promised them to imitate their faith and patience. Would they please ask God to have the star appear again?

It did. Next morning came a night cable: EVERYTHING READY FOR FIRST CONCERT MARCH TWELFTH COPENHAGEN.

Our new faithful friends helped us in closing the house and getting the family on the right train to New York. The Drinkers sent their chauffeur with the car for Georg, the baby, and me.

In New York we all assembled at Carleton Smith's house, and from there we went to the boat. Last kisses and good wishes, then shouting and waving, and then the *Normandie* was towed out into the open sea. Soon the skyscrapers disappeared in a golden mist, and we found ourselves on the way to Europe.

The *Normandie*! What a noble boat, and what a wonderful crew! Although we were only third-class passengers, the French Line went out of its way to make our stay as enjoyable as possible. We got a pass with which we could stroll at any time all over the boat. We were invited to eat in the tourist class, and for our rehearsals a special drawing-room on the first-class deck was assigned to us, adjoining the wonderful winter garden. The third-class cabins were much more luxurious than our places on the *American Farmer* had been. But nicest of all was the behaviour of the crew. The stewards and stewardesses, the waiters and officers were all so polite that for four short days we almost forgot that we were poor refugees with a very uncertain future. On board the *Normandie* we were treated as celebrated artists. People knew about our Town Hall concert and we were asked to give a gala performance on the last evening together with René Le Roy, the flutist. Champagne was served free of charge afterwards. The boat itself was a dream of beauty, and the size was such that it took me eight minutes from my cabin if I wanted to reach the upper deck with Johannes for some fresh air. I felt like asking: When will this town arrive in Europe? When we had barely learned which passage to take to reach the Chapel Number 1, the Movie Number 2, or the Swimming Pool Number 3, it was time to get ready for Southampton. But four days was not too short to create a love for the boat and its crew, and when, years later, we learned of the dreadful disaster the *Normandie* had suffered in New York, we felt as if something terrible had happened to an old close friend.

VI. *In Sight of the Statue of Liberty*

From the day in March when we left on the *Normandie* to that day in October when we again set foot on American soil we learned a lesson, the greatest of them all. In Bible English it is called: " Be not solicitous," and translated into everyday language, it means: " Don't worry."

We started out by worrying.

" What shall we eat, what shall we drink, what shall we put on?" These must be the very elements of human worries, as Our Lord picks them out when He says: " Be not solicitous for your life, what you shall eat, nor for your body, what you shall put on." Then He explains how useless it is if we *do* worry, how it gets us nowhere: " Can any of you for all his fretting add an inch's growth to his height? And if you are powerless to do so small a thing, why do you fret about your needs?" After having told us how senseless it is to worry, He tells us what to do. We should look at the lilies, how they grow. Your Heavenly Father knows well what you need. Therefore, seek first the Kingdom of God and all these things shall be added unto you.

And this half-year was set apart for teaching us this lesson, that we should never forget it in the future.

There we were, a group of twelve people and a little baby who, for the next seven months, had no home, and except for six concerts, which would provide for three weeks' living, did not know the answer to the question: what shall we eat, what shall we drink? The political horizon was filled with dark clouds; the outbreak of war seemed imminent; the atmosphere in Europe was full of suspicion and mistrust; we didn't know a soul in the Scandinavian countries, nor any of the languages; the permission to stay was carefully restricted by every country to the time necessary to give our concerts. Europe was just waking up to recognising " tourists " as " fifth columnists."

It would have been easy for God to show us His plan for this period, how there would be enough concerts, enough money, extensions of our stay, helpful people, generous invitations, new friends, and new love. But then we again would not have learned that most valuable lesson, so He left us in the dark, and gave us only one thing at a time.

In this way we passed the time until the end of May in Denmark, Sweden and Norway. When our prolonged extension had almost expired, an invitation from Holland with permission to stay for twenty-eight days at the country home of friends took care of the month of June. In July we dared to pay a short visit to Austria. The men of our party, however, stayed away. Back in our old home we learned with horror what one short year can do to an invaded people, how it had embittered some while it changed others, and falsified their way of thinking and living. We learned the shocking truth that " home " isn't necessarily a certain spot on earth. It must be a place where you can *feel* at home, which means " free " to us. Soon we met our menfolk in St. Georgen, south of the border, where I fulfilled my promise and carried little Johannes up the hill and lit a big candle in the shrine of Our Lady. For August and September we had our engagements in Sweden. But not all of these were neatly put down on a list in advance. No, each concert brought forth the next one, when an excited member of the audience invited us to his home town for a performance. By then we were well advanced in our course: " Don't worry." It really would have been a waste of time. All the practising and rehearsing of this new art we needed badly when in September, 1939, the war broke out. All frontiers were closed, foreigners were asked to depart, concerts already promised were cancelled. But we had learned by then that the Heavenly Father knows what we need. More than before, we tried to concentrate on " Seek ye therefore *first* the Kingdom of God " in doing our daily duties, rehearsing the programme for the next American tour, taking care of all the little chores of everyday life, and trying most concientiously *not to worry*. At the moment before our last permission to stay in Sweden expired, Mr. Wagner again advanced the money on the next concerts and sent the tickets for the SS. *Bergensfjord.*

When, on October 7, 1939, we finally docked in Brooklyn, Hedwig said with disappointment in her voice:

" In spite of the war, this crossing was not dangerous and not a bit exciting. Nothing unusual happened."

Photographers and newspaper men crowded on board, searching for sensational stories. Our picture was taken, too: The Trapp Family Alone, and The Trapp Family With Kirsten Flagstad, who also happened to be on the *Bergensfjord.* Then we saw Mr. Snowden, our friendly guide of the first year in the crowd. He waved and called, " Welcome home! " and then it was our turn with the Immigration Officer. Rupert had an immigration visa this time, whereas the rest of us were all on visitors' visas.

I was so relieved and so grateful after all these months of uncertainty to have reached the haven again, that when my turn came and the Immigration Officer asked me the fatal

question: "What time do you intend to spend in America?"
I didn't answer as I was supposed to: "Six months, sir, as my
visa says," but I simply blurted out: "Oh, I am so glad to be
here—I want never to leave again!"

Their whole attitude changed. The members of the Trapp
Family were held for the very last, and then they were questioned and questioned again; but nothing we said could undo
the dangerous impression my most unwise outburst had
created: these people don't want to leave again.

Everybody was gone; we were the only passengers on
board. But we were not allowed to leave. A tall policeman
came and watched us, and all we could do for the rest of the
day was play shuffleboard among ourselves and admire
beautiful Brooklyn. We didn't understand yet why, but we
were prisoners, and so Hedwig had got her highlight for this
trip after all: to-morrow we should be taken to Ellis Island.

A large motor-boat came, and our policeman took us over
to the island with the large prison building, where the doubtful
people from foreign countries were scrutinised. Lucky Rupert
went to the Hotel Wellington and started from there to try to
get his family out of jail, because jail it was. When the huge
door was closed behind us, the door which had no knob on
the inside, we were led into a hall as big as the main waiting-
room in Grand Central Station.

It was one of those beautiful, hot October days, Indian Summer; but tradition on Ellis Island has it that on October 1 the
central heating has to be started. The windows, high up and
barred, could not be opened, and the temperature was around
eighty degrees.

"Could I get out with the little ones into the fresh air?"
Martina approached a warden.

"Every day for half an hour after lunch," was the answer.

We still didn't understand why we were there. We had been
told by some officers of the ship that our papers were not quite
clear, and it was only for some formality that we were being
taken to this place. But we couldn't remember having done
anything wrong. It must be a misunderstanding, and Rupert
would come in the afternoon and get us out. So we tried to
make ourselves at home on two large benches facing each
other. With the help of our suitcases we boarded up a corner,
and as there was absolutely nothing else to do, we started to
sing. It is always good to rehearse. Soon people grouped

around us, and it seemed that their strained faces looked less
worried after listening for an hour to our music. Then we
started to talk. There were Spaniards, Jews, Greeks, and a
large group of Chinese. We learned that the Chinese had been
here already for eight months. Most of the people had been
here for weeks Goodness—and our first concert was supposed
to be on the fifteenth. A lady from Poland said:

" At least it doesn't cost anything; it's all paid by the State.
And if America doesn't let you in, the ship line on which you
came has to take you back in the same class, at its own cost,
to the port where you started out. It won't cost you a cent."

How terribly consoling! That meant another third-class
passage on the *Bergensfjord* to Oslo!

" And if that country in Europe doesn't let us in, what
then?" asked Werner.

" Well," said the lady cheerily, " then the ship has to keep
you. There is an Italian family on the ocean travelling for the
eleventh time between Le Havre and New York. And it
doesn't cost them a cent."

What a prospect!

One of the wardens came, a fat lady with greasy hair and a
stern look, and handed each one of us a sheet of paper where
it said in German:

" Information: You have been asked to come to Ellis
Island as there is some doubt concerning your passport. You
will come before the special hearing as soon as possible, and
you can plead your cause. If you can't speak English, you
will get an interpreter. There is no reason to get excited. You
will be treated very politely." Then it said in capitals:
" DON'T TALK ABOUT YOUR AFFAIRS WITH YOUR FELLOW PRISO-
NERS "; and at the end it added: " Please be patient. We
don't want to keep you a moment longer than we absolutely
have to."

Then it was time for lunch. We were lined up by twos and
filed through the door, which was opened with a special key
from the inside. As we passed by, the fat lady tapped each
one of us on the shoulder, counting. Georg disliked this extremely.

On long tables the food was served in tin plates, everything
on one plate.

After lunch we were taken out into the yard by twos. The
yard was closed in by a high wire fence, and what should we

see greeting us through the bars from a very short distance, but the Statue of Liberty! The half-hour was very short; the whistle blew and we had to go back in.

Finally Rupert came, and he didn't look very cheerful.

"One of you must have made the remark that she wants to stay in this country. That makes you all suspicious, and the authorities don't want to let you in. That's what Mr. Wagner was told."

Soon Rupert had to leave. The visiting hour was over. We asked him to call our different friends to help us out.

Johannes had started to walk while we were alone on the *Bergensfjord* on that last day. Now he practised walking all day long. He was not quite nine months old, but was very strong. Between singing and playing with Johannes the long hours passed. We filed through the door again for supper, and afterwards we had to take all our luggage and were led upstairs into a large dormitory. The windows were small slits up on the wall, and the door had no knob on the inside. The bright lights were left on the whole night, which made sleeping hard, and every so often the door opened and the warden came in and counted noses. Each time Johannes woke up and cried unhappily.

Next morning we were awakened at six o'clock. The newspapers had heard of the Trapp Family at Ellis Island and sent reporters and photographers. From time to time a policeman came in and called a name, the name of the lucky one who should go into his hearing. In the afternoon Rupert reported that he had called Mr. Drinker, who had promised to do what he could. How quickly one gets used to things: to be marched by twos, to eat from tin plates, to be counted numberless times a day and night, to windows next to the ceiling and doors without knobs. Father Wasner could say Mass each morning, but only we were allowed to attend, no one else.

Mr. King, the big boss of Ellis Island, came to visit us. He was especially nice and said that even Toscanini had been here briefly, and many other famous artists, and we should not worry. In the afternoon Elizabeth, Carleton Smith's wife, came with a big basket of fresh fruit and newspapers with our picture: The Trapp Family Playing Recorders on Ellis Island. What publicity! Elizabeth assured us that our friends were working busily to get us out.

We were singing a good deal now, because the people were

so happy about it. It took their worried thought away from their own problems. We were getting very popular on Ellis Island.

On the fourth day we were pretty much at home, with a daily routine, during the day rehearsals, recorder practice. Father Wasner was working on a new composition. We wrote letters back to Sweden, letters of thanks. Quietly we waited for our hearing. We had been told from all sides that this was merely a formality; we just had to wait for our turn. An extremely nice letter from Mr. Drinker helped a great deal to cheer us up. In the afternoon the door opened again, and this time *our* name was called. The policeman led us over to the court-room. There we took a solemn oath that we would tell the truth, the whole truth, and nothing but the truth, and then the long questioning started. For two and a half hours we (I particularly) were questioned. Why had we come? What did we intend to do? Where did we intend to live? On what boat did we intend to leave again? We didn't know? Didn't we have return tickets? Didn't we intend to leave? And so on. After we had told the truth, the whole truth, and nothing but the truth for two and a half hours, the judge said he didn't believe us, and we were dismissed.

" And the *Bergensfjord* is sailing to-morrow," went through my mind.

Our companions were eagerly awaiting the outcome, and when they heard what had happened, all looked very gloomy. Each time a prisoner is released, they all gather around him and applaud heartily while he is let out the door. This they had intended to do with us. But quietly we all sat down again and—started to sing. It was the only thing to do if we didn't want to cry. In the middle of a song Georg was called out. He came back shortly afterwards, and his beaming countenance spoke the word: we were FREE. Our friends had approached their Senators and Congressmen, vouched for our honesty, and word had come back from Washington to Ellis Island and the misunderstanding was cleared up.

It was touching how our fellow prisoners selflessly shared in our joy. First endless applause while we got hold of our bags; then one more song; more applause; another song, and finally our best *Jodler* at the end. Outside Rupert was waiting, and in the motor-boat we waved over at the Statue of Liberty, this time from the other side of the fence.

VII. Learning New Ways

Now we were really in America, and although I wouldn't have dared to whisper it to myself even on top of the Empire State Building or in the middle of Central Park at midnight, for fear the Immigration Officer could hear it again, I knew this was for good.

A touching reunion with the Hotel Wellington! For the first time I noticed that there were green carpets in the lobby and that the bellboys and elevator boys wore a handsome purple uniform.

A great many other things I seemed to discover all anew, and many times my family exclaimed:

" But, Mother, don't you remember from last year?"

No, honestly, I didn't. It seems that an expectant mother is more occupied with herself, taking in from the outside world merely the bare essentials.

The first concert was in Town Hall, New York, on a Saturday afternoon. It was a week-end, and one of those balmy days in the autumn when the foliage in the country is a riot of colour, and people simply didn't feel like staying in town and listening to Palestrina. Result: a small audience. Further result: a disappointed manager, who had thought we were a better " drawing card " than the box-office receipts showed.

For the week-end of our Town Hall concert our Philadelphia friends had come to New York. How wonderful to see them again! The Crawfords offered most kindly to take the little ones into their home. Rosmarie and Lorli could go to their old Academy again, which was not too far from the Crawfords' home. The parting was always a bitter moment for all of us ; but at that time I still thought children had to go to school, and everything else had to be sacrificed to this fact. Later I was to learn better.

That was the year of the World's Fair, and we spent some exciting days on the grounds, which seemed like a book of fairy-tales.

What that word " drawing card " meant, we were to discover in a painful way during the next weeks.

In a short time we learned to know some of the largest auditoriums in this country with a seating capacity of between 2,500 and 4,000, and we always had ample opportunity to meditate on the colour of the upholstery; in one place, a silvery grey, in another, a deep red, or a warm golden yellow; because it was not disturbed by human forms—the huge halls seemed practically empty.

An otherwise large audience of eight hundred or nine hundred got almost entirely lost in that vast space. What was the matter? Well, Grandpa Wagner had "invested quite some money in the Trapp Family Choir," and now he wanted it back. That's why he had them sing in large halls; but he forgot to tell the people about it. From our short encounter with publicity we had learned sentences like this: "You can't tell the people often enough. You just have to rub it in, or they forget." For these people in Hartford, Connecticut; Harrisburg, Pennsylvania; Raleigh, North Carolina; or Washington, D.C., it was not a question of forgetting, but of getting acquainted with the fact that their presence was requested at the first concert of the Trapp Family Choir in their town. Quietly we came and quietly we left, and Mr. Wagner got more and more disgusted. At that time he used pink stationery. At each hotel and at each concert hall those pink envelopes awaited us, filled with gentle reproaches about how badly we had done the last time. This is not exactly a tonic before a concert.

We got more and more nervous and discouraged. We knew we had rehearsed very conscientiously. This "Missa Brevis" by Palestrina *was* a masterpiece, and we *did* sing it well. You just feel such a thing. We also knew that the people who had come to our concerts went away deeply moved, and their words of appreciation were sincere. But something seemed to be wrong with us—what was it? We tried so hard, even if so tired, to be nice and jolly at the reception—to please everybody; still, the pink envelopes came in greater numbers.

At our first visit at his office Mr. Wagner had received us with the news that so far he had been able to arrange only twenty-four concerts out of the forty. This time it was due to the war. But there wouldn't be any difficulty in booking the rest as soon as we had started to sing. Now the pink letters threatened there would be no more dates if the halls continued to remain empty. It was very disheartening.

Otherwise, we had a wonderful time. There was the big blue bus again with the same driver, who continued in his friendly way: " Let me explain something to you." But this time with our advanced English we understood much more of what he explained.

He noticed with satisfaction that in another point, too, we were advanced: that was our luggage. In vain he had tried to explain to us that when he had driven the Don Cossacks from coast to coast, each one of these grown-up men had carried only one suitcase.

" And these kids don't seem to get along without three bags every night," he had sighed.

I hadn't argued more about this with him for the simple reason that I hadn't enough English words to argue with. Otherwise I would have tried to make him understand that I had to unpack my three suitcases every night, put the little stacks of nightgowns, shirts, panties, etc., neatly into the drawers, my different framed photographs, alarm clock, New Testament, Missal, rosary, candle-holder, and little vase with flowers on my night table ; hang the dresses in the closet, and so on. It is just as well I didn't even try. I am sure he would never have understood that. But now with the help of the Crawfords' attic, a lot of stuff was left behind, and each one of us made his entry into and exit out of the daily hotel with only one big, and one small bag.

This time my camera was not packed away, but at my right hand always.

" Please—stop! " I would cry at the most inopportune moments, when the driver was just overtaking a big truck on a well-populated highway. Then when we finally managed to halt, I ran back and took a picture of such an exciting item as a huge roadside advertisement, shouting to the world that you can't live without a Ford.

Or I took an American graveyard on the roadside: simply stones stuck into the grass—no little hills covered with flowers, no shrines, no iron or carved-wood crosses ; these cemeteries didn't look as if they were frequently visited and tended. There were no seats or benches beside the graves. There was no wall around the graveyard, and no tender love hovered around the place, and this made Martina exclaim:

" I wouldn't like to be buried in America."

In Gettysburg we took snapshots of the battlefield, of the monuments and cannon. In Europe every ancient town has such a memorial as this, but in America it is the only one we remember.

In the South we were enchanted with the Spanish moss and the cypress trees growing out of the water. And with the Negroes. Bashfully at first, later more and more encouraged by the always hearty and kind reception, I asked whether I might take a picture of this old grandma rocking on the porch with the cutest little darky on her lap, or of that group of sturdy coloured boys picking cotton or harvesting peanuts.

What a different kind of sightseeing! This time it was not cathedrals, galleries, or museums. This spectacle was prepared directly by the hand of God: these huge oak trees, these cypress swamps, these endless woods in the Blue Ridge Mountains. They were not man-made, and neither was the Natural Bridge, nor the caves in Virginia, nor Niagara Falls.

" How does it happen," mused Agathe thoughtfully one day while we were riding through the endless pine forests in North Carolina, admiring the bright red soil, " that I feel at peace and quite at home here in America as long as I am in the wilds? The minute, however, traces of civilisation appear, these roadside advertisements, for instance, or these ugly wooden houses—oh, it makes me so unhappy! It spoils the countryside, and then I don't like America."

Funny—I felt the same way, and we found that the others did, too. There was some disharmony that man had brought into the ravishing beauty of this country.

" If I think of the villages in Europe," said Rupert, " in the Alps or in France or England or Scandinavia, there the houses fit into the landscape, and the people do, too. They seem to be a part of it."

" Yes," said Werner, " that's true ; and those old farms at home look so nice and well kept, with flowers all around. Look ! " and he pointed through the window. We were just passing a run-down farm with rickety barns. " Why don't these people take better care of their houses for their children and grandchildren?"

" Ah," put in our driver, who had listened to our spirited conversation, " that's where you make a mistake. Who wants to live in the country with children and grandchildren? They just want to make some money, for instance, cut down some wood or get a few good crops, and then move back to town and take it easy."

"You mean," gasped Hedwig, "that the people on these farms won't live there for ever?"

"Sure not," he laughed, and his mere tone of voice said, "you crazy Europeans."

"Who wants to work hard from dawn to dusk if you can make more money much easier in a factory in the next town?"

Well, of course, that solved the riddle why so many houses were not painted.

Anyway—this side of America was very strange to us. We had to learn much more about this country and its people before we could fit the many little pieces together.

Our next stop was Hartsville, North Carolina. There we would learn some more. There was no Catholic church at the place, but on Sunday morning the priest came from the next parish in his car and said Mass in a private home, and we assisted at it. Afterwards we all had breakfast together, and Father Plicunas, the friendly priest of Lithuanian extraction, wanted to show us his church.

"Come on, let's run over. It's just around the corner," he insisted, and packed his car full of as many Trapps as possible. Off we went at hair-raising speed, forty-five miles to his rectory.

"But you said it was . . ."

"Yes, just around the corner. Why—that's nothing. My parish is . . ." and he quoted a fabulous number of miles, length and width, the size of at least three dioceses in Europe.

More and more as we rode along we were impressed by the foremost quality of America; it's terrific size.

One day in December as we drove through the lovely winter woods and were admiring the increasing beauty of the landscape as we came farther north, the "Let me explain something to you," was heard again.

"Now we are entering the State of Vermont. No use looking out of the window. This is not a progressive State. All they raise is gravestones."

The last of our twenty-four concerts was in Philadelphia in the Academy of Music in the afternoon. It was two days before Christmas. Afterwards we were invited to dinner at the Drinkers'. Harry Drinker received us radiantly.

" I have a house for you just across the street."

After supper we all went to look at the house. It was furnished, and he really meant it, we could move in immediately.

" Instead of paying me in cash, pay me in music." And so it happened: a most perfect exchange of goods. Each one gave what he had; and we sang for him and with him the master works of the sixteenth and seventeenth centuries which he hadn't discovered yet, and both parties were truly happy.

VIII. The Miracle

The inevitable happened. After Christmas came one more pink letter containing a cheque for the rest of the money due to us, and notifying us how much Mr. Wagner esteemed us as artists of first rank, but that he did not think we were made for American audiences, and he did not see his way clear to the renewal of his contract, but he wished us God's choicest blessings for a successful future.

That was a deadly blow.

Georg and I went to New York to talk to Mr. Wagner, but he only quoted sadly a five-figure number, the money he had lost on us.

" You will never be a hit in America. Go back to Europe. You will be a great success there."

Back to Europe, with the Swastika stretching its black spider legs all over the map.

Very depressed, we went to the Wellington after a little supper at the Chinese Cafeteria. In the lobby we met the husband of an artist whom we knew. They also had come from Austria some time ago. Perhaps he knew the secret of appealing to the American public, and we confided to him our troubles. Something gleamed in his eyes which now, years later, I can distinguish as the genuine joy of getting rid of a rival. He talked very earnestly and very persuasively.

" Mr. Wagner is perfectly right. You must go back to Europe. Let me advise you: go right away before you spend your last dollar. Your art is too subtle. People here will never

understand it. This is no place for you. Go back to where
you belong and be happy. In three days the *Normandie* sails
again. Let me help you to get tickets. May I call for reservations?"

This was perhaps our darkest moment. The star had
vanished altogether. But how grateful was I when Georg said:
"No, thank you, I can do that myself," and rather stiffly we
parted.

Then we sat upstairs in our room and looked at each other.
What now?

"Our Bishop said that it was the Will of God that we go to
America. So many people have told us since that our music is
more than just earning our living. We must keep on singing.
Let's look for another manager."

At the time of our first Town Hall concert we had made
the acquaintance of several managers. One of them I still
remembered very clearly, a Mr. F. C. Schang from Columbia
Concerts, Inc. When we had met him, he had talked about
the English Singers, whose manager he had been. The very
way he spoke of them impressed me. It was not cool and
business-like, but warm, personal, respectful.

"It must be nice to work with a manager who feels that
way about his artists," I had thought then. Now this came to
my mind.

Next morning we called Mrs. Pessl to find out how one
approaches a manager. So far, managers had approached us,
and we didn't know anything about the other way around.

"Well, that's easy," she answered. "All you have to do is
ask for an audition," and she explained to us what that was.

With trembling hands I dialled CIrcle 7-6900 for the first
time and asked for Mr. Schang.

"Am mother of Trapp Family Choir," I informed him in
my halting English. "Want to ask audition. Will be possible?
When?"

"Georg, he sounds awfully nice," I said happily. "Right
away he said a week from to-day."

Quite consoled, we went back to 252 Merion Road, which
from now on was our address. No more "c/o Management
Charles Wagner"; a real address of our own.

Anxious faces awaited us, and great was the joy when we
told them: "A week from to-day."

We rehearsed as never before. Three hours in the morning,

three hours in the afternoon, and an hour after supper. We chose the most difficult and intricate pieces, and perfected our performance in most concientious work.

The big day came, and we stood on the stage of Steinway Hall. Our audience consisted of Mr. Schang and Mr. Coppicus, the two managers of the Metropolitan Music Bureau, a division of Columbia Concerts, Inc. Mr. Coppicus had heard us once in Vienna.

We sang the very best music in the very best way we could, as solemnly as possible, as was fitting for Bach and Palestrina. We sang for half an hour ; then the gentlemen arose and went out. They sent word back that they felt very sorry indeed, but they did not think they could manage the Trapp Family Choir.

Silence.

In the train going home we discussed what it might have been that made them refuse us.

" Perhaps we should have sung Josquin des Prés instead of Palestrina. That's even more difficult and would have shown better what we can do."

" Or we should have played more on the recorders. Mr. Schang seemed to like them."

" Next time let's do . . ." I said.

" What do you mean, next time?"

Into Georg's tired eyes came a faint hope.

" Surely you don't want to give up now," I said belligerently. " What else is there to do? We'll study some more, ask them for another audition, and next time they'll take us ! "

It didn't even occur to me that we could have given auditions to other managers in New York. Two weeks passed in which we rehearsed " Alle Psallite," an organum of about A.D. 1500, the motet " Ave Maria " by Josquin des Prés, one piece by Dufay, and a difficult trio sonata by Telmann for alto and tenor recorders and spinet. Then we felt up to the occasion and wrote to Columbia Concerts, attention Mr. Schang, for another audition. We held our breath waiting for the answer, which came by return mail: the first envelope with the weighty words, " Columbia Concerts, Inc." The answer was most cordial: " Come any time. Let us know twenty-four hours ahead."

We fixed the date. The evening before, we couldn't go to sleep, it was so exciting. To-morrow our fate would be decided. If they refused us again, we would have to ask the

Department of Labour for permission to earn our living as maids and cooks.

Again we stood on the little stage in the Steinway building. This time there were more people present: girls from the office and others. If a shy smile had crept in between numbers the first time, it certainly was suppressed on this occasion. The quaint chords of the sixteenth century couldn't afford such worldly gestures.

My heart started sinking when one girl after the other quietly left the room. Also the gentlemen left. We were waiting. Then I was called out and informed by Mr. Coppicus' secretary that it was definitely "no."

I just couldn't believe it, and I couldn't bring myself to break this cruel news to my family.

"Will you please wait for me at the Wellington," I said to them cryptically and disappeared. This was my very last chance. I at least had to find out *what* was wrong with us. I asked my way through to the nice young lady who had just talked to me.

When I had found her, I said: "Why Mr. Coppicus not take us?"

She looked so kind, so sympathetic; she took me over to the window and explained in a low voice:

"Mr. Coppicus said the Baroness has absolutely no sex appeal. They will never be a real attraction."

"Oh," said I, and looked blank, and then quite hopefully, "thank you very much indeed."

"Sex appeal." I memorised the words. For heaven's sake, I mustn't forget the precious phrase before I found out what it was. I had been too proud to admit to the girl that I didn't even know what it was that I lacked so badly, but I would find out.

But how? Well, in a book store. Around Christmas I had been in Scribner's on Fifth Avenue and remarked on their vast music department. It must have to do with music, of course. "Sex appeal," I murmured from time to time as I walked the blocks over to Scribner's. Now after Christmas it was quite empty, and right away a nice-looking young man wanted to know what he could do for me.

"Music," I said, and he led me over to the big alcove which was lined from floor to ceiling on three sides with books on music. After a little searching, I discovered that they were

arranged alphabetically. Quickly I moved over to " S ":
" Shostakovitch ; Sibelius ; Strauss, Johann ; Strauss, Josef ;
Strauss, Richard ; String Quartet ; Symphony." I read all the
titles aloud to myself, but " it " was not there.

The young man came.

" Can I help you with anything?"

" Yes," I said somewhat haughtily. " Book on sex appeal,
please. Need it for concerts."

Why did he disappear so quickly and never come back?

Scribner's had disappointed me. I really had thought they
had a book on *everything*. All I could do now was go into the
lion's den and find out right there. So back I walked to
Steinway Hall. On the way I mused to myself whether " sex
appeal " was something you put on your head, whether it is
part of your appearance, whether you buy it by the ounce or
by the inch. Shortly afterwards I found myself on the
fifteenth floor of 113 West 57th Street, face to face with Mr.
Schang.

After having shown me to a seat, he was leaning back in
his swivel chair, and with a big cigar he produced a smoke
screen between us. What a moment! All of a sudden I
became conscious that this was my last, my very last chance,
and there was my bad English.

" Why you not take us?" I started out.

He didn't answer right away. Then suddenly he sat up and,
taking the cigar out of his mouth, he started to explain.

" It has nothing to do with your musicianship, I want you to
understand. Already at your Town Hall concert I recognised
you as good artists. Still, it's the worst programme I've ever
heard. That programme. *That programme!* That piece by
Bach was forty-five minutes! That's for a few music en-
thusiasts, but do you think ordinary people want to listen by
the hour to quaint ancient tunes? And the recorders! They
sound like a calliope. But by far the worst thing is your
appearance—solemn and deadly serious, you come and go
like a funeral procession. No charming smile and no good
looks either," and he continued in real disgust: " those long
skirts, high necks, hair parted in the middle, braids in the
back, shoes like boys, cotton stockings! Can't you get decent
store clothes so one can see your legs in nylon stockings, get
pretty, high-heeled shoes and put a little red on your face and
on your lips?"

" No," I said gravely, " we can't." And I was choking-full of explanations as to why we couldn't, but I knew I would get hopelessly tangled in long English sentences.

Silence.

" This is—last word? " I finally ventured to ask.

" Yes."

The battle was lost. All of a sudden I felt very tired. The strain had been great ; the rehearsals of last week, the excitement of the morning, and the tension of the last minutes. And this was America, of which everyone had told us—here you can say what you want, do what you want, wear what you want. An urgent desire took hold of me to let this man in front of me know how I felt. All was lost ; I couldn't spoil anything any more. If I couldn't say it in words, I'd say it anyhow.

And I took a thick book lying on his desk, slammed it on the table, looked at him as crossly as I could manage, and said :

" I thinked—America free country. *Is not!* "

After this annihilating speech, I turned and walked out. My tears he should not see.

While I was waiting for the elevator, the nice young secretary tapped me on the shoulder and asked me to come back into Mr. Schang's office.

" Maybe after all you'll make it all right," said an altogether different Mr. Schang—" win over the American audience at large, I mean. I'd like to try for one year," and he sounded genuinely interested. " But it will need a great deal of publicity and advertising, and that is expensive. Could you spend —let's say—five thousand dollars on advance publicity? "

" Will try," I said, and then we shook hands.

All I let them squeeze out of me at the Wellington was : " Mr. Schang is almost sure that he will take us ; not quite, but almost." Then I lapsed into silence and prayed for the money. In the bank we had exactly $250.

The same evening we went over to the Drinkers' and sang with them for two hours. Afterwards I told my story.

" If we can advance five thousand dollars, he will take us," I finished, avoiding looking at my family, but looking pleadingly at Mr. Drinker. Would he have an idea?

There—while Sophie was still laughing to tears about me at Scribner's, Harry Drinker's voice could be heard :

" I'll lend you half the money if you find somebody for the other half."

I closed my eyes in excitement, and also in order to think hard.

When I opened them again, I said: " Mrs. P."

That was a rich lady whom we had met at a concert at the Cosmopolitan Club in New York, and she had said with such genuine cordiality: " If you ever need any help, let me know."

Mr. Drinker went to the telephone and called Mrs. P. She said " yes." The miracle had happened.

The very next morning—he had said there was no time to lose, it was late in the season—I stood in Mr. Schang's office and handed him two cheques, each one for $2,500, and said simply:

" Here, borrowed for a year."

There was great quiet in the room until a warm and sincere-sounding voice came from behind deep blue clouds:

" Congratulations!"

Again I wanted so very badly to " say something." I pressed his hand, and he must have seen in my eyes what was in my heart when I said:

" You not regret—never—I r-r-r-really mean it!"

When he walked with me to the elevator, he said:

" I believe in you as musicians, but now we have to try to coin the gold lump of your artistry into practical currency, so that everyone may take something home from your concerts.

" For this we shall start by changing your name. ' Trapp Family Choir ' sounds too church-y. I am the manager of the ' Trapp Family Singers.' "

IX. Merion

When I arrived in Merion Station, I didn't go straight home, but stopped first at the Drinkers' house. The last twenty-four hours I had lived—we all had—in a pink fog. Things were too good to be true. As they slowly began to sink in, a deep gratitude took hold of me, and not only gratitude, but also a new feeling of responsibility. There were people—Mrs. P., Mr. Drinker, Mr. Schang, who, while believing in us, risked some-thing. Not only should they not be let down, but some day

they should have real reason to be proud of us. Now we
simply *had* to become the best artists in our field for the sake
of these people who trusted in us.

And this I had to tell to the Drinkers before going home.

There we experienced in our own life what other people's
trust does to you. It releases new powers; new depths in your
soul, hitherto unknown to yourself. It sharpens your will and
fixes it on the goal—it helps you to do the impossible. That's
the way God works with us. He always gives us another
chance. Why do people use this magic wand so little? It
would transform this world into a paradise.

A new life had started for us when we entered the "house
across the street." Our application for extension of temporary
stay had been granted this time on account of war conditions
in Europe. It had to be renewed every six months, but no one
would be forced to leave the United States during the war.
And we had a new manager in whose hands we felt secure.
Those troubles of last year did not cloud our sky any more.
With new strength and vigour we reorganised our life.
Johanna took over the kitchen; Hedwig was in charge of the
laundry; Agathe started to sew; Maria took charge of the
mending and darning; Martina, the housecleaning; the boys
brushed the shoes of the entire family and helped with the
dishes; Georg did the shopping; I took care of the correspon-
dence; and Father Wasner, of the book-keeping. From the
day we had left Austria Georg had asked Father Wasner to
take over the handling of the money. During all those critical
years when we were in debt, we felt we hadn't the right to own
anything individually until we had paid back every cent we
owed. Therefore, the incoming money and the incoming bills
went to Father Wasner, and everyone, Georg and I included,
who needed money for one thing or the other, went to him.

At that time the little girls wanted to start learning to play
instruments, which didn't seem to go with their being at
school. At that very moment I happened to meet in Philadelphia a former teacher of mine from Vienna. Now she was
over here, a refugee too. It was almost incredible, but how
lucky we both felt! She was looking for a home, and I, for a
teacher. So she came and stayed with us and became one of
the family as Tante Lene. Very soon we noticed with amazement how much time the little ones had to practise the piano,

the violin, the recorder, and still spend hours every day out-of-doors.

Mr. Schang had suggested that we give two Christmas concerts in Town Hall. That meant an entirely new programme, and we started working on it. Father Wasner went to the big libraries in search of Christmas motets. When he brought them home, the different parts had to be copied before we could start working. Then we had to get acquainted with English and American carols, for many of which Father Wasner made new settings.

It was the day before Christmas when we moved into our new home, the little house with the blue shutters. Very kindly, a neighbour came over to find out whether she could do anything to help.

" Yes," I said, " can you please tell me where I can get a goose? You see, at Christmas one has to eat a goose if one can afford it at all."

Good-naturedly the friendly lady, whose name was Betty, herself drove me to the Reading Terminal Market in Philadelphia to get that indispensable Austrian goose. She obviously didn't want to spoil Christmas for me. But that was my last day of vacation.

Directly after Christmas school started. This was not grade school any more with our bus driver as teacher ; this was high school, and these were the subjects: American Past, American Present, American Living, American Thinking ; and Betty was the teacher. Soon we were good friends. From what I had told her in my halting English, she had made the hair-raising observation that I was floating around in a dream world, in which money and what it stood for had no part. As far as Americanisation went, Betty saw with sharp eyes that we were freshly hatched baby chicks with eggshells still sticking to us: eggshells of European thinking and believing. Out of pure helpfulness she decided that something had to be done about it. First she took care of my English, which still showed strong traces of my two first teachers: Dr. Johnson and the driver.

" Betty, who are the two guys over there?" I asked the very first morning, pointing to two dignified gentlemen.

" But—Maria! You can't say that. That's very poor English."

Oh, I was sorry, but I definitely remembered Dr. Johnson

having told me that " guy " is just another word for " gentleman."

" And never say ' O.K.' That's vulgar."

" O.K., Betty," I said.

" But Maria—that's very vulgar ! "

How often would she have to say that?

Now I would have to learn to unlearn. No more " gee
whiz," " golly Moses," " jeepers creepers," "gosh," "oh
shucks," " boy oh boy," " jump in the lake "—at least not
when Betty was around.

But this was only one part of my education and at that a
minor one. To make, eventually, a good citizen out of me, she
would have to make me money-conscious to teach me to
appreciate the nickel of which there were twenty needed to
make a dollar.

Desperately she tried to explain:

" You are not rich any more, Maria. You are poor, now,
don't you see?—poor."

What a sad truth, and how cruel to state it aloud like that!
And, quoting Dr. Johnson once more, " If I never see you
again it's too soon ! " I went into my room and bewailed my
fate with real tears that these Americans were just hard-boiled
hard-hearted, didn't understand us, never would and wasn't it
awful ! Betty with her sound common sense never even
dreamed how my sensitive heart shrank each time at the word
" poor."

Another thing we had to learn from scratch: that no work,
as long as it is decent, can ever disgrace anybody. We were
still so Europeanly prejudiced, that we didn't want to be
caught at manual labour. When company came and we were
busy in the kitchen, pantry, or basement we went out the
back door and came in the front door, not to give away the
secret that we had been working. What a blessing however,
that we had no money at all, and simply had to jump in and
swim. I remember the sad number of fellow refugees whom
we met occasionally in New York. One such refugee had been
a director or inspector or professor in Europe, and now, of
course, he was waiting for a " leading position." He had
brought with him a little money, too much to die with, and too
little to live on ; but it kept him, unfortunately, from starting
all over again from the bottom. And there they were, huddled
together in shabby apartments, starving cold, but still wearing

old fur coats and leather gloves and wasting precious time
waiting for that "leading position" which might never come.
This misfortune we were spared. We just had to learn the
hard way and that is one of the things we are most grateful
for now. Now when we are driving the manure spreader on
our farm and see a smart Cadillac drive up with some unexpected company, we only wave and shout: "We'll be right
with you!" without the slightest shade of embarrassment.

But that was not so on that morning in Merion. The night
before, we had been invited for dinner at a friend's house, and
my partner on the left had been an extremely nice-looking
young man in evening clothes. The next morning a coal
truck came with a load, and who can describe my horror when
my elegant young man, black all over, started to shovel the
coal into the cellar. I was quite bewildered and looked away
discreetly, not to embarrass him. Embarrass him? Why?

"Good morning, Baroness. Don't you remember me?" he
shouted through the rumbling of the coal. Well, he wanted to
get into the coal business, and had started from the bottom.
What a completely different world, but what a wholesome
one!

Betty rejoiced when I cheerfully announced one day that I
would rather *walk* into town (ten miles!) to save the fare, and
almost tenderly she started to caution me not to overdo my
thriftiness, only to be most cruelly disappointed by the finishing of my sentence: because I wanted to buy a colour film.

"But you can't afford that, Maria. Don't forget, you are
poor."

And now something funny happened. Without being the
slightest bit offended, I looked at her triumphantly and said
sweetly:

"No, we are not poor. We just haven't any money."

Johannes was so cute now with his blond curls, waddling
like a penguin all over the place. If I wanted to take coloured
pictures of him in that state, I just had to do it then, and
couldn't wait until we might one day have real money in the
bank. Johannes might be in college then. This I tried to explain
to Betty, but I didn't succeed. I thought if I showed her my
coloured slides, that would make my point clear but——

"You have a projector, Maria, and a screen?"

"The screen was a present, Betty, but the projector "—and
I lighted up with eagerness to show off what I had learned

most recently—"the projector we bought, and the sewin
machine, and the victrola, and the washing machine, withou
any money. American instalment plan buying is somethin
wonderful. Only five dollars a month—just imagine! In thre
years they will be really our own."

Betty was torn between feeling proud of her hopeful pup
and mad at the projector. The sewing and washing machine
she let pass right away. The victrola I had to explain as bein
absolutely necessary in our business. We *had* to listen t
other choirs. All right then. But the projector remained a sor
spot.

Our life did not allow much social activity, but there was
small circle of people with whom we loved to spend ou
Sundays and free evenings. And there were the Drinker
across the street. Nothing was more gratifying to us than t
have found such genuine music-lovers. Harry's enthusiasti
"Let's do it again!" still sounds in our ears, and his radian
smile whenever we performed for him for the first time one o
our newest motets or songs was applause in itself.

Nothing demonstrates more his sincere love of music tha
the fact that he had made, besides other translations, nev
English translations of the entire vocal works of Johann
Sebastian Bach. These translations are a more correct render
ing of the German originals, especially those taken from th
Scriptures, and are more singable.

Another dear friend whom we met in those days wa
Madame Marion Freschl, a famous voice teacher with a fin
grasp of the problems of the voice. In those critical moment
which occur in every singer's life she always came efficientl
to our help.

Again we were fortunate at this time in beginning an asso
ciation with Miss Alix Williamson who has since handled ou
publicity so well.

One morning in early May Father Wasner remarked at break
fast:

"We have not quite fifty dollars left in the bank."

There were still four months to the next concert tour, an
one thing was sure: fifty dollars wouldn't take us to Septem
ber. Next came a family council. Recently we had seen a
exhibition of Pennsylvania Dutch handicraft, which had bee
very interesting, and we had noticed that the items sold fast

As there was nothing and nobody to sing for at that moment, the only other suggestion we could think of was: " Let's have a handicraft exhibit, too."

The different Christmas and birthday presents had shown that there seemed to be a talent for handicrafts in the family. Let's find out. The next two weeks were devoted to the most concentrated work in leather, clay, wood, linoleum, paint, and silver. At one of the Drinker singing parties we had learned to know the sisters Smith, one of whom was a sculptor. Eleanor and May became the most faithful and devoted helpers now. Where to get the materials ; where to have the clay baked ; how to find a place for the exhibition ; how to advertise it ; they helped us with all these most practical factors The exhibition proved such a success with so many orders coming in, that we were seriously advised to repeat it in New York.

Reverend Mother from Ravenhill lent us the station wagon in which the whole Trapp Family Handicraft Exhibition drove to New York. With the children's furniture, the carpentry work which had been done by Georg and the painting most successfully by Martina, who showed great skill in peasant art (she was also the creator of lovely trays, wooden bowls, and boxes) ; really artistic work in clay by Johanna ; very original jewellery by Werner ; leather work of all kinds by Hedwig ; wood carving by Maria ; linoleum cuts by Agathe, we felt we had an unusual collection of objects to sell. Rupert and I were the unskilled ones. We did the exhibiting.

Soon there were more orders than time to execute them, and September was reached without our having had to contract more debts.

Now we were well on the way. We had learned that work —whatever it may be—honours you and makes you free. Further, we had found out that as long as you are willing to work, America is still the land of unlimited opportunities. It is up to you to use them. And we had also found out that this was the only way to become American, a part of this nation of pioneers: to be a pioneer yourself.

X. The Fly

September came, and one day a big bus stopped in front of the house on Merion Road. This time it was a red one, the newest type with a motor in the rear. The same bus driver was here again, the old faithful, and started to load. To his great delight, we had decided to take Johannes along with us. He loved the baby dearly and rearranged the bus for him.

Tante Lene and Martha would stay behind with the little girls. Martha was a school friend of our Maria from Salzburg. She had been with us in Sweden as a baby sitter to take care of young Johannes during our lengthy rehearsals. When the war broke out, she couldn't return home, but came along with us to America.

By then we had found out that school can be taken care of at home, but we still thought that it was bound to a house. Later we would learn that it can very well take place on wheels.

A friend of the family had offered to come along and help us take care of Johannes while we were rehearsing, and during concerts.

How altogether different was this farewell from the other years! The first time we had had to lug around all our belongings with us and deposit the children in a strange boarding-school; the second year we could leave them in the house of friends, and a corner of their attic housed part of our goods; this time, however, we left them in our own home, surrounded by friends who would keep an eye on things. Slowly, slowly, the tree with the ten branches which had been plucked out by the roots and taken across the ocean into a new soil, started to root again. It is always an experiment to transplant a full-grown tree. One doesn't know whether the roots will take to the strange soil. What a relief when it shows that they do!

After a tearful farewell we went first to New York—Hotel Wellington, of course! This year the carpets were red and the uniforms, bright frog-green. The next day we were to give a concert in a New York college, and Mr. Schang would be

present. This was the first concert under his management, and
the first one of a tour of sixty-five, which would lead us from
coast to coast. What an important and exciting moment!

F. C. Schang was no stranger to us any more. We had seen
him several times in his office, and he had also visited us in
Merion. Out of his vast experience in the concert business he
had given us the most valuable advice in building up new
programmes which would contain something for everybody,
for the housewife in Michigan, the farmer in Kansas, the
rancher out west as well as for the music scholar. Our programmes in the past had been mostly in Latin and German.
Now we added English numbers. Among the English madrigals and folk-songs we found some wonderful pieces like
" Sweet Honey-Sucking Bees," " Early One Morning," and
" Just as the Tide was Flowing "; and among the old American folk-songs we found hidden treasures. Our programme
now had five parts: first, sacred music, selections from the
ancient masters of the sixteenth and seventeenth centuries;
second, music played on the ancient instruments: recorders,
viola da gamba, spinet; third madrigals and ballads; fourth,
Austrian folk-songs and mountain calls; fifth, English and
American folk-songs.

I had admired Mr. Schang many times for his unique ability
to master every situation. It was perfectly incredible how he
could always say the only thing which should be said at the
moment. Now we were at the college, and Sister Mary Rose, a
saintly nun, was in charge of the concert; I felt genuine
curiosity creeping up within me: what would Mr. Schang
do to make Sister Mary Rose happy? He couldn't kiss her
hand, he couldn't tell her how much he liked her gown—*what*
was he going to say? This would be his first meeting with a
nun.

There he was.

" Sister Mary Rose, may I introduce Mr. Schang, our
manager?" A few nice words went back and forth, and look
—here we go!

In a voice vibrating with genuine admiration, F. C. uttered
the weighty words:

" Sister Mary Rose, in all my life I have never heard such
perfect diction!"

We got a return date.

This concert was a new experience. We tried very hard to

put into practice the very good admonitions our new manager
gave us before the concert:

"Don't be formal; smile, relax, forget about the audience.
Simply sing for the fun of singing. Be at ease; don't look so
pained; relax, don't worry."

But if you have to try hard to be informal, if you have to
force yourself to look relaxed, that to begin with is not the
real thing. The worst of it was that *he* was in the audience;
he, the one person among all the people of the U.S.A. whom
we wanted most to please and satisfy. But all the same, the
concert turned out to be very successful. Mr. Schang smiled
all over, congratulated us time and again on the great
difference in our stage appearance.

But the next day when he came to the Wellington to say
good-bye, as the bus was waiting outside all ready to take us
to the West Coast, he added:

"There is something you are lacking, and I can't put my
finger on exactly what it is. There is something between you
and the audience; but I know that if you try hard, you will
find what it is."

That word "lacking" stuck with us. From now on we
watched for what we should do; most critically so. After
every concert we sat together and discussed it. Was it the
coming and going, the standing, the smiling and bowing?
Georg, our most faithful helper and companion in the concert
business, sat in the first row every evening and added his
observations. But all along, we knew we still hadn't found it.
The concerts were good, very good; the people liked them and
said so; but . . .

We were heading for Los Angeles and driving on Highway
66. The great highlight of this trip was for us our first meeting
with the Indians, the real Indians, about whom we had read so
much in Europe. We had all been brought up on Carl May, a
German, who had written many books about those great
heroes of the Wild West. His books were devoured by every
boy, and also by many a girl, and every one of us had once
cried over Winnetou, the great chief of the Apaches. And
now we would meet his blood brothers. Our hearts beat
higher long before we came to New Mexico; but finally it
said on the map: "Pueblo Laguna," and I was ready with
cameras for both moving and still pictures.

Finally I said to the driver: "When is Pueblo Laguna coming?"

He answered casually: "Oh, we passed it a good ten minutes ago. Why?"

"Passed it? The Indians? Our first Indians? Just passed it like that?"

I was so disappointed, I could have cried. I went back to the very rear of the bus to hide my feelings. But above the driver's seat was a mirror, and the driver's eye could see easily what was going on within me. He was sincerely sorry. Never in his life had he thought that anyone could want to take pictures of Indians, something so unprogressive; but, well, she took pictures of Negroes, too, didn't she? He turned the bus around, and back we went to Pueblo Laguna and met our first Indians, nice, friendly people, who looked at us as curiously as we at them. They had never seen Austrians in their national costume, either. We admired their beautiful church, bought some of their quaint pottery, and sang a few Austrian folk-songs for them, and I was permitted to take pictures, with hands trembling with excitement. One was a picture of baby Johannes with his white-blond curls, embracing a little Indian boy of his own age with straight, bluish-black hair. There was something about the Indians which moved us deeply that first time, and every other time we met them, something so dignified and so sad. A strange sensation of sympathy and understanding passed between us.

On this trip we saw some of the most dazzling phenomena of nature: the Painted Desert, the Petrified Forest, the Grand Canyon, the sand desert of California. There was little time to spend in each place, but every day our admiration grew for this country of wonders.

Then we were in Los Angeles, the "suburb of Hollywood," and we were disappointed. Somehow the world of the films had enveloped the whole area around Hollywood, and the atmosphere was one of artificiality and unnaturalness.

Then we greeted the Pacific Ocean for the first time on our way up the coast, heading for Seattle. In Santa Barbara we spent a wonderful day with Lotte Lehmann. The Indian missions, the redwoods, Yosemite Valley and Sequoia National Park, Golden Gate Bridge, Carmel-by-the-Sea, more redwoods, finally the lagoons of Oregon, the peaks of the snowy mountains, and the beautiful bay of Seattle—it was all like a dream; the vastness of the country and its riches, its wild beauty and its proud spirit.

We had sung many concerts, but we were still hunting for the missing link.

Then we wound our way back and finally came to Denver, Colorado. We had been forewarned that the society sponsoring our concert was very high-brow in a musical sense, and expected a very classical programme. This they would get. We omitted the ballads and folk-songs and gave our best in a most serious type of music. At the end of the performance I felt suddenly sympathetic with the few among our listeners who might not have been so high-brow as the others.

On the way out to take a bow, I whispered to Father Wasner: "I'd like to sing a *Jodler* now."

As this was not on the programme, it had to be announced. All announcing was an additional pain, accompanied by blushing each time.

I stepped forward and said: "We shall sing as an encore now one of the mountain calls from the Austrian Alps, known as *Jodler*," and we started.

In yodelling one has to take a deep breath and then hold out for long phrases at a time. We were just in the middle of it when, oh horror! a fly started circling around my face. I watched it, cross-eyed, and got panicky. I knew very soon I would have to take a deep breath, and what if . . . A simple move of my hand would have chased it away, but that's it. To move your hand leisurely on the stage whenever you want, and wherever you want, it is necessary not to be rigid with self-consciousness and sweating with stage-fright. We took our deep breath, and it happened. In went the fly and, of course, down my "Sunday throat," where it got stuck. I felt like choking. Again, a good cough would have helped. But to cough the right way on the stage is much, much harder than to sing the right way. I outdid myself in not coughing, but I couldn't help turning purple. I happened to have the leading part in this *Jodler,* the melody; but that mountain call had to be finished without it, because I was struggling between life and death. My brave children tried not to pay any attention to their choking mother, and when they were finished, I was, too—with the fly. I felt terribly sorry for everyone, but mostly for the audience, who had been cheated of their encore

I forgot that I was on the stage and embarrassed and facing people. I only felt I had to apologise and make amends.

So I stepped forward and said quite naturally:

"What never happened before, has happened now: I swallowed a fly."

I was perfectly amazed at the success of this simple statement. The people laughed and laughed and laughed. When they had recovered, I informed them that we wanted to sing another encore to make up for the spoiled one: this time an Austrian folk-song, and I explained:

"It describes how a young hunter climbs up in the rocks for hours, looking for, and finally finding and shooting, a . . ." I wanted to say *Gemse*, the only word for which I knew was "chamois"; but somehow I got mixed up and said "chemise."

I was perfectly dumbfounded. Was that such a joke in America? I couldn't see anything *so* funny, and looked questioningly at my children who—can you believe it?—were shaking with laughter, too. When finally the worst had passed, I started. For a whole line I was alone; the others were to fall in later; and while I was singing by myself in full, loud yodel tones, Rupert, the mischievous one, whispered to me what I had said. To remain serious now and go on singing was almost harder than not to choke with the fly. I could have skinned Rupert in front of the whole audience.

But—the incredible had happened. The missing link was found: the audience and we had been for some precious minutes one whole. The spell was broken. Now we had found the bridge. Very soon we could say truthfully to our audiences:

"We don't consider this a concert; but we rather feel as if we had taken out one wall of our living-room at home, and you are all our guests at a musical party."

Quite informally we explained interesting details of the numbers to be performed, and the people assured us afterwards that they had quite forgotten that they were in a concert hall.

"You have made us feel so much at home."

Three cheers for the fly!

XI. Stowe in Vermont

We had to be back East in time for the Christmas concerts.
And when Mr. Schang heard us again in Town Hall, he was
all smiles.

"Now you've got it—you've got it! I always knew you
would," he exclaimed. "It sounds like an altogether different
show, and looks so, too," he added pointedly. He had finally
convinced us that the artificial, glaring light of the stage
required artificial means merely to make one look natural and
not like a fainting ghost.

"Some of your girls look green as spinach. You don't
want the audience to be unquiet about their not feeling well,
do you?"

No, we didn't, and so some of us with a less ruddy com-
plexion submitted to the use of make-up in order to look
natural. These Christmas concerts turned out to be a real
success. Everybody was satisfied, and when the first season
under Columbia Concerts' management was over, we had
reached the goal. They were not disappointed that they had
taken us on their list of artists. We had not let anybody
down. More and more requests for concerts came in, and the
second tour was already planned for ninety-six, and the third,
for over a hundred concerts.

". . . And all these things shall be added unto you."

Now we were living through the second part of the promise.
All these things: friends, the ability and the opportunity to
work. We were able to meet our debts at the appointed times.

From September through April we were travelling constantly
with only a short stop around Christmas.

In the first touring year, for lack of the necessary money,
we had had to go to the cheapest hotels we could find. The
mere atmosphere in these places was depressing. You always
felt like sneaking in and sneaking out. In the second year we
couldn't stand that any more. We still hadn't any money, but
we had learned of the existence of cabins and tourist homes.
Of course these places were never large enough for such a big
group, and so we had to split up every night, which made it
difficult for the bus to deliver and collect us. Sometimes there

were no eating places near—it was rather complicated, although more satisfactory than the low-grade hotels. This way of travelling was stopped by Schang.

He insisted: "You must eat and live decently if you want to do a good job on the stage," and he was right. Those lunches for thirty-five cents at the diners on the roadside filled one's stomach for the moment, but didn't give any energy. That's why we had been so absolutely exhausted after the first concert tour with eighteen concerts ; much more so than after the one with over a hundred.

Everything was fine, except for the one sad fact that for the greater part of the year we were separated from our little girls. They had meanwhile made great progress on their instruments, and one day the question arose: shouldn't they be on the programme now? Fine, wonderful. But what of school? Couldn't we try to take a teacher along and have school in the bus and in the hotels? Well, there was nothing like trying. Tante Lene had a young friend, Betsy, who was willing to try, and on the next coast-to-coast trip Betsy came along with Rosmarie and Lorli, and Tante Lene accepted a teaching position at Ravenhill, leaving Martha alone with Johannes in the house.

Now the whole family, only the baby excepted, was together again—on wheels—and when we came back from this fifth American concert tour, we celebrated a great feast at home: we had paid the last cent of our debts, and we still had some money in the bank, after five short years.

That meant that this summer we wouldn't have to stay in Merion. When this sentence was pronounced aloud during lunch, the whole family broke out into cheers.

These past Philadelphia summers had been a real penance for us northerners. The combination of heat and moisture is something unknown to people from the Alps ; the moisture was such that the wallpaper peeled off, and the shoes under the bed became mouldy overnight. Our heavy woollen costumes with close-fitting bodices, our heavy shoes and stockings had not been designed for this climate, but they were still all we posessed in the line of dresses. So far, that had never been a problem as the money question came foremost. We were all still wearing what we had brought from Europe, but the things were starting to get threadbare. So one day we went shopping in Philadelphia, and in a wholesale store we found material and patterns almost exactly like the ones at home, in cotton. Agathe, our seamstress, opened a workshop, everybody helped, and for about twenty dollars in all everyone got two light summer cottons. Every item had to be sewn at home. The dresses, the blouses, the aprons, even the men's socks were knit at home. For our own red stockings fashion came to the rescue. All of a sudden it was the latest rage for all college girls to wear red or green stockings in exactly the pattern we were used to. When low-heeled shoes also came into fashion, we were all right. It would have been difficult to make shoes at home, although Hedwig had already begun to try it.

Usually around this time of the year in May our friends began to talk about their summer plans, whether they would go to the seashore or to the mountains, and by the middle of June they would all have said good-bye. For us country people it got harder and harder to live in a suburb, even in such a nice one as Merion. We tried to get out on the highways for a hike. But owing to the kind-heartedness of the American, every other car stopped and asked whether we didn't want a lift. When we branched off from the highway on a side road and wanted to sit down somewhere for a picnic, a sign on a tree invariably said: " Private—Keep Out —No Trespassing." After several attempts, we gave up hiking.

Now a great thing happened. Mr. Schang had said right at the beginning: "Don't you think you would save money by making the tour in your own cars?" It had taken us two years to digest the suggestion, but now, all of a sudden, two large cars presented themselves for a very reasonable price: a seven-seater 1935 Lincoln Continental for $400 and a large Cadillac for $500. For twelve people with all the concert and private luggage we needed heavy cars. Here they were, and we took them. Little did we know the difference in cost of repairs between a Ford and a Cadillac, but we were to learn that in the near future. At first we were drunk with the feeling of having advanced so high as to be car owners. Georg and the boys got drivers' licences, and the next tour would be easy.

The Drinkers had invited us before to use a cabin of theirs in New Jersey in the woods on the Rancocas Creek. We had been there once, and it was a most delightful place, that spacious bungalow on the bank of the quiet river with the strong current and the low, black cedar waters. But there was always the transportation problem. Now, however, with the cars, the whole world was open to us, and we accepted most gratefully the renewed invitation and settled for a couple of weeks on the Rancocas. There we found all the possibilities for exercise: hiking, swimming, canoeing, cutting wood.

Back in Merion, the question arose: where did we want to spend the summer? Somewhere where it was cool, that was understood—but where? On the wall in the living-room was a big map of the United States with little dots all over it, showing where we had given concerts. This map was now the centre of interest, everybody having his own ideas and wanting to return to the spot he or she particularly preferred in all our trips. No one was astonished that Georg wanted to go to the seashore, to salt water. My special attraction had been New Mexico and the Pueblo Indians, and couldn't we please get tents and camp in a Pueblo? Father Wasner preferred his love-at-first-sight, Kentucky. The boys were lured by the Rocky Mountains for some climbing—everybody had his very own ideas and fought for them.

Then one day a letter arrived from a Mr. R. from Stowe in Vermont, saying he had heard we were looking for a summer place. He had a tourist house equipped for twenty people, and was sure we would like it there. The price was reasonable, just exactly what we could afford, and the plans for the seashore, Kentucky, and New Mexico were postponed for some other year.

Our two big cars were packed, the house closed for the summer without any regret, and we went up north into that State which had been introduced to us by our driver as not worth while looking out the window for, as " they only raised gravestones."

The farther north we came, the more the countryside reminded us of Austria. Finally we drove into Stowe, passed through the village with the friendly white church and its beautifully pointed steeple, out towards Mount Mansfield, as the tourist home called " The Stowe-Away " was in that direction. From the moment we entered, everything seemed to be waiting for us: the score of pleasant, sunny rooms, the lawn around the house, little cabin in the rear, and the view—the view! For years we had looked on to a suburban road with cars passing by; and now it was like home; mountains and space and sky, meadows, fields and trees.

Across the road was a wide brook with swimming holes, and all around were woods and pastures, the most ideal hiking country. Now we could walk again. We walked the three miles into the village when we needed anything; we walked up Mount Mansfield many times and through Smuggler's Notch and down to Bingham Falls and over to Mosglen Falls, around Round Top, and into Stowe Hollow.

It was a wonderful summer.

The longer we stayed, the more we liked it, and the more difficult it was to think that one day we would have to pack the cars again and drive back into city life.

One day a friend came visiting on his way from a lecture trip in Canada back to the States. He also had been a refugee, but he had been longer in the country than we and knew more of its ways. We told him what a nightmare it was to go back into the city.

"But why don't you buy something and stay in Vermont?" he asked.

"Just because we haven't the money," we answered.

"But you don't need money if you want to buy a farm." He seemed amused that so much naïveté. "All you do is make a down payment, and then pay by and by."

From this moment our life was changed.

Once more we had a short meeting, the last one on that subject. Should we buy store clothes or a farm?

"But why buy store clothes now?" asked everyone rather impatiently. "People are used to us the way we are—nobody seems to mind—America is a free country—and how much would it cost anyhow?"

When we found out that walking shoes, street shoes, evening shoes, nylon stockings, underwear, six summer dresses, four winter dresses, an afternoon tea dress, evening gown, suit, skirt with several blouses and pullovers, summer coat, winter coat, hats to match, handbag and umbrella would run up to five hundred dollars apiece, which meant four thousand dollars for us all—that settled the question. That much money we didn't have anyway, and it would be a shame to waste it on clothing.

So we decided to buy a farm in Vermont.

I read once that bees can smell flowers in bloom even across hills and dales and male butterflies find out about a female of their own species over sixty and seventy miles. Something similar must be the case with real-estate people. We hadn't told a soul outside the family, but catalogues started to come in, cars stopped in front of the house with agents who had heard we wanted to buy a farm in Vermont. The peaceful days when we played croquet on the lawn and lounged in the shade of the trees, sipping our coffee, were now gone for good. The fever had seized the family, and our sole occupation came to be looking at the property of other people who, for one reason or the other, wanted to get rid of it.

So far, we had learned English and American, which, as I had found out, were two distinctly different languages; but now we discovered that there existed another idiom, the one used by real-estate people. " Good—very good—excellent " mean one thing to you and another thing to a real-estate agent. After visiting the twentieth farm, we had learned by experience. If the buildings on the place are called " in excellent condition," then it is worth while looking at them. If they are ' in very good repair," you don't risk much when you go through the house. But if they are only " good," you'd better stay at home. They might not be there since the last storm. Then there is the inevitable " rushing trout brook." If you are lucky, you find a thin trickle between the stones; but mostly you aren't even that lucky. You just look at the stones and they are dry.

Up and down we went in the State of Vermont. We saw " a valley of your own," which was highly recommended by one of the agents; but we would have to be Indians, or Eskimos in the winter, since the whole valley was densely wooded, and didn't even contain a cottage. Then we were shown the ' dream castle," an old stone foundation next to which stood a little farm-house. As it was too much " dream " and too little ' castle," we declined it. A " spacious log cabin nestled in woodland " was offered us. This turned out to be an old shack, uninhabited for ten years, at least a mile away from the nearest road. We saw a " charming hilltop farm " with a ' sweeping mountain view." This looked fine until we discovered by chance that three months of every year the water supply ran out completely, and water had to be carried by hand from the nearest pump half a mile away.

We almost bought something near Brattleboro, a terrific number of acres—2,800—of woodland, a road leading through a gorge-like valley with a few houses and sunshine, most probably between June 10 and 30. We even went so far as to bind the bargain with one hundred dollars. Never did we spend one hundred dollars better than when we got out of the deal. In spite of the thirty-acre lake on that property, Georg shuddered when he thought of that dark, dismal spot.

"I want sunshine and penlty of it," he sighed.

That settled it.

Finally, when we had looked at most of the " bargains " and couldn't find what we wanted, we started to hate the mere words " real estate." The farms in good locations with nice houses were far too expensive, and the ones we could have afforded were in all stages of disrepair. We gave up.

One day in August a car stopped outside The Stowe-Away, and in came a gentleman. He took off his straw hat and introduced himself as Mr. Burt from Stowe and sat down. My family was out somewhere, so I was there alone for the conversation.

"Nice day," Mr. Burt started.

"Very nice," I agreed. "Wonderful haying weather. How is the haying going?"

"All right, I guess."

Silence.

"Are there many tourists in Stowe?" I didn't really want to know, but I had to say something.

"Not too many."

Silence.

"It must be beautiful up here in winter."

"Yes," Mr. Burt agreed, " it is."

So far, he had rested his arms on his knees and kept twiddling his hat. Both of us were watching it in fascination. Now he changed the hat's direction, turning it the other way, and said:

"Are you singing much these days?"

"No," I said, " we are taking it easy. This is our first vacation in America."

"Oh."

Silence.

What in the world could I say next?

Then something dawned on me.

" Where do you want us to sing, Mr. Burt?"

The hat stopped twirling.

" Yes," he said, " that's it." He sounded genuinely relieved.
" That's what I really came for. You see, last week the Army
took over a former C.C.C. camp outside Stowe, and we have
been asked to entertain the boys ; so we thought of you people
and wondered whether you would give them some kind of a
performance."

" But surely, gladly. When?"

The date was fixed for next Saturday, and we would be
called for in Army jeeps.

The next Saturday two Army jeeps stopped in front of the
house, and a Captain Hunt and another officer drove us over
Barrows Road through an enchanting little valley to the camp.
What a nice place for a camp! The barracks stood together
on a flat spot on top, and there was something which looked
almost like an amphitheatre with a few more barracks below.
Soldiers everywhere. We sang from the bottom of the
amphitheatre, which was a former gravel pit overgrown with
green, and the soldiers sat all over the slopes. The stars came
out, and the music sounded more beautiful than in any concert
hall in the world.

After the concert we were asked whether we could sing a
Mass for the soldiers. Next Sunday was to be our last Sunday
in Vermont. We agreed readily to come. Again the jeeps came
to get us and drove us through the valley. This time it was
morning, and even more beautiful. It was one of those wonderful, warm autumn days with an incredibly blue sky. On the
way back Georg asked the driver to stop for a moment.

Then he pointed up to the last sunny slope and said with
emphasis :

" A place like this ; that's where I'd be happy."

And five days later that sunny slope, which belonged to a
large farm, was our own.

The very next morning a man knocked at our door.

" I heard you wanted to buy a farm," he said. " I want to
sell mine. Why don't you have a look?"

Although we had given up the idea, there couldn't be any
harm in looking at one more place, and in the afternoon we
drove behind the farmer, who showed the way. We drove as
far as the little white schoolhouse, and there was a sign:
" Luce Hill." That's where we branched off. Up and up it

went, and the farther up we went, the more beautiful became the view. Then we were on top of the hill; and when we got out of the cars, we knew: this is the place. What a panorama! Three valleys lay open before us, and as many as nine mountain ranges stretching into the blue distance. We had been in all forty-eight States; we had stood on many a top of the Green, White, Blue, Smoky, and Rocky Mountains; and in Vermont we had travelled up and down the State and seen many hills and dales, but never had we come across anything like this.

For a while we stood in silent admiration, until Georg whispered into my ear:

"For heaven's sake, look at the buildings!"

A quick glance told me that they were "in fair repair," which didn't disturb me the slightest bit.

"Oh, Georg," I exclaimed, and my arms were around his neck, never minding the farmer and his numerous family. "We can build a house and barns, but we can never build a view like this!"

"We shall let you know in three days," Georg said to the owner, and we drove back to The Stowe-Away.

For all of us it had been love at first sight, and Georg's remarks about the buildings I couldn't take too seriously. After all, hadn't he liked the spot first? That was his "sunny slope." I understood perfectly, however, that he felt how serious the step was. The place was to be our home, and we must never have to regret that signature.

The only thing to do was pray; only thus would we find out the Will of God. We turned an empty room into a chapel. We put up a crucifix on the wall, and two candles were lit, and one member of the family was there for an hour at a time. We all took turns for three days and three nights. Then we had one more meeting, all of us together, the family and Father Wasner, and in perfect peace and unison we all said the same: we hadn't found the place, but the place had found us.

On Thursday we met at the Town Clerk's office and solemnly received the deed, all of us together, as a joint possession. Then we went up our hill. Rupert and Werner felled two trees from our woods and made a Cross twelve feet high. This they carried up to the highest point on the hill behind the house, and we all followed, singing and praying. On the top the Cross was planted, while we sang a hymn of thanksgiving. In California we had learned that the Spanish missionaries had thus taken possession of every new spot on the coast.

One has to have lost a home oneself to appreciate the words: " home sweet home."

XII. A New Chapter

Once more we set out on the concert tour to the West Coast; but this time everything was different; we owned a farm! Now we had a place where we belonged; we also had pictures which we carried around with us. In the joy of our heart, we had to show them to everybody. We still have those pictures, and when I look at them now, I understand fully why a really good friend of ours in the Middle West, after careful study, said slowly and deliberately:

" I hope you like that place."

The view, which was what we really had bought, didn't come out on the photos very well, and what did come out was not too dazzling. But it was with us as with parents of a new-born baby. In pride and exultation it is shown around: " Isn't it lovely?" No, it isn't. That red-faced little dwarf isn't lovely at all, but none of the friends has the heart to say so aloud. The same was the case with our friends who had not been up on Luce Hill on that glorious September day and were confronted with only the pictures of a shabby little house and crooked barns. But they all wanted to share our enthusiasm, and bravely broke out in those exclamations which we wanted to hear.

One of the greatest things in human life is the ability to make plans. Even if they never come true—the joy of anticipation is irrevocably yours.

While on our way out west, this was our royal occupation. As the neighbouring farm had proved to be a terrific bargain when it was offered to us for sale, we had " bought " it, too, and now owned almost seven hundred acres. And what were we going to do with them?

Vermont is a dairy country. The most obvious thing for us would be to go into the dairy business and build—eventually —a big barn for a hundred and fifty cows, which our place

could feed, as people had assured us. The first thing we would
have to decide was: which breed of cows.

"Our neighbour at the foot of the hill has Jerseys," said
Hedwig. "They look lovely, just like deer; and some of the
best farms around Stowe have Jerseys, too. They say the milk
looks almost like orange juice, just yellow with butter fat."

"Yes, but I have heard that Jerseys suffer a great deal from
diseases. Ayrshires are supposed to be much more hardy,
especially for a hill farm," said Agathe.

"Why not Holsteins?" asked Martina. "They are twice as
large as your lovely Jerseys. Mr. H. told me his cows give an
average of fifty to sixty pounds a day, which makes about $2
times 150, makes $300 a day, $9,000 a month, and $108,000 a
year!"

"And how much do those elephants eat?" asked Maria. "I
was just reading here," and she pointed to one of the U.S.
Government pamphlets on agriculture, "that the Brown Swiss
are comparatively new in America, have practically no disease,
don't eat so much as the Holsteins but give the same amount
of milk, are very hardy . . ."

"But they are twice as expensive," said her father.

"Last year you sent us postcards from the West, huge herds
of cows with such funny faces—a white strip down the nose.
Why not those?" Lorli wanted to know.

"Or the other ones," said Illi, "the dark black ones."

"Hereford and Angus seem to be westerners. I haven't
seen them anywhere around Stowe," said Georg.

This conversation was going on in the Cadillac. In the
Lincoln they were discovering meanwhile that Vermont fifty
years ago had been the wheat granary of the East, and in addition the sheep country. Government pamphlets went from
hand to hand, and the discussion centred around different
breeds of sheep.

Whenever the inhabitants of the two cars met, at meals, for
instance, or after the concerts, there was always a spirited exchange of ideas on the one and main topic: the farm.

"How many men shall we need to work?"

That important question was raised one day. Father Wasner had been born and raised on a farm, and he knew more
about farming than any of us.

"Ours was a good-sized farm," he said, "about a hundred
and twenty acres. We had seven people and three teams all

the year round, besides my father and brother; and during haying and harvesting we had fifteen."

"Then," I mused, "with twenty-five or thirty hands and five teams around the farm we should be able to do it."

"No, I don't think they do things that way in America," said Georg, who had read more than we. "Look at this."

He also had some pamphlets from the Department of Agriculture—on farm machinery. And now our vocabulary was enriched by such words as: "side delivery rake," "hay loader," "seeder," "corn planter," "blower," "manure spreader," and "tractor."

"That way we'll do it perhaps with three men and one team."

These words merely "increased our word power." At that time they didn't mean a thing to us, since in our day those things didn't exist in Austria. Very few individuals, indeed, owned seven hundred acres. In the whole neighbourhood there was one single silo, and that had turned into a point of sightseeing. Tractors were a great rarity and much talked about.

With altogether new interest we looked at the countryside as we crossed the Middle West; and the longer we looked, the less we liked it. Miles and miles and miles of corn fields or wheat fields—always the same crop. Later we came into the ranch country, and there were thousands of acres of pasture land; and when we were in California again, we passed through orchards with thousands of apple, or cherry, or orange trees. But it was always "or"; never "and." Now we saw clearly the difference. At home in Austria a farm was a self-sustaining, independent unit. You tried to grow a little bit of everything: for the people and for the animals, and a little extra to sell in order to buy the few items you couldn't grow, such as coffee, tobacco, and cotton material. The wool of your own sheep was spun at home and woven or knitted. The pigs supplied you with smoked meat for the whole year, and lard, besides. For sweetness you had your honey. The flax of the fields provided all the linen. Eventually you slaughtered some beef cattle or a sheep or some geese, ducks, or chickens, to get variety in your menu. In the orchard behind the house you had cherry, apple, and pear trees. and in a protected corner, even some peaches and grapevines. In the vegetable garden was a corner for strawberries, raspberries, blackberries, gooseberries, and currants. From your own rye you baked that delicious black bread, and you always kept enough grain for next year's seed. That way, each farmer on his homestead was an independent little king in his own realm. And after we had weighed dairy farming against wheat raising, or sheep breeding, or fruit growing, we all settled contentedly on doing none of the " or's." We wanted a little bit of everything as it was at home. Each one of us chose right there and then a favourite department: Martina, the pigs; Johanna, the sheep; Hedwig, the cows; Maria, the garden; Agathe, the bees; Georg, the machinery; Father Wasner, the orchard; and I, the horses.

This choice was made on the edge of the desert at Death Valley, entering California. We were eating in a nice western-looking inn, and our spirits were high. All of a sudden I stopped and looked at the boys.

" And how about you?" I exclaimed. " What's the matter? What do you choose?"

There was a moment of hesitation, and then Rupert said:

" Mother, we have to tell you: Werner and I received a letter from the Draft Board to-day. We have to be ready to be called."

Deep silence followed these words. What each one of us had secretly dreaded, now had happened. I looked across at Georg; he was studying the pattern of the tablecloth.

A cloud had passed over the sun of our happiness. For a short while we had forgotten that there was raging the most cruel war in history. We had become farmers in spirit, and farm work means raising, bringing forth; not destroying and annihilating. Now we had been brought back to the present day with brutal force.

In Los Angeles we had to go to register as enemy aliens and had to be fingerprinted. Fingerprinting had so far existed in our minds only in connection with detective stories, and we felt like semi-criminals.

When we stopped at the Grand Canyon on the way back home, I heard somebody whisper behind our back:

" They are Dutch from the East Indies."

" Georg," I said, " please look at the newspapers. The East Indies must be invaded." They were.

That incident reminded us of the time during the war when Hitler was making such fast progress in invading country after country. We in our quaint costumes attracted attention where-ever we went. Upon hearing that we were refugees, people immediately associated us with yesterday's invasion. Alter-nately, we were thought to be Danes, Norwegians, Poles, Croatians, or French.

One day, back in New York it happened that in an over-crowded cafeteria I couldn't find a seat. I tried to balance my tray and eat standing up. Suddenly a lady rose from her seat, silently took my tray out of my hands, indicated her vacant seat, cut the meat for me, and motioned me, still silently, to eat. Deeply embarrassed, I tried to gulp the food down at super-speed. With cheeks still full, I hastily got up and said:

" Thank you very much."

" Oh, not at all," my benefactress replied beamingly. " I was only too happy to do something for the poor Finns."

Before we reached the Continental Divide petrol rationing set in. There we were with those lovely cars of ours, each one doing ten miles per gallon. Our allowance was only the minimum amount, allotted to all private cars. This wouldn't even get us out of Colorado. From now on we had to visit the local rationing board in each town, explain our situation, and ask them to help us to get back home.

We had reached Chicago when the local Draft Board sum-moned Rupert and Werner.

The boys, who hated leaving the family at such a critical moment, were still the bravest ones.

" Mother, remember the old saying: ' If God closes the door, He opens a window.' You'll see that everything will turn out all right again. It seems to be God's Will that we go."

" And God's Will hath no why " went through my head.

We were back East and had finished the concert tour. Georg and I, two girls, and the two boys went up to Stowe to prepare for the family moving. The boys started immediately to cut firewood before they had to report for training. It was the beginning of March and still bitterly cold. In the deep snow nothing else could be done.

On March 9 Georg and I drove the boys to Hyde Park, our county seat, where the new draftees assembled. Not much was said on that trip. Each heart was filled to the brim with the one wish: God bless you!

How dry eyes can get when they are not allowed to cry!

In the silent group of elderly parents, brides, and children we watched the small local train disappear around the curve, waving "God-speed" and trying not to be afraid of the future.

It never rains but it pours! F. C. Schang had tried for months to get into the Army. When I came to the office with a heavy heart to talk over what was to be done now the boys had left, he received me radiantly in a Captain's uniform; this was his last day in the office. My knees grew weak. In this most critical moment of our career as singers we would have to do without the support of the one man who had believed in us and had helped us to build up our nation-wide reputation. I went to a florist and came back with twelve red roses.

"That's one from each of us, Freddy," I said; because now I was not only talking to the great manager, before whom I had once trembled in my boots—I was also talking to the man with the warm heart and the irresistible laugh, the quick wit and the brilliant mind, the personality whom you are proud to call your friend. Very European as we still were, we had many, many acquaintances from coast to coast, but only a very few whom we called friends. Freddy Schang was one of them.

When he saw how hard it all was for us, he grew serious and came over from behind his desk.

"Thank you, Maria," he held my hand. "I feel sure that the Trapp Family Singers, who have weathered many a storm, will also survive this."

There was a request at the office for one belated single concert in Bethlehem, Pennsylvania, ten days hence. The office pointed out to us that this was a chance to try to see whether or not we would be able to sing without the boys.

Of course, we had to try. This seemed like an unsurmountable obstacle: first, the finding of genuine music written for a women's choir; and second, the learning of it by heart in practically no time. Father Wasner did the impossible. In one sweep through music libraries he came home with motets by Vittoria and Palestrina for equal voices, and also precious rounds by Mozart, Haydn, Beethoven, and some songs by Schubert and Brahms for women's voices. Besides that, he arranged some of our old numbers for the new ensemble. From then on, we hardly took time to eat and wash dishes. Once more the house on Merion Road resounded with music. The closer the day came, the more discouraged we grew. We missed the boys so much ; not only in singing, but everywhere, all over the house. There wasn't the same joyous spirit of rehearsing. It was subdued, serious, dutiful. When the day came, we drove over to Bethlehem, knowing that if this concert was not a success, our singing had come to an end. Columbia Concerts would have no more use for us ; and there was a $12,000 mortgage on our place, and a run-down farm to be built up, which would cost a lot more money.

At that time we knew over two hundred pieces by heart, but each one was for mixed voices all of which didn't do us any good now. It added to our excitement and tension when we discovered several well-known faces from the New York office among the audience ; they also knew of the importance of this performance. And all this happened not in some corner of the United States where there hadn't been many concerts before, and the people would most probably like whatever we did ; no, it happened in Bethlehem, where we had sung a year before, and where the audience was composed of singers and music lovers. The world-famous Bach Festivals had educated these people to a high taste in music. If we could please them, we would be all right.

With the help of God we came through with flying colours. I was told that it wasn't an average, good concert ; it was one of those outstanding, excellent ones which one remembers for years. When we sang Brahms' " The Day Has Come When Thou and I, My Dearest One, Must Say Good-bye," the audience was in tears ; and when we sang finally " The Orchestra Song," it got the people to their feet, they clapped and clapped and clapped. And that makes the success of a concert: to keep the audience between tears and laughter. The art of your music must be so convincing and so strong that it makes people forget themselves. It must take them out of that everyday state of mind. They had cried and they had laughed, and they wanted more encores than we had prepared. The performance was a great success, and Columbia Concerts was satisfied. Half dead but relieved, we went back to Merion the same night, after having sent a telegram to the boys, saying: BATTLE OF BETHLEHEM HAS BEEN WON! Whereupon Western Union demanded to know whether this was a code.

No, it was the truth. It marked the beginning of a new chapter. God, Who had closed the door, had opened a window.

XIII. The End of a Perfect Stay

The next days were full of commotion and unrest; the packing and moving from Merion. Three happy years we had lived in the shelter of this house, which seemed much larger inside than outside. Trying times had been followed by easier ones, and each one of us left many memories within its walls. This had not been an ordinary three years. An important metamorphosis had taken place within us. It changed us from Europeans, not yet into Americans—that is a matter of growth and development that takes time—but into people who wanted to become a part of that nation. We could never understand those refugees who seemingly underwent a magic transformation aboard ship, which they had entered as Europeans and left as ready-made Americans, finding everything wrong which they had left behind, and everything " swell " and " O.K." in the States. It had been a slow and painful process with us. One cannot love what one does not know. The more we knew about America, the country and its people, the more we felt a strong, warm love grow in our hearts. For instance: there was a war going on, and we were registered as enemy aliens; but not only were we not locked up in a camp, but we could go about our business unmolested, while wearing our foreign costumes and talking our native tongue on the street and in the trains and elevators. There had always remained some German numbers in our programmes, and never had the audience minded that. This attitude was completely unEuropean, this lack of prejudice was heart-warming. The Americans never seemed to ask, " Who are you?" but " How good are you? Let's see." They give you a fair chance to give your best, and then they accepted you for that, whether you came from Poland, Russia, England, or Austria. And on that day when the boys were leaving we felt that the country our boys would be fighting for, and perhaps dying

for, we wanted to be *our* country. We declared our intention
to become citizens. We were allowed to go to Toronto,
Canada, and enter the United States, this time not as visitors,
but as immigrants. Now we had a quota number, and had to
wait five years to become citizens.

The little house was bulging with furniture which belonged to
us, the family who had arrived with a few suit-cases and four
dollars in cash.

It happened like this. Once we met the publishers Sheed
and Ward, Mr. and Mrs. Frank Sheed from England, who also
spent the war years near Philadelphia. We found we had
many things in common, and from then on, spent many
delightful hours together.

On my first visit to their house I exclaimed:

" Oh, what beautiful rugs! "

This item of furniture the little house on Merion Road
didn't contain.

" Oh, " said Maisie Sheed, " they are from an auction. This
one was eight dollars, and this, five dollars, and this one here
was the most expensive: twelve dollars. "

They were beautiful old oriental rugs, one even a Bokhara
like the one in the living-room in Salzburg, and Maisie Sheed
told me that there was a place in Philadelphia on Chestnut
Street, Samuel T. Freeman's, where there were auctions every
Wednesday. You got good things there very reasonably.

" I always go on Tuesday first to look over what they have.
Then I mark down the numbers in which I am interested, and
then I take just as much money with me as I want to spend.
As you have to pay cash, you don't run into temptation that
way. "

I could hardly wait for next Tuesday. And then I started
out to investigate and discover what was behind the name of
Freeman. There were three very distinct worlds: the basement, the ground floor, and the second floor. The basement
contained a lot of junk. It looked like a receptacle for the
contents of other people's attics; many washbowls and
pitchers, mattresses, pillows, and bed springs, and dozens and
dozens of oversized pictures in old-fashioned frames. The
second floor—what a difference! Very expensive furniture,
illustrated catalogues which showed its origin abroad. Wedg-
wood china, crystal glass, and acres of expensive carpets.

Then there was the ground floor, a hybrid of the other two. The majority of the items on sale was mediocre, but there were one or two first-rate pieces, unrecognised by the crowds. I looked all over the huge room.

I returned the next day to the auction with five dollars in cash. Very soon I was seized by that fever which comes while one watches bidding. A tall young man by the name of Bill was the auctioneer. His sonorous voice held the audience spellbound. The voice had many shades. It could sound matter-of-fact, sympathetic; it could plead; it could get outraged: "What, only four dollars for this easy chair? That's a darn shame!" And sure enough, he would frighten somebody into $4.50. The voice could sound reproachful and then die down to a whisper, which it did now.

"This sideboard, genuine pearwood lined with green felt, four dollars. No one gives more? No one gives more than four dollars for this wonderful piece of craftsmanship? Ladies and gentlemen, if you go to a lumber yard, the lumber alone will cost you three times as much! Who gives more?"

"I," I said, unnecessarily loud, and when everybody turned towards me, I wished I were inside that sideboard.

A benevolent glance from Bill's eyes hit me, and "Five dollars, sold!" made me the owner of a genuine pearwood sideboard.

That was the first of many Wednesdays to come. Bill, who had learned that I was a refugee without a table or chair to my name, helped me with all the organ-like registers of his voice. Obviously I was the only refugee in the place. My competitors in bidding were mostly second-hand dealers, and somehow I seemed to deserve preference over the professional. When I, very timidly in the beginning, indicated by raising my hand that my heart was set on a certain bed, sofa, chair, table, carpet, etc., Bill's voice immediately dropped down to contempt:

"And here, ladies and gentlemen, is one of those pieces . . ."

"One of those pieces" seemed to mean, "whoever takes that junk home is an outright fool," and no one wanted to show such lack of discrimination. Almost invariably I got my piece for a very reasonable price, always under ten dollars. Other people go to the races or to ball games or to Friday Symphony Concerts. I went to Freeman's whose ground floor was a heaven of bargains. Soon the place on

Merion Road was filled until it couldn't swallow any more. That was before we had bought the farm, and my husband got worried.

When the family sighs became louder and more frequent, I decided to get me an accomplice, and after I had once lured Father Wasner into Freeman's, he succumbed to the charms of the place immediately. That time we bought, for practically nothing, six old carved-wood statues of Apostles, a couple of large crystal vases, and a bunch of silver spoons.

After we had bought the farm, the situation grew worse, as the house on the farm was about half the size of the one in Merion, and where could we put all these things?

There was a large cow barn on the upper farm, and that's where we were going to store the furniture for the moment. And now we were packing it into a big van, destined for Stowe, Vermont. These days we were packing from morning till night, and interrupted the packing only for a hasty lunch. We never had to prepare supper, as there was a farewell party every night; at the Smiths', the Crawfords', and at many another friend's house.

And finally, at the Drinkers'. Once more we sat around the large dining-room table with Harry at one end and Sophie at the other, with me next to him, and Georg and Father Wasner next to her, the family in between; and in came one of those giant turkeys which Harry carved with such elegance that watching him was at least as much pleasure as eating the turkey. Once more we sat around the fireplace in the large music-room and sang. This time there was no " let's do it again." We wanted to sing every piece once which we had ever done together and that was a large order. Once more Emily came in with a tray of ginger ale, beer, and pretzels. And then there was that awkward situation which arises invariably when your hearts are full of emotions that cannot be pressed into words. We were so grateful to the Drinkers, for their trust and all their efforts ; and the Drinkers, we could feel, were pleased that we were on our own feet now, and we knew that they would miss us, their neighbours across the street. It was the early Pennsylvania spring, forsythia blooming all over the place, all the trees budding, and the robins, fat as ducks, busy with their nests.

" Spring is such a good time to start something new," Sophie said.

Then we grouped once more round Father Wasner and sang Bach's Chorale of Thanksgiving. This we didn't sing with the Drinkers, we sang it for them.

As I crossed the street looking at the moon which stood bright in a cloudless sky, I couldn't help thinking:

" Even if Harry and Sophie don't believe it as literally as we do, how pleased they will be one day when Our Lord says to them: 'I was a stranger and you took me in. As long as you did it to one of these My least brethren, you did it to Me. Come, enter into eternal joy!'"

XIV. The New House

Early next morning we left for Vermont—for home. North of Rutland there was snow; and after we had passed through Burlington and come into the mountains, there was lots more. When we reached Stowe, we came into a real blizzard.

The dark floor in the living-room of our house was partly covered with a thin layer of snow (" like sugar on a cake," as Johannes remarked), because windows and doors did not shut tightly.

" That's very good for sweeping," exclaimed Hedwig, taking a broom and demonstrating how well you can get after the dust that way.

The man who had lived with his family on the lower farm, which we had bought, too, had remained there and was now our farmer. He had helped the men when they came with the furniture. All we had to do was put up enough beds for the first night. While Georg went down into the small cellar to make a fire in the one-pipe hot air furnace, we ran to and from the barn with parts of beds and mattresses and pillows. The beds *were* pretty large and the house *was* pretty small, and it was only twenty degrees above zero and rather chilly. Johannes discovered a register in the living-room floor. Lying flat on his stomach, he pulled a chain which opened the furnace, and he could gaze right into the flames. When he let the chain drop, it made a loud bang. What a delightful heating system; not dull and invisible as in a city house. Then Martina came in with a lighted kerosene lamp. My enthusiastic exclamations of how cosy it was, like the old days, couldn't shatter Georg's stony silence. Poor Georg. He couldn't see any of the romance of all this. I knew he was genuinely troubled about the shabby little house, into which we really couldn't fit for longer than a week-end, " and a week-end in summer with picnics out-of-doors, I mean," he had said. The crooked barns, the boys gone, and not much money, with half a year to go before we could make any more, and how many concerts would we get without the boys—this nobody knew. It was a picnic supper that first night with paper cups and paper plates, which were burned afterwards in the furnace while Johannes pulled the chain. After supper there was a knock on the door, and the farmer came in.

"The sap is running," said Theophile ; " we have started to tap."

We looked at each other, and finally Georg said:

"What is running?"

And Theophile had to explain to us new-comers all about maple syrup and how it is made. We had never heard of it in Europe, and now, without even a warning, we were making it ourselves.

The next morning we started out on the loveliest time we had had in America, the weeks in The Stowe-Away included: our first sugaring season. Theophile and his eldest boy went with the team and the gathering tank on the sled. Our girls helped collect the sap, and Theophile showed Georg the rather intricate process of boiling it. Georg and I were in the sugar house, and we loved it.

This was the beginning of spring in Vermont, much snow still around, and the horses had to force their way, breast-deep when they started to break in the sugar road. But by noon the sun got warmer. It thawed from the roof of the sugar house, and little rivulets were running all around the sugar bush. Some unprotected places on the slopes were already bare, and an early spring flower raised its dainty head. The first birds could be heard through the woods ; spring was in the air and filled one with new energy and joyful anticipation. Feeding the fire with those heavy, big logs and handling the cans with maple syrup made our backs ache in the evening when we walked back towards the house, very tired but satisfied. Maple syrup is a cash crop. It was the first money we made on our farm. Then Georg counted the gallon cans as the stack grew, down in the cellar. There were already over a hundred, and each can would bring $3.60. I was very happy, because the occupation in the sugar bush kept Georg away from the house, the sight of which was a thorn in his flesh, and his work got him into better and better spirits.

Cold weather set in again, the first run was over; an awful blizzard kept us in the house. There would be no sugaring, Theophile told us, for a few days. When we were all in the house at once, it didn't need much persuasion to see the point: it was too small for us. There was an architect, Alfred, living in Stowe, whom we had consulted about the condition of the buildings before we bought the farm. He had assured us that they were in good enough repair to be fixed for our personal needs. This architect was a godsend for us, as he had lived more than half of his life in Europe, especially in our Austrian Alps, talked our language fluently, and knew very well the part of the country where we came from. Very soon his family and ours were on most friendly terms.

On this particular blizzard day we called Alfred on the telephone. Although we had no electric light, we had a telephone, which we had not used so far. This was a machine screwed to the wall. One had to stand on tiptoe to be able to speak into the mouthpiece, but it was a telephone. I took the receiver, and great was my astonishment when a voice said:

"And how do Grandpa's new teeth fit?"

I hadn't had any experience of a party line before, didn't know what was going on, and listened entranced to the sad story that the teeth didn't fit at all, and Grandpa was losing them all the time. Finally I got Alfred on the line and informed him that our cabin was slightly too small, and what could he do for us?

"Oh, that can easily be arranged," I heard his cheerful, reassuring voice. "You just raise the roof and build another story. You'll have plenty of room."

Further, he advised us to see Mr. Sears, a very good carpenter in the village. We called Mr. Sears, who promised to come and see us as soon as the blizzard was over. That was next day. We explained to Mr. Sears our need and Alfred's advice, and asked if we couldn't start right away. He looked a little doubtful as the weather was still very cold, but when he saw our pleading eyes, he gave in and on the same afternoon we started to rip open the roof.

Georg, Maria, and Hedwig went whole-heartedly into carpentry, and soon most of the roof was gone, and a new construction of two-by-four's indicated the new lines. On the fourth day there was another blizzard, which kept Mr. Sears at home. At noon we were all sitting in the kitchen, which was in the ell, eating lunch, when all of a sudden we heard a terrific crash. We jumped up, and when we opened the door into the living-room, we stepped into the open. Most of the house was gone. It had fallen, chimney and all, right down into the cellar. A few broken walls were still standing, but the roof was definitely gone. As if this had been the goal to be accomplished, the blizzard almost at once died down, after having covered the whole mess with a thin film of new snow. At this moment the telephone rang. It was our ring—Ring 3. I went into the open air. The telephone was still hanging on a piece of wall. Alfred's cheerful voice inquired how things were.

" I wanted to say, don't open too much of the roof at one time," he warned. " On a stormy day that might not be too good."

" It won't bother us any more, Alfred," I said.

" Oh," he seemed to beam, " congratulations! Are you that far already? But that was fast."

" Why don't you come and see for yourself," said I and hung up. Then I called Mr. Sears.

" Mr. Sears, can you tell me what one does with a fallen-down house?"

" I'll be right up," said a hasty voice.

An hour later an architect and a carpenter stood at the grave of their plans and tried to hold hands with the bereaved. What was going to happen next? My poor husband looked broken.

" Now, Georg," I said, " I am really glad for your sake. You hated the idea of putting a new patch on the old frock, as you called it. You didn't trust the foundation, you didn't like the whole idea. Now we'll build a new house and make it exactly as we want it."

" Build a new house—where's the money, may I ask you?"

" Bah—money! Didn't somebody once say that a nation is worth exactly as much as it is willing to work? What is good for a nation is good for a family, and that way we are worth millions."

Architect and carpenter agreed that the next thing that

S.M.   G

would have to be done was to tear down what little of the
house was still standing.

"And now, Alfred, please make us a plan of an Austrian
farm-house, and if we all work together, we'll have a lovely
home very soon!"

I was astonished that the always-happy-sounding, cheerful
voice only said "Well," but it rather sounded like "W—e—e
—e—e—l—l," and then: "There's a war going on and the
War Production Board has forbidden any new building to be
erected. We'll have to see about the regulations."

While the sugaring went on, some of the family worked in
the sugar bush, while others learned the use of crowbars in
tearing down walls, in separating boards. Under layers of
wallpaper we found a newspaper from the year 1832. The nails
were hand-made; the boards, very wide; the beams, hand-
hewn. We tried to keep as much of the good old material as
possible to be used in the new building. Alfred had found out
that the war building regulations permitted one to build on to
an existing house, and this fitted our case if anyone dared to
call the remaining ell a house. There was the kitchen with a
woodshed behind downstairs, and two rooms upstairs. One
room was inhabited by Father Wasner; the other one by
Georg, myself, and little Johannes. These rooms were not
heatable. When the snowstorms raged outside, dainty little
pyramids formed on the floor, as the roof leaked. That was all
right as long as what came down from the sky was snow.
Later when the weather grew warmer and it started to rain,
we needed an umbrella and a few buckets in each room. But
that was after the sugaring season, and there were plenty of
buckets to use.

We had to make an application, and the War Production
Board sent a commission to investigate the necessity of the
planned construction. All we had to do was show them
round; first, the small kitchen, which also served as dining-
and living-room for twelve people; then, the two remaining
bedrooms; then, the dormitory for all the girls, which was
above the horse barn in the hay loft; and finally, the arrangement under the horse barn, which was a substitute for the one
bathroom for a mile around, which, with the rest of the
house, had gone down into the cellar. The gentlemen whole-
heartedly agreed that the necessity for new construction was
urgent, and our petition was granted.

When the sugaring season was over, we proudly counted 363 gallons. The clearing-up of the ruins now made it necessary to carry the cans into the cow barn. Agathe had found time between chores to make a lovely woodcut for a label, saying: " Pure Vermont Maple Syrup from the Trapp Family Farm." We were deeply impressed when we read that for the first time.

Now the buckets had to be washed and stored for the next year. The evaporator was turned upside down, the smoke-stack packed away indoors, the sugar house closed up after a final "sugaring-off party " with Theophile and his family. It had been a lovely time. On the same afternoon Theophile broke the sad news to us that he had bought a farm of his own and he was going to leave us, but he recommended that his brother be given his place. We were glad that Theophile had found a place he liked, but we were sad to lose him. A few days later Ovila came with a family of seven children, the oldest, eleven.

It was Sunday afternoon and the whole family had gone down to the farm-house to help the new-comers move in. I was sitting outside just enjoying myself ; I intended to go down a little later. As I felt cool, I started to go upstairs to get my jacket. When I walked through the kitchen, I could hear footsteps upstairs. I knew definitely that all our people were gone. Who could that be? There it came over to the stairs, and I could hardly believe my eyes when a tremendous big skunk came waddling down the stairs. I had heard enough about skunks to make me politely retreat. Slowly he came down into the kitchen but, oh horror! didn't walk out through the wide-open door, but settled under the ice-box. I ran down to the farm-house to tell the others, and when we all came back home afterwards, the black-and-white tail was sticking out from under the ice-box. We all tiptoed and whispered in order not to frighten the dangerous guest.

He apparently liked it there, and for days he came and went, so that finally he became so tame that he drank milk out of a bowl and looked for food in our garbage pail. One day he came back with a family. As the ice-box was not big enough, they settled under the house. But one cannot tiptoe and whisper for ever, and once in a while something dropped on the floor, which was the roof for the skunk family. Then Mother Skunk quietly gave the defence signal: " Let us spray," and unanimously we cursed the one who had dropped that fork, or whatever it happened to be.

Real spring came to Vermont. The last snow was gone, and after a few days of warm rain and another few days of hot sun, the whole countryside was changed within a week. A new coat of green covered everything, green in all shades, from the tender, yellowish green of the new foliage to the more intense green of the grass on the slopes, and the dark spots of spruce and pine. The air was full of new melodies we had never heard before. Every day brought exciting discoveries. The first trillium was found in the shade, dutchman's breeches, dog-toothed violets, quaker ladies, all were new to us, new and exciting.

Spring in a suburb is tame and well-groomed, like everything in a well-kept suburb. But spring out in the country in its wild beauty is something which almost tears one's heart out. What abundance, what generosity of nature! So much of everything; of flowers, of buds on the trees, of water trickling in innumerable springs down the hills, making the brooks in the valleys roar with joy, of sunshine falling in heavy, warm folds from the cloudless sky. You feel some of this elementary renascence within yourself. Your chest widens and so does your heart. You are full of new plans and new life, and your heart is willing to love everything and everybody with new zeal. Our living quarters gave us plenty of chance to live out-of-doors, and that way we enjoyed to the utmost the first spring on our hill. Every morning when we saw the sun rise behind Elmore Mountain, bathing our hill in its light while the low valleys were covered with thick, white fog, and every night when it went down behind Nebraska Notch, our hearts filled with exultation and thankfulness that we had bought this place, this hill, this view.

All we needed now to complete our happiness was a decent place to worship. Chapels were not mentioned among necessary constructions, so we couldn't think of building one now; but next to the old horse barn was the newest building on our place, a chicken coop, uninhabited. After a lot of scrubbing and whitewashing, it looked and smelled clean, and the walls were covered with thick curtains. Georg made an altar and Maria made a tabernacle; we put two benches along the side, and carpets on the floor, and then we approached our Bishop for permission to reserve the Blessed Eucharist. The permission was given, and the Feast of Corpus Christi was celebrated in joy and glory on our hilltop. The Bishop had graciously lent vestments and a monstrance for this our beginning. Two priest friends had arrived from Washington and helped now to celebrate this great event. For the first time since the creation of the world, the Blessed Sacrament was carried over this hill. When Father Wasner raised the monstrance in Benediction, he showed the Lord this corner of Vermont, and as in the very first days of creation: " God saw all the things that He had made, and they were very good."

With Holy Mass in the morning and Benediction in the evening, the days were framed from now on, and what rich days they were!

After the snow had gone, we started first to clear up round the house. Twenty-four big truckloads of rusty old wire, parts of machinery, beer and whisky bottles, three broken-down cars, and tin cans were taken down to the city dump heap. After a wilderness of old fence posts and wires was taken away from round the house, it looked much better, especially when the old apple trees broke out in blossom. Only the old ell still looked like a broken tooth. From the left-overs of the main house Mr. Sears built a nice, roomy cabin outside on the lawn, which served as dining- and living-room very well all through the summer.

Mr. Sears had long since turned from mere carpenter into an all-round factotum. He knew absolutely everything, from where to buy this and that to how to make elderberry wine or how to collect and dry fresh ferns to fill a cushion against rheumatism.

During the last year in Merion when we needed more time for rehearsing, we had looked for part-time help for the kitchen, and had found a coloured maid. Her name was Aunt Bea, and she was of such a sweet disposition that we all grew very fond of her. Aunt Bea had cried when we moved away from Merion, and had said: " Whenever you need me, just tell me. I'll come with the next train." As far as help was concerned, we really needed Aunt Bea. It would have released a whole person for working on the house. But where to put her? Mr. Sears, as always, had the answer. He remade the woodshed behind the kitchen into three dear little rooms. One more thing we needed: a bed not so wide as the ones we had bought.

"Why don't you go to an auction," Mr. Sears said, and showed me how, in the back of *The Burlington Free Press*, auctions were announced daily; two, three, or four. The mere word "auction" had a sweet sound to my ears, and I picked the nearest one and set out to buy a bed. Georg had such an innate aversion too buying second-hand things that he didn't want to come along. I would have found the place easily by the number of cars lining the road, and there was the place, with all the farm machinery displayed and the auctioneer standing on the manure spreader, pointing with his stick at the various things. They were through with the cattle when I arrived. I had hardly taken a place at the outskirts of the crowd, when the auctioneer eyed me and addressed me sweetly over the heads of the others.

"And you, lady, what do you want? I'm sure we have it."

It was embarrassing to be so suddenly the centre of attention.

"A bed," I said and blushed.

His whole face was one expression of condolence.

"Oh, but we have no beds. But I have something for you, lady, I have a horse."

"But I don't want a horse," I said, horrified. "I need a bed!"

"Lady," and his voice grew stern, "I told you once already, I have no bed. But look at this horse," and he came down from his throne leading a brown horse over to me. The horse was shy and bony and very big. "This is the horse for you, lady," and that tone of voice didn't allow any contradiction. "Topsy is twelve years old, and exactly what you need. In all your life you haven't met such a bargain," and he whispered in my ear: "You can have her for forty dollars."

I was absolutely inexperienced in horse prices, but forty dollars sounded even to me very little. Taking my hesitation —I was desperately thinking how I could make it clear to him without hurting his feelings that I absolutely did not want a horse—for an assent, his jubilant voice rang through the air:

"One brown horse sold—forty dollars!"

Merely to collect myself, I bought a few other items: a few chains for a quarter, a bag of salt for a dime, loads of rope for a nickel, two more crowbars for another dime. Slowly I drove home. The family was sitting at supper.

"Did you get the bed?" Georg asked me.

"N-no."

" Did you buy anything else—antique furniture?"

" Yes—I mean no," and a little too hastily and too exuberantly for the occasion, I told about my bargains in rope, chains, and salt.

It made Georg suspicious; he put down fork and knife, looked at me straight, and said:

" And what else did you buy?"

" A horse."

" A what?"

" A horse, Topsy. The best horse on the market for forty dollars. Twelve years old."

" And Aunt Bea? Are you going to put her on Topsy, or whatever the name is?"

Now everybody laughed, and I felt better.

" Aunt Bea can have my bed," Martina came to my rescue. " I'll gladly sleep on a cot."

A few days later we got Aunt Bea from the station in Waterbury.

We also got Topsy and put her in the stall next to Prince and Lady. I had taken over the horse barn, and jealously I cared for " my " horse now, giving her double portions of oats, grooming her morning and night a little more than Prince and Lady, the team, and very soon Topsy became fat and round and strong.

After all the remains of the old house had been cleared away, we started one bright summer morning with the new one. Alfred had made a beautiful plan of a Swiss chalet.

First we had to dig the cellar. The old one was much too small. Again Mr. Sears advised what to do. We needed a scraper and a man who would handle it with the team. The scraper we found on a neighbouring farm for ten dollars, and the man we found, too: Cliff. He was helping his old father on the farm, but he had time to spare. Cliff knew all about horses. When he saw my interest, he showed me how to harness them, explaining the different parts of the harness and reins. After a few days he encouraged me to get a harness for Topsy and a second scraper. From then on Cliff worked with the team, and I with Topsy, who was ambitious and jealous, and wanted to be as good as the team. For a little while things went fine. The scrapers went into the loose soil as if it were butter, and the slope in front of the house vanished rapidly, until the topsoil was gone. Then came hard-pan, and it was hard hard-pan. The scrapers only scratched it. Mr. Sears sighed deeply two or three times, produced picks the next day, and from then on, all of us had to work with picks until the loosened dirt could be scraped away. That was a slow process and a backbreaking one. The summer days grew hotter, and often we were interrupted by heavy thunderstorms. There was no bulldozer anywhere near, and for eight hot weeks Georg, Father Wasner, the girls, Mr. Sears, Cliff and I worked our way deeper and deeper until the excavation for the cellar was finished.

At another auction we had brought home three lovely little pigs, as Aunt Bea had cried out about so much good garbage going to waste. These pigs grew fast into pets. They were called Petunia, Violet and Suzy. Aunt Bea and Martina completely lost their hearts to them, and the piglets grew almost while we watched them. The skunk family had left, as there was too much commotion around the house, but we had two cats and a dog and, on the lower farm, another team and fifty-two head of cattle.

Haying time was in full swing when the scraping was over, and Oliva was very glad to get the other horses to help. Now Topsy and I mounted the one-horse rake or the hay tedder, and Topsy acted very intelligently on the large meadow behind the horse barn. She worked very slowly the long stretch across to the other side, but the very moment we turned, she almost galloped back to the barn, only to be turned around and mourningly wind her way in the other direction. What a feeling that was on the rake, surrounded by the sweet-scented hay, the shiny body of "my" horse in front of me, reins in hand, happy as a queen.

Meanwhile, the Trapp Family had completely dropped out of newspapers and magazines, and they had begun to wonder why. But one beautiful summer day two reporters came up Luce Hill, a lady and a gentleman. She was the writer and he, the photographer. They wanted a story on what the Trapps were now doing.

"Come and see," I said. "We have no time for posing, but you can take pictures of everything you see." So they took pictures of the building, of Martina with the pigs, and Agathe with her beehives, and Maria in the new vegetable garden, and Hedwig in her out-of-door laundry under the apple trees, and Johanna on the tractor, and me with the horses. After we

had spent a hot day haying and they had followed us
patiently around up and down a sloping meadow, we all
finally rested in the shade and drank cider.

Mr. Sears had got two helpers besides Georg, Maria, and
Hedwig, and they were working on what they called "forms."
They looked to me like huge wooden walls. Then these forms
were put in the cellar hole and pressed and counter-pressed
by a whole forest of two-by-fours.

Then one day Mr. Sears didn't come. He didn't feel well.
He never returned. From his sick-bed he still gave us advice
as to what to do next. When he died, we stopped all work.
We were mourning for our first and best friend in Stowe, the
one who had guided our beginnings in the country with an
almost paternal love. In our Sunday best we accompanied
him to his last rest, and sang once more his favourite song:
Brahms' "Lullaby."

Now the going was hard. We missed Mr. Sears all over the
place. As if to make up for Mr. Sears' absence, Alfred came
more often, and one day the forms were ready.

A runway was built, and Alfred said:

"Now we need a cement mixer."

We rented one from a man in Waterbury Centre. Then we
needed wheelbarrows. We borrowed some from the town.
Then we telephoned for sand, gravel, and cement. We found
we needed another carpenter who knew exactly what, when,
and how to mix. The last was the hardest of all, but finally
we persuaded Mr. R. In the beginning he came in the evening
until he had finished another job ; then he came a few days a
week, and finally, he took over. Trucks came with gravel, and
others with sand, and a hundred bags of cement were piled up
in the horse barn. In the middle of it all stood the cement
mixer, and on a bright and shining morning in August Cliff
started the motor, and the mixer began to turn. Mr. R. had
given us the recipe: one shovel cement, two shovels gravel,
and three sand, and enough water—and he showed how much
is enough ; then you turn the wheel and the mixture empties
into the wheelbarrow and you start all over again. One
cement, two gravel, three sand. I was at the mixer, and somehow I got the fixed idea that if you put in more cement, the
cellar wall will be harder and better. So I secretly put in more
cement. Whenever I look at the cracks in the cellar wall

now, I know who is responsible for them. Each visiting guest was put into overalls, adorned with a shovel, and told " two gravel, three sand," while I took care of the cement.

Guests *did* come, and they were all wonderful helpers. Everything would have been just fine if it hadn't been for the cement mixer. When all was lined up: four wheelbarrows and three men (or girls) with shovels, one would hear all of a sudden a stuttering noise from the motor, and then silence. One cry, " Cliff!" and Cliff would come and try to persuade that temperamental mixer to run ; take it apart, put it together, kick it finally with his heel, and all of a sudden, without any special reason, it was on the go again. So it went off and on many times a day, but the walls grew, and one day the corner stone of the new house was solemnly placed by Father Wasner and sunk into the wall, together with a Latin inscription on parchment and a bottle of holy water.

Meanwhile, many letters had gone back and forth between the boys and us, and great was our joy when they came home for their first furlough, two privates, looking very handsome in their uniforms. They came just at the time when the cement was dry enough for the forms to be taken off, taken apart, and used again for the rough floor. The whole family hammered along on that rough floor, and then it was finished. There was a big party with singing and folk-dancing on that new floor of our new house. We were singing in four parts again. From now on we marvelled at American speed in building a house. In no time the studs were up, and the rough floor of the second floor was laid and the studs were up for the third floor ; and the skeleton of the roof was going up before the boys had to leave again for Camp Hale in Colorado—they had volunteered for the mountain troops—so they got an idea of what the house would look like eventually. It was very hard to see them go again.

A real fever for work had taken hold of us. We were either hammering along or boarding up the walls or laying a floor, or we were in the hay or on the other side of the hill in the berry patches, for there was an abundance of berries that summer. We had found an old sugaring pan which we put up under the old apple trees beside the house and used for canning. Guests could now choose whether they wanted to help on the building or in the hay or in the berry-picking or canning. Besides all this, the large vegetable garden needed

pickers for peas and beans, and the first apples, those delicious
Duchesses, were ripening.

All of a sudden, time seemed to fly. The days grew shorter
as September came around. We had to cut out several hours
a day for rehearsals again. In a few weeks the concerts would
start, and the roof was still not boarded up, not to speak of
the shingles.

One morning Mr. R. mentioned that the people in Stowe
were in trouble. The roof of the schoolhouse was leaking, and
there were no funds.

" Do you think a concert by us would bring enough?"

His face lit up.

" I guess it would."

By now we had learned that a true Vermonter will hardly
ever say flatly " yes " or " no." He'll say " why not?" or, " it
seems so to me," or " I guess it would." It had to be done
quickly because the roof should be mended before school
began. A few nights later we were standing on the stage of
the Town Hall and singing our new programme—the programme without the boys. The concert had been sold out on
the first evening after it was announced. The tourist season
was over, and there were only townspeople and farmers from
the neighbourhood. And now something happened which will
always remain unforgettable to us. After the last encore, one
of the men sitting in the first row got up and started to come
up the stairs to the stage, and everybody else followed. The
whole audience. They passed by and everyone shook hands
with us in a sincere and heartfelt way, as if to say: " Now
you are one of us. Welcome home!"

This was on a Wednesday. The next Saturday two pick-up
trucks drove up to our place filled with young boys, each one
with a hammer, led by Mr. Page, the teacher of carpentry and
handicrafts in the high school.

" We have come to help *you* out now," said Mr. Page, and
that was all the explanation he gave.

In the next moment he and his boys were all over the roof,
and a furious hammering could be heard for the next few
hours. On Sunday they came again, and some more cars with
townspeople with hammers, too, and next Saturday and Sunday again. At the end of each visit we served coffee, cocoa
and doughnuts, and we began to believe in the old fairy-tale
which tells of those little dwarfs who finished a half-completed

work secretly by night. Three days before we had to leave on
our tour the roof was shingled, the windows and doors were in,
the outside of the house was covered with tar-paper—we were
ready for the winter.

While that most cruel of all wars was inflicting deeper and
deeper wounds on humanity, a little group of people in a
forlorn corner of the mountains had discovered how to create
that Good Will to which is promised Peace on Earth.

XV. Concerts in Wartime

A few days before we had to leave on our concert trip I went
down to Stowe to the drug store. Casually I opened the latest
issue of *Life* magazine and—stared myself in the face. There I
was, with Prince and Lady, and there was Georg, and there
was Martina decorating the shrine of Our Lady with flowers;
and there were haying pictures, and I had a vision of a hot
summer day and a couple from New York, hot and exhausted,
following us all over the place; and we had had no idea that
this was for *Life* magazine.

When we arrived in New York at Pennsylvania Station, a
porter ran up and said:

" And how is Johannes? I saw his picture in *Life*."

That accompanied us this whole trip. Once in Ohio, we
somehow had managed to lose our railroad tickets, but that
copy of *Life,* which we had with us, served as identification.

In New York we received at the office a thick manila
envelope with long strips of green and red railroad tickets and
an itinerary the size of a little booklet, saying:

Leave New York, Pennsylvania Station ....
Arrive Haverford ....

Leave Haverford ....
Arrive Pittsburgh ....

Leave Pittsburgh by bus ....
Arrive Dayton ....

and so on. Between " leave " and " arrive " there were hours

of time. Sometimes they were filled with a concert; sometimes
we would just have to wait at a bus terminal or a railroad
station. It was all new to us, as we knew American railroads
only from Philadelphia to New York. It was 1943, our sixth
American concert tour, and the war was at its height. The
whole nation seemed under arms; on the streets, in the
dining-rooms, in the hotels, and on the railroads, one saw
only men and women in uniform; very few civilians.

A few weeks later we felt ourselves—uniform or no uniform
—members of the home front. To give our concerts was a
part of the programme to keep up morale, and with the type
of our music—soothing, consoling, uplifting—it had become
a rather important part, as dozens and dozens of letters from
Army and Navy camps and all kinds of audiences assured us.

Rosmarie and Lorli now took an important part in the
instrumental section, both playing recorders very nicely; and
little Johannes was with us, too. He was just starting to learn
to play the recorder, and this important musical education
could not be interrupted for six months each year. He had his
lesson every day with Maria. He was now four and a half
years old.

This travelling by rail proved to be extremely strenuous,
especially with young children. If, for instance, we had to take
a train after a concert in order to reach a certain town in time
for the next performance, it meant standing on a cold,
draughty platform, waiting for a train which was late, sometimes far beyond midnight. Once this happened in Illinois,
and when the train finally came, it was one o'clock. Each one
of us had his ticket with a Pullman reservation for his berth,
and we said good night before we entered the different
sleepers, everyone set on getting as much sleep as possible.
Mine was Lower 8. I opened the curtain, took my heavy bag,
swung it once, up and down, aimed, and threw it on the bed.
At the same instant I heard a low moan, and out came the
upper part of a man, eyes rolling wildly. His ticket also read
" Lower 8 " for the same car. It had been sold twice.

After a concert in Oklahoma a Colonel came backstage and
congratulated us on the performance. Born in Hungary, he
felt himself a close countryman to us. He took us all with
him, and we had a lovely evening together. He and Georg

discovered friends and acquaintances in common, and when
we finally said good night, he had become " Uncle Ferdinand."
Next day he came to the train, and just before the last good-
bye, he took one of the eagles from his uniform and pinned it
on little Johannes' soldier's cap, a gift from brother Rupert.
Half an hour later some soldiers passed through our car on
the way to the dining-car. The first one, wanting to please the
little boy, stepped up before Johannes, saluted, and said:

" Colonel, may I request a furlough?"

Johannes fixed his big blue eyes on the soldier and said:
" Yes, thirty days."

The lucky soldier fished into his pocket and counted out
thirty pennies for the gracious little Colonel. I went on reading
in my book ; then I suddenly discovered there was no
Johannes next to me any longer. Alarmed, I got up and
looked all over the car, ladies' room, men's room, the next
car, and finally found him in the third car, busily selling
furloughs all around a crowd of highly-amused privates, his
little pockets full of pennies.

The concerts went very well indeed. Not that we didn't miss
the boys, or that the audience didn't miss them ; but we had
to do without gasoline, without tyres, without sugar—so we
also had to do without the boys. It would almost have been
awkward to have them with us. One would have felt like explaining or apologising to the other mothers. In the letters
which went to our soldiers in Camp Hale we were glad to be
able to relate some hardships, too. We wouldn't have wanted
to have a high time, no complications, no deprivations, while
the boys went on manœuvres and slept in the open at thirty
below, and were longing for us, just as we were longing for
them.

XVI. Trapp Family Music Camp

During that first concert tour by railroad, we took a few
weeks off at Christmas for a much-needed break, because
afterwards we were to go to the West Coast and not come
back until May.

What a home-coming it was! When we left the train in

Waterbury, it was thirty-six below zero, to go down to forty-five the next morning. The snow was singing under our feet when we stepped out of the taxis which had carried us up the hill. Instead of the steps which now lead to the front door, there was a kind of broad ladder; and instead of a front door, there was a thick carpet. As no inner walls yet existed, our curtains had come in handy. Alfred had draped them around the big living-room. In the fireplace roared a blazing fire. The two sofas with the swan's-down cushions for thirty-five dollars each were standing there on the rough floor covered with Freeman carpets. The statues of the Apostles on the mantelpiece—oh, how wonderful it all was! Everything seemed to fit perfectly into the new house. On a ladder one reached the second floor, which was a yawning floor one large dormitory with a corner partitioned off for a temporary chapel for that winter. There we celebrated Christmas very happily in our new home; it was overshadowed only by the great yearning for the boys. This was the first Christmas that the family had not been all together.

Soon afterwards we armed ourselves with hammers and nails again, helping to erect partitions, board up walls, and lay floors. In good weather the others would go ski-ing. As my back bothered me a little more as the years went by, I had given up ski-ing for good. One morning Mr. R. brought news from the village.

"They're going to tear down the C.C.C. camp."

That was the very camp in which we had sung for the soldiers that first summer in Stowe. When I heard that the camp which had looked so different from all the other Army camps we had visited since, was to be torn down, a pang went through my heart. The mere thought disturbed me all day, and before the men went home, I said to Mr. R.:

"Isn't it a pity to tear down the camp? What could one do to preserve it?"

"Oh, nobody has any use for the place. If you want it," and he laughed, "just make an application to the State."

When the others came back from the ski-ing, they brought a guest along: Mr. Burt from Stowe, the man with the straw hat. They had met him at the Toll House, and he had stayed with them the whole day, showing them trails; finally, over a cup of tea at the Octogon, Martina had said to him: "Mr. Burt, you have been just like an uncle to us"—which delighted

him so much that he asked whether he couldn't keep that title
So it was "Uncle Craig" from then on. I asked him to stay
for supper and extend his "uncle" qualities also to me, as I
had had a brain wave. During supper I explained what a crime
it would be, to my way of thinking, to tear down a good camp
which surely could still be used.

Uncle Craig busied himself with his plate and seemed to be
thinking. Then he looked up and said quietly:

"The State Forester is coming to Stowe to-morrow. He is
the one in charge of the camp. I might bring him up, and
you could talk it over."

Next day Uncle Craig came again and brought Mr. Perry
Merrill, the State Forester.

First, we talked about the winter and the ski-ing and the new
house; and when we had reached the dessert, which was
Schmarren, Uncle Craig said:

"Mr. Merrill, the Baroness wants to talk to you about the
camp. She has certain ideas."

And then a great silence settled over the dining-room. Mr
Merrill made some encouraging noises and looked at me; not
only he, but my whole family looked at me, very interestedly
and very curiously; and if I could have looked at myself, I
would have done the same.

"What am I going to hear now?" I was wondering.

So far, it had been an intense pity and sympathy towards
that good little camp which was about to be torn down. But
now I was supposed to have certain definite ideas. Well let's
see.

"You see, Mr. Merrill—I mean to say—what I want to
explain is this . . ."

While I was stammering, the one question zigzagged wildly
through my head: what, *what*, WHAT can one do with a camp?
and there was my answer: Song Weeks. And I listened to
myself explaining to Mr. Merrill.

"When I was a young girl, I attended, several times, so-
called 'Song Weeks.' We met somewhere out in the country,
groups of between fifty and a hundred, and we spent eight or
ten days devoted to music-making and folk-dancing. I haven't
seen that done in America yet. Couldn't we start them in that
camp?"

Quite exhausted, I put down my fork and wiped my face.
Mr. Merrill immediately liked the idea.

" That sounds like a very wholesome recreation, and that's what we want to boost in our State. The type of people who might come for such a thing are exactly the ones we want to draw to Vermont."

Now *I* was looking down at my plate, avoiding the eyes of my family. Hadn't I started something now? Yes, I had.

" Inasmuch as there is no other party interested in preserving the camp," Mr. Merrill went on, " I can assure you that you will be granted a lease from the State of Vermont. You will have to make an application, and then a lease will be drawn and will be signed by me and approved by the Governor and five other officials. You can work on your plans right away; and how about going down after lunch and having a look at the camp?"

Well, well! That camp seemed like an orphan clinging to the one person who had talked in its favour, not wanting to let go any more.

So we went down the hill, Georg, Father Wasner, and I, with Mr. Merrill in Uncle Craig's car; the rest, on skis. We met at the camp. It looked lovely in this wintry landscape. There were eight big barracks on top of the hill, one on the slope, and two more at the bottom. Although the barracks were completely empty and exactly alike, Mr. Merrill opened each single one for us. They were large and bright and airy.

" They seem to be in good condition," said Georg finally.

Greatly delighted, I noticed the undertone of satisfaction in his voice.

" This was the kitchen and dining-room, and this building opposite the others was their recreation hall. Everything else was used as dormitories except the little one over there, which was the infirmary, and the extra long one on the slope, which was the guardhouse."

" The ex-guardhouse would make a fine chapel," said Father Wasner.

" We'll get you a little steeple with a bell," promised Hedwig, the practical one.

" I don't see why we couldn't leave the arrangement as it was, with the dormitories, recreation hall, kitchen and dining-room," said I.

The others had gone on trips around the buildings on their skis. Now they came back.

" Mr. Merrill," inquired Illi, " I haven't seen a single wash-room in the whole camp. Where did the soldiers wash?"

" Maybe in the brook like Boy Scouts," answered Johannes.

" Yes, but . . ." continued Illi.

" Oh, I found that," said young Lorli unashamedly. " It's behind the barracks and has seventeen seats!"

Mr. Merrill and Uncle Craig suppressed a smile, and then Mr. Merrill said:

" Of course, you will have to do some readjusting for your purpose. But I am sure we can find plumbing fixtures some-where in the State for you to put in. Whatever we can do, we'll be glad to help you."

When he saw the excitement of the family, he smiled and said:

" Now, I expect your application, and it's granted as far as I'm concerned."

" Then the camp is yours," whispered Uncle Craig.

" Look, look!" cried little Johannes.

What a spectacle! A wonderful, complete rainbow extended from the top of the hill across the camp. Funny—there had been no rain or snow that whole day. We stood and gazed: the snow-laden trees sparkling in the sun, the camp tucked in between the hills looking so snug and peaceful, and over it all the rainbow, the old token of peace. I took Georg's arm and pressed it.

" Let's take this rainbow for a good sign."

Soon we were on the road again on the way out west. In New York we explained to our publicity manager in general terms that we would run a music camp in the coming summer, and would she please announce it. Soon afterwards 100,000 green leaflets went out in all directions, saying: " You are invited to enjoy a holiday of music-making with the Trapp Family Singers during the coming summer at the Trapp Family Music Camp in Stowe, Vermont." There is always a magic in the printed word.

During long hours riding in trains and buses I had plenty of time to consider what I had done, and what I told myself about it wasn't always flattering. There—our house on the hill was only one-third finished. An O.P.A. and a War Pro-duction Board had to be consulted for every single door-knob and every inch of pipe. Was this new project necessary? Did

I have to start more trouble? More headaches all around? When I looked at my husband, I dissolved into one act of contrition. Not a single word of reproach had come from him, but when he thought himself unobserved, he looked tired and discouraged. The boys had just been sent overseas. That anxiety was wearing him down, too. We were again deep in debt, and little as I minded that, he hated debts. And now I had heaped another burden on his shoulders. We would have more uncertainty, more anxiety, and more money to borrow. That weighed heavily on him.

But the leaflets were out, and the folders were on the press, giving a description of "a typical day at the Trapp Family Music Camp" as we were planning it. Now we had to go on.

This train from Phoenix to Los Angeles had only Pullman cars, and for a day and a half we enjoyed being together in one compartment. With pencil and paper we started: what do we need for the camp? The most important thing: hot and cold running water in the barracks for washrooms. That meant so many feet of pipe—or was it better to say it in miles, as the water had to come from the top of the next mountain. We were counting on eight dormitories with three showers, four washbowls, and four toilets for each dormitory. A hundred and twenty persons, therefore, would need a bed apiece, equipped with mattress, pillow, and two blankets; the supply of bedding alone would run into a large sum. How many plates, cups, glasses, forks, spoons? Partitions would have to be made—how about the timber? Metal of any kind was the scarcest of all. How about the pipes and fixtures? The barracks would have to be painted inside and out, and . . .

And then I was glad that we had arrived in Los Angeles and had to get out. There was not much we could do from there anyway, except make another application to the War Production Board.

This was an unusually long tour. The time was getting shorter and shorter before the people would be coming to enjoy their vacations at the Trapp Family Music Camp. We had already received a hundred and four reservations from real persons who wanted to come that summer and had paid a deposit of ten dollars each.

At last we were back east. We rushed home and over to Montpelier, and Mr. Merrill handed us the lease and wished us the best of luck. That was May 24. As our folder in-

vited people for July 10, that left us but little time to conver
an abandoned C.C.C. camp into a comfortable place fo
music-making.

Mr. Merrill had told us the good news that he had foun
a number of washbowls and toilets and a couple of truck
loads of timber. The rest he was sure we could get. Th
rest——?

There was no time to lose. To our great disappointment
the War Production Board informed us that we were no
allowed to use anything new; even timber we had to ge
second-hand. That was a blow. We put an ad. in the pape
and watched every auction, carrying home eagerly every single
two-by-four we could find in somebody's attic. In the mean
time some of us roamed through all the second-hand stores ir
Boston and New York for washbowls and toilets, for hot
water tanks and electric fixtures, but pipes we couldn't ge
second-hand. Another application was refused. Precious time
went by. A commission came and investigated the place to see
whether it was a necessity for the war effort. We tried to explain that it was necessary in the same way as good concerts
and everything which helps to keep up morale. And so the
application for the pipes was granted.

Every day the telephone was busy.

"Uncle Craig—where can I get . . .?" and the silence or
the other end of the line grew longer and longer. Finally we
had the necessary men; but the painters couldn't start until
the carpenters were out, and the carpenters couldn't finish
because the plumbers were still working, and the plumbers
couldn't do a thing right now until the pipes came from
Boston or New York.

But how many other things we had to think of! Our folder
promised the future campers that we would sing with them
out-of-doors down at the brook under the cool shady trees in
the grove, where it would always be cool, even in July and
August. That called for benches.

"Uncle Craig—could you possibly imagine where we could
get benches for, let's say—for a large number of people?"

The faithful one could imagine. There was an auction at
Mosglen Falls with benches on the list. We got them.

More and more as I came to talk with different people
about camps in general I learned that such recreation spots
were not at all unusual in these United States; but I was told

that two things were essential for a camp: the camp manager and the cook. None of us had ever been in an American camp or seen one from within, so I simply took for granted all I heard and went on another trip to Boston; this time not to visit wrecking companies, but employment agencies. Within three days I was told that I could count myself extremely lucky to have found a camp manager who was reported to be most efficient and experienced. Before he would accept the position, however, he wanted to see the place. He would come within the next few days.

They had also found a cook for me, who was supposed to be perfect in Viennese, French, American, and Chinese cuisines. She asked one hundred dollars a week, and wanted to bring her husband along.

As I was in Boston already, I continued to hunt for pots and pans, chairs and blankets. I had to go from one store to the other, grab here a dozen blankets, there six pillows, and in a third place, a bunch of spoons, hoping to find matching forks and knives somewhere, anywhere.

Then came a day which I shall never forget. After I had come back from Boston, I was standing in one of the barracks, talking to Mr. Steele, our plumber. Martina came in with two visitors.

"These gentlemen are from the War Production Board," she announced.

Soon I found out that these gentlemen *were* the War Production Board, and they didn't like us at all—anything connected with the name Trapp, whether it was the Trapp Family Farm, or the Trapp Family Music Camp—too many applications.

Sternly they looked around and pointing to the newest partitions, they said:

"This is new timber."

Well, it was and it wasn't; and tried to explain that we had bought it for the farm half a year ago, and now had bought it second-hand from the farm for the camp. But that didn't make it any better. One of the gentlemen waved a six-page folder in very small print before my eyes and said:

"Didn't you study that? Don't you know that you have transgressed the law?"

I had seen the folder before, but it was in such medieval English with "heretofores" and "wherewithals," references to schedules or provisions, which were "superseded by . . ." and "further amended . . ." that I could never make out what it was all about.

Both gentlemen were very stern, and one said now, firmly:

"You are to stop all activities here and on the farm, and you are summoned to appear at the main office in Montpelier on Tuesday for a hearing."

With a long, sympathetic look Mr. Steele, the plumber, slipped out. That was Saturday, and it was a long time until Tuesday; a long time in which to think and be sorry.

At the main office in Montpelier I was informed that, having wilfully transgressed the law, paragraph so-and-so, I was to be fined $10,000 in cash and must serve one year in jail, and did I have anything to say in my defence?

Whereas my English, according to my own estimation, was quite good enough for most occasions, unfortunately, it grew worse and worse when I got excited, and this I was now: excited. Who would ever lend me $10,000 to pay my fine? And would Columbia Concerts ever take us back after a year in jail? And what would my family say, and Freddy Schang, and the Drinkers, and all the other friends? My imagination ran riot. The more I tried to talk composedly and quietly, the more I stuttered and stammered. I tried to explain that I had not *wilfully* transgressed the law.

"And gentlemen," I said, "I can't serve my penalty all at once. Will you allow me to do that in instalments? Half a year I must have to earn the money to pay my fine. The other half I can spend in jail. I think I can do it in two years."

After this heroic speech I was exhausted. One single tear stole out of the right eye and rolled slowly down my nose, and there was nothing I could do about it.

Was it the tear, or had the gentlemen meanwhile received an impression of my well-meaning harmlessness? They withdrew for a moment, and when they entered the room again, they were very different. I should relax and not get excited, and things would be ironed out. They saw that I didn't want to cheat the government, and they would be up on Luce Hill late this afternoon for another investigation. I could go ahead.

They came and were very human. We showed them all over the place, house and camp, and explained all the purposes of each. Then it was supper-time, and we asked them to stay for an Austrian meal, goulash with beer and afterwards,

Apfelstrudel. After they had convinced themselves that there was really no dishonesty involved, they stopped being fearful officials and were very friendly. Next morning we could continue our work, and I wouldn't have to go to jail or pay that fine, either; but the gentlemen went all through that leaflet of the War Production Board with us to avoid future misunderstandings.

The two boys had landed safely in Europe. They were not supposed to say too much, but from their letters, we gathered that they were in Italy, and enjoying it.

Amid all the hustle and bustle of the preparations for the camp, there fell one beautiful family feast: Johannes' First Communion. He was only five, but since the days of his early babyhood he had been present with us at Holy Mass in the morning, and day after day the sad moment would come when little Johannes was the only one who did not receive the Blessed Bread. At the age of three he started begging for it. When he was told that he must wait until he was able to make real sacrifices to show his true love, he wanted to know what a sacrifice was.

"Do something you don't want to do, like eating your spinach without yelling," explained Lorli most readily. "Or don't do something you want to do; for instance, leave those sweets for me."

And the little fellow set out on the road to perfection by trying to curb his likes and dislikes. When the small chapel on the farm was installed, a new hardship had been added. Every Saturday evening the family would sit on the bench outside while one after the other went in to Confession, and Johannes was always told to keep quiet and out of the way because he was too young. But now the great day had come. He knew all he was supposed to know, and had shown good will through a lengthy period of time, and the Bishop gave permission for his First Holy Communion on Corpus Christi day. The evening before, Johannes went down to the chapel to go to Confession for the first time. This he couldn't keep to himself.

"Now it's *my* turn," and at the word "my" he beat his little breast. "Now, it's *my* turn; now *I'm* coming for a change!" he shouted all over the place.

Next morning he knelt in his red altar-boy cassock and surplice at the altar steps, a burning candle in his hand, to receive his Lord and Master into his young heart. A radiantly happy boy sat in the place of honour at breakfast afterwards, his plate decorated with flowers and heaped with little gifts.

It was but two weeks before the camp was to open. Not a single house was finished. The whole family worked together feverishly. The beds had been promised by a department store in Boston, and the kitchen equipment by one in New York, but nothing had come so far. Again we lived in hope.

On a rainy morning we all assembled in the camp kitchen for a family council about the rusty Army stoves and the oily, filthy cement floor which was cracked in many places. The kitchen was the sore point of the camp. The paint had scaled from the drab, tin-covered walls. It was entirely empty except for those huge stoves and some benches, on which we were perched. We didn't look very hopeful on that particular morning. We were all engaged in painting, and it could easily be told which one was painting the red floor in the chapel, or the white window-sills in some of the halls, or the green flower boxes. From our seats we were looking disgustedly around the kitchen, when the door opened and one of the workmen said:

" Somebody wants to see you."

A beautifully groomed, handsome, middle-aged man lifted his hat and after a cheerful " Good morning all around," said: " Could you please announce me to the Baroness?"

Goodness—the camp manager! This camp kitchen was the last place in the world in which I wanted to meet him, but there he was, and there *I* was, and in that attire! Too late. Here was the precious man on whom the entire success of our camp would depend, as I had been told. But let's hope for the best, for his imagination, for his sense of humour—after all, there *is* a war going on, and the camp will be finished in ten days, because it must.

Courageously I stepped forward to greet and introduce him. My apologetic remarks he took most graciously, and said:

" Never mind, never mind. Could you kindly show me the camp now?"

" But this *is* the camp!" the girls chorused in amusement.

" And this is the camp kitchen!" little five-year-old Johannes cried at the top of his voice. " It isn't quite finished," he added.

" Not—quite—finished——! You—don't—mean——! "

I saw plainly that he needed a change of atmosphere, and suggested:

"Let's go over to the recreation hall."

Hedwig stopped me.

"No, Mother, I'm sorry, I'm painting there."

Where else could we go? The dormitories were out of the question, the future chapel looked like a log cabin inside out, and as for the many lovely places under the trees and at the brook—the rain was pouring down. The taxi was still waiting outside. Soon I discovered why. The chauffeur wanted to know what to do with the two elegant pigskin cases, the tennis racquet, and the set of golf clubs.

I suggested that he drive up to the farm for a cup of tea. Once at the farm I quickly changed into my best and, trying to be charming as never before in my life, I painted a glowing picture of the future camp.

He listened politely, and then he suddenly discovered that for some important reason—how silly that he hadn't thought of it before, he would have to go back to Boston on the next train!

"But you will come a few days before the camp opens, won't you?" I repeated the question now, for the fifth time at least.

"If I can possibly manage it, I shall, of course. I shall write you a note first thing when I reach Boston."

Two days later I held his letter in my hand. Among other things, he said—and I still have his letter:

"I had no idea you were not ready to operate. When I think of obtaining, shipping, installing and testing out equipment only for your kitchen by July 10—this is absolutely impossible. I strictly advise you to return your deposits and wait for next season to start RIGHT. To be perfectly honest, Madam, I doubt whether it is in your line to operate a camp . . ."

Return the deposits? Impossible, sir; every cent was spent already.

What a blow! But I couldn't get into mourning merely for lack of time: the cook had arrived in Waterbury! This time it was a beautiful, sunny day. The lady cook showed much more understanding and real imagination than the well-groomed manager. The kitchen was freshly painted, and the stoves were just being cleaned with kerosene. After I had showed her around, continually explaining what this and that place *would* look like in eight days, we finished our business talk on the new benches under the trees at the brook. The gracious lady consented to come for seventy-five dollars a week under the following conditions: that she and her husband be given a three-room apartment close to the kitchen, that she have a large electric dough-mixer, an electric meat-cutter, a stainless-steel coffee-urn, a stainless-steel sink, a gas baking oven, so and so many aluminium pots and pans. . . .

I was so grateful that she was willing to come at all, that without looking at the list, I promised that everything would be ready. Overnight I went down to New York and spent the whole day buying kitchen equipment. I didn't ask for prices any more. The main thing was—I got it all. Footsore and exhausted, I fell on my seat in the train the same evening to go back to Vermont, feeling as if I deserved the Congressional Medal.

Every day I grew prouder of my family. The girls started to paint and hammer as early as five o'clock in the morning, and worked through the day and evening until ten o'clock or later. If I wasn't in New York or Boston or Montpelier in one of the offices, or on the train, I looked over the camp anxiously and counted the objects which hadn't arrived yet. There were only five days more to go, and the beds hadn't come. Pillows and blankets had arrived, but there were no beds to put them on; and the china was lying about because the kitchen cupboards were not yet ready.

Georg was busy at the farm; the haying season was in full swing, and plumbers and electricians were working in the house. He couldn't help me much now, or so he thought; but the tight clasp of his hand once in a while and the reassuring twinkle of his eyes were the greatest help at that moment.

Father Wasner had his hands full, arranging the chapel and sacristy, ordering and copying music, numbering one hundred folders, making programmes for the singing sessions of each day, and trying to obtain recorders.

The different houses at the camp had to be named. The girls suggested names of composers, the great masters, Johanna, who was very good at lettering, wrote the signs in white paint on green boards: " Mozart Hall," " Palestrina,"

" Schubert," " Beethoven," " Stephen Foster," " Haydn," and " Brahms Hall." Then we came to the naming of the dining-room. Father Wasner opposed violently our calling it " Johann Sebastian Bach Hall " ; that was a disgrace in his eyes. But it had to have a name. After the day's work was done, the girls went through a music encyclopædia, and with a yell of triumph they discovered that Rossini, the composer of *The Barber of Seville,* had been a baker and a cook. Not even Father Wasner would find any objection to calling the dining-room " Rossini Hall."

Two days before the camp opened, half the beds were there. Two early guests came. Hastily we put them up on the farm.

July 10: The guests were expected on the evening train. The Governor of Vermont, the local worthies of Stowe, our friend, the State Forester, and everyone from the village who wished were invited for the formal opening of the camp at seven o'clock in the evening ; and still half the beds hadn't come. It wasn't funny any more. Eighty-four people expected to sleep this very night, and I was still many beds short.

Among the guests who had arrived by different buses earlier in the day, there was a gentleman who noticed that I was alarmed about something. As I was running about the place, he stopped me, put his hand on my shoulder, and said kindly :

" All that matters now is that your boys and our boys come home safely. Isn't that right? "

That saved the day for me. Not only that day, but very often afterwards when I was in trouble, I repeated those words, and they worked every time.

The plumbers had gone, the carpenters had gone, the electricians and painters, too. The dormitories and private rooms looked lovely, shining with cleanliness. The chapel was finished ; it even had a little steeple. In the recreation hall was the small camp store, equipped with toothbrushes, pencils, stamps, and postcards. And at last but not least, the kitchen had emerged from the state of an ugly larva into a most beautiful butterfly. In the shiny kitchen floor were mirrored scores of stainless-steel pots and pans and ladles. There was the coffee-urn, the baking-oven, an oversized dough-mixer, an electric meat-cutter, a brand-new kitchen table seven by seven feet, and a brand-new kitchen cabinet. The large refrigerator was stuffed with hams, ducks, chickens, and veal, and the pantry looked like a medium-sized country store. And in the centre of the kitchen dwelt the most imposing object of all—the lady cook, with a tall, snow-white cap and the air of a Dowager Empress. Her husband was unpacking their luggage in the newly created three-room apartment furnished with maple furniture, according to their wishes. Four girls waited on the Empress.

If only that second shipment of beds would come. One couldn't even telephone, because they had been shipped by truck, and the truck was " on its way." For heaven's sake! During the formal opening ceremonies, while we were singing the National Anthem, Georg was supposed to raise the flag slowly—and we had forgotten to buy a flag! It was five o'clock, too late for the stores. Georg rushed down to Stowe and borrowed one from the high school for this night.

My secretary was busy writing names on little white cards to be tacked to the room doors and over the beds in the dormitories. The express office called to tell us that a few huge packages were waiting for us. Thus the three dozen white aprons came just in time for the young waitresses, who had started to set the tables for the first meal.

Around six o'clock Governor Wills came. How I would have liked to stay with him, looking relaxed and cheerful; but a lady was looking for her luggage, which she had sent a week ago, and in the kitchen they had discovered that I had forgotten to purchase a tin-opener—what about the tomato juice then?

Little Johannes, sitting on a tree, watching the highway down in the valley, suddenly yelled:

" The buses are coming!"

Our guests had arrived. My husband, the girls, and I welcomed them. Then Governor Wills opened solemnly and formally the Trapp Family Music Camp. Everyone joined in singing " The Star-Spangled Banner," and slowly the flag rose over our camp for the first time. The Governor addressed the guests and welcomed them in the name of the State of Vermont. The local worthies followed in welcoming them in the name of the town of Stowe, and my husband welcomed them in the name of his family.

After the opening ceremonies we ushered the guests into the dining-room.

" Dear Lord," I prayed most fervently, " and here they are

going to stay until You have sent the remaining beds "; and I asked the waitresses to be very, very slow.

The incredible happened again. Before the glasses were taken off the tables, the truck arrived, and everyone helped to put the beds up; and when the guests left Rossini Hall, strengthened and refreshed, everything was ready. Camp guests and townspeople grouped themselves on the lawn around the flagpole, and we gave them a little welcoming concert under the stars. We couldn't help thinking back to that first starlight performance in the same place two years before, and as we looked up into the sky, we saw flashes of green and golden light darting upwards—northern lights. It reminded us of that crisp winter day when it all had started, and we felt as if we were still standing under the rainbow.

When I came out next morning, my secretary was already waiting with a harassed expression.

" I'm so sorry to disturb you—but we have no water in the camp. The spring has run dry; the water supply is not enough for all the people."

The guests were already streaming into the dining-room. I had only two minutes' time, and then I had to " say something." With a knife I tapped on a glass, and then I announced cheerfully:

" Ladies and gentlemen, will you please get your music and also your towels ready. We want to give you this morning the sensation of a shower in the wilderness. The buses are on their way. We shall have a picnic at Bingham Falls."

And so we did. While the whole camp was enjoying a hot summer day at the cool waterfalls, making up for the lack of a morning bath, Mr. Steele, the ever-helpful, brought an electric pump, made a temporary pipeline from the brook into the houses, and supplied the bathrooms with brook water, leaving the spring water for washbowls and kitchen.

From then on things went smoothly.

Every morning and every afternoon we sang with our guests the immortal music of the old masters down in the grove near the brook. We sang the folk-songs of many nations. We sang choral works of the classical masters, and it was pure joy to witness how persons who had never before sung to any extent, could derive such deep satisfaction out of learning those wonderful pieces. Every night we all danced folk-

dances on the lawn. One day we took them up the highest
mountain in the State of Vermont, Mount Mansfield; on
another we showed them one of the loveliest lakes of the
neighbourhood, carrying along music and food. Every excur-
sion was a success. Every night after Benediction in the chapel,
we sang a few motets and hymns to give those hearts present
a little more chance to enter into the spirit of prayer. There
was so much to pray for.

XVII. Snapshots of the Camp

The first camp summer was over. Everything had been done
now for the first time, and we could feel how a tradition is
established. The arrival of the guests for every Song Week,
the picnics, the camp routine, and the last evenings would
repeat themselves year after year, until some day somebody
would say: "We always do it this way."

The break up of the camp was very touching. There were
funny surprises during the last evening meal. Little groups
performed short scenes from camp life. After that, Maria's
recorder class gave a short concert, showing what could be
done in just nine days of teaching. We all laughed to tears
when the beginners, trembling with stage fright, produced out
of pure nervousness funny little shrieks while playing "Mary
Had a Little Lamb."

It showed again that the recorder is the ideal instrument for
any adult whose childhood musical education has been
neglected. If someone discovers on his fiftieth birthday, that he
should have taken piano or violin lessons at school, he will
hardly want to start them, for fear of not getting very far; but
he will always miss it—to be able to "make music" himself.
That's where the recorder comes in. After six weeks of faithful practising, even the oldest pupil can play folk-tunes quite
nicely. The combination of soprano, alto, tenor, and bass
recorders gives a lovely mellow sound. There is no limit to the
literature which can be played, beginning with easy, four-part
setting and going through the vast realm of madrigals and
motets. Some will get more ambitious and find out about the
wonderful literature written for the recorder: sonatas by
Telemann, arias by Bach, etc., real virtuoso literature, too.

There are untold riches in that little instrument, which can be had for less than twenty dollars.

And it really happened. People who had started out with " Mary Had a Little Lamb " in that first camp summer, and who came back year after year, are now playing Bach and Telemann, to Maria's pride and joy. They themselves have spread their enthusiasm among their friends, and the forgotten recorder is enjoying a revival all over the States.

After the recorder concert by Maria's class, we all went down to the chapel. Once more we prayed together in thanksgiving, and then we sang for our guests once more by candle-light their favourite songs: " The Children's Blessing," " The Lord is My Shepherd," " The Virgin's Lullaby."

After that we went over to the little dell where we had given that historic concert for the soldiers, and a huge bonfire was lit.

Next morning three big buses came to take our guests to the train. When the buses were filled, they lined up abreast, facing us, and the place resounded with the round: *' Viva, Viva la Musica!"* each bus taking a part. Many a tear was shed. Everyone was sorry that the Song Week was over.

The Trapp Family Music Camp had turned out to be the answer to the question which had been asked hundreds of times backstage after a concert, at parties, and in letters:

" How could we do what you are doing: sing in our family?"

In that ten-day course we try to make people acquainted with as much musical literature as possible, from easy beginnings to complicated cantatas and fugues. The excuse, " We couldn't possibly sing—we have no piano," is being dropped, as we usually sing down at the brook or under the old butternut trees outside the recreation hall. Besides the singing, we also try to revive those beautiful old folk-dances of all nations, and we try to show our friends at the camp that the best recreation is when one does things oneself with others joining in: singing, dancing, playing games, telling stories, reading aloud, enacting those wonderful old folk-customs throughout the year, following the maxim: " A family which sings together, plays together, and prays together, usually stays together."

Our age has become so mechanical that this has also

affected our recreation. People have got used to sitting down
and watching a movie, a ball game, a television set. It may be
good once in a while, but it certainly is not good all the time.
Our own faculties, our imagination, our memory, the ability
to do things with our mind and our hands—they need to be
exercised. If we become too passive, we get dissatisfied.

What a great joy and satisfaction it was when the campers
became so enthusiastic about everything that they didn't want
to wait a whole year until they could meet again. They
founded the Stowe Singers, a group of people who would
meet once a month to sing and play the recorder together.
There was a chapter in Boston, in New York, and later also in
Montreal.

Funny things happened at times in the camp; for instance, that
one morning when the ladies, sopranos and altos, were singing
too loud—oh, much too loud, and Father Wasner, throwing up
his arms, implored them:

"Reduce, ladies, reduce!"

Or that other time when the whole group of one hundred
and twenty people was congregated for the afternoon singing
and, while Father Wasner was detained on the telephone, a
lady entertained the others with a little cloth monkey, which
she made do all kinds of funny tricks. Next to her the concert
pianist, Fritz Jahoda, was standing with his little daughter
Eleanor, four years old. Suddenly the child's clear voice was
heard:

"My Daddy says you look exactly like your monkey!"

In the camp we had a question box. Towards the end of the
Song Week one evening would be devoted to answering and
discussing questions.

"What do you think about popular music?" was one of the
most frequent questions.

Father Wasner would attend to the questions concerning
music. With emphasis he would declare:

"The mere word 'popular' means 'of the people,' but
these tunes going under that name have nothing at all to do
with the people. They are artificially made up by some indivi-
dual, put on the market with the aid of great publicity, and
after two years they are completely forgotten, which only
shows how little popular they have been. Neither the words

nor the music express the true sentiments of the people. That's why they have no strength to survive." And then he always pleaded: "But there is such genuine folk-music in this country, marvellous folk-songs throughout the hills and dales of New England and down the Appalachian-Mountain range, the cowboy songs in the West and the Negro spirituals in the South. These are the ones which deserve the word ' popular,' as they come out of the people, and will live through the centuries."

Another much-asked question was:

"Why does the Trapp Family not wear American clothes?"

We explained that after the First World War the people in Austria returned to wearing their national costume for economic reasons. It is so much less expensive. You have two or three wool dresses for the winter and three or four cotton ones for the summer, and that lasts you for years and years. You change the white blouses and the coloured aprons according to week-days or holidays. In a family with seven daughters that makes a great difference. We love our dresses for still another reason besides the money question, and that is that we don't have to bother about the fashion of the day; whether frog-green or cardinal-red is the latest rage. It has become an all-round agreeable and practical situation for us, saving money, time, and peace of mind.

"And what are you going to do about your girls marrying? Do they meet young men? Do they have boy friends?" was the third of the most popular questions.

As far as marrying went, my husband and I had started in Europe to say one Hail Mary together every day for each one of our children in order that they might find the right mate in life. As for meeting people—who met people more than we with all those parties and concerts, invitations, and now with the camp? But things were altogether different here from what they had been in Europe. I had always felt sorry for my girls because they didn't have that wonderful experience I had had when I was young and in our Catholic Youth Movement. Those large groups of young boys and girls meeting together for singing and folk-dancing and long hikes and discussions—what pure joy, what a wonderful thing! Such groups didn't seem to exist here.

One day seven young men walked into the camp and introduced themselves as students from the University of Montreal.

They had head us in a concert there and wanted to meet u
all again. The moment I saw them, I was startled. In the
shorts and their brown knees and rucksacks, they reminde
me very strongly of the type of boy I had always wished m
girls to know. They happened to come at a difficult time whe
we were short of help all around the camp. Would they sta
and help us out? Four weeks later when they finally had to g
home after their long stay with us, I realised how true th
word of Our Lord is: " Whatsoever you shall ask the Fathe
in My name, that will I do," " Whatsoever," He had said, an
He meant it. A mother had asked for the right company fo
her children, and there it was. Singing, dancing, hiking, camp
ing, discussing and praying together had filled all the spar
time of the last weeks The young men still come back tim
and again. They bring their friends. We have met the
families, and some of them have stayed on our hill an
become members of the larger family.

It was during the second camp summer, 1945, that one da
in August we were told over the telephone that the war wa
over. One of us ran down and rang the bell of the chapel, an
when all the people had gathered outside on the lawn, we tol
them. I shall never forget how impressed I was that there wa
no great shouting, no loud rejoicing, but one by one, they a
filed into the chapel to give thanks.

Then came a telegram that our boys were coming hom
from Italy. Not only the whole family, but also the whol
camp participated in arranging their welcome. These boys ha
become a sort of symbol for all the others who were expecte
home now, sooner or later. They had become " our boys.
The large hay wagon was decorated with garlands and flower
Georg drove the team. Little Johannes was riding ahead o
his pony, Popcorn, the girls and I in our Sunday best, on th
wagon. So we awaited the boys at the edge of the cam
property. There they had to get out of the car and into th
wagon and, accompanied by one hundred and twenty cam
guests, they rode on in triumph. What a day! Only then
saw how much Georg must have suffered in silence all thes
anxious years of uncertainty, now when the burden ha
dropped off his shoulders.

After the first joy and happiness of being together again ha
quieted down, the boys began to make plans. Rupert had pu

side his personal plans for so many years, had sacrificed his medical career to the necessity of keeping the family going with our concert work; and we had appreciated it deeply. The war had shown that he was not indispensible in that work any more. Now he could think of getting his American degree of M.D. He enrolled at the University of Vermont and went to school again.

Werner, within whom the farmer and the musician were always fighting, decided to stay in concert work and work on the farm between times.

Once we had three girls in the camp. They came from a family of ten children. They became such close friends with our girls that they came back the very same summer, together with Father, Mother, and the rest of the family. They were wonderful people, and we had so many things in common! Later somewhere on our concert tour I got a letter from Rupert in which he complained how lonely he was, and wasn't there anyone I knew whom he could visit.

"Yes," I said, "I do know somebody. Why don't you go and see the Lajoies in Fall River."

The next thing was a radiantly happy announcement of his engagement to Henriette Lajoie, which we received while on our in Seattle. Three cheers for the camp!

XVIII. Trapp Family Austrian Relief, Inc.

When Joseph, the young son of Jacob, was taken into Egypt, it was against his will. There his beginning was very hard; but after years of much trouble, he succeeded in winning the confidence of the people and their king, and his exile turned into glory. Oftentimes he may have wondered for what this new name and new fame were given him, until one day he learned through travellers that a famine was raging in his homeland, and his people starving to death. Now he understood, and with the help of his new countrymen, he could use his new power to help his people at home.

Something similar happened to us. *Our* beginning in *our* Egypt was a hard one; *we* also succeeded in winning the confidence of the people in the new country; and as we built up a new name and new fame, with *us* too, exile turned into glory. Also *we* wondered at times what it all meant, until one day we, too, learned that in the old homeland a famine was raging, and the people starving to death. That was the answer and most happily could we turn now towards the old home and with the aid of our new countrymen, help the old ones.

It happened like this.

In January, 1947, a few days before we had to leave for the West Coast again, a letter arrived, addressed to the Trapp Family Singers. It came from the General of the American Army of Occupation in Austria, and the letter described briefly how terribly hard, how heart-rending the suffering of the Austrian people was. And then the letter pleaded: Could the Trapp Family Singers perhaps do something for Austria during their concert tours?

This was a call, a summons. The letter was read aloud in the family, and a council was held. For this we would have to incorporate. The very next day we went to our capital, Montpelier, and founded the Trapp Family Austrian Relief Inc. A document with the seal of the State of Vermont testified that this corporation was founded for the purpose of " general help and relief to poor, displaced, and unfortunate people of all nationalities and creeds in the United States and elsewhere," and that it was "not organised for profit, but exclusively for charitable purposes." The first meeting of the association was held at the law office of Mr. William N. Theriault. At this meeting by-laws of the corporation were discussed and unanimously adopted, and the board of trustees was duly elected by unanimous vote: President, Georg von Trapp; Vice-president, Maria Augusta von Trapp; Treasurer, Reverend Franz Wasner; plus two additional officers: Secretary, Johanna von Trapp; Clerk, Werner von Trapp. It was also voted that the corporation procure a corporate seal and a rubber stamp.

Now we were permitted to collect food and clothing and money from coast to coast, and *contributions could be deducted from the donor's income-tax*. That impressed us. We had been told that big firms, factories, and also individuals made at one time terrifically large contributions to charities for that very reason. We saw ourselves heading for millions in collections. We also had a leaflet printed, which we intended to distribute among the audiences of our concerts. In this we

aid that our native country, Austria, which so many
Americans knew and loved, was in the gravest danger.

"The country which gave to the world a Haydn, Mozart,
Schubert, Johann Strauss—a 'Silent Night'—may perish if we
don't all help together and act now"; that "everybody is informed about conditions in the larger European countries, but
hardly anybody knows what is going on in Austria . . . where
her people are just about to give up courage and hope." We
told them that "all over Austria the population suffers from
lack of practically everything and in Vienna conditions had
reached a climax of misery." Then we said: "Let a social
worker tell you about her daily attempts to do the impossible"
—and we quoted from actual letters we had received.

"Our railroad stations have been shattered by bombs. In
the ruins live thousands of displaced persons, waiting for trains
to take them no one knows where, while hundreds of new
ones arrive daily. The dying and the dead, the badly sick with
high fever, and little children are lying together between the
shattered walls. We have no accommodation for these poorest
of the poor. When the new transports arrive, we usually find
little babies with diapers frozen to their emaciated bodies,
children dressed in newspapers or old rags kept together by
string and pieces of broken wire, and the grown-ups in all
stages of exhaustion and starvation. Usually these people have
been in that box car for two weeks or longer without any care.
It is absolutely impossible to describe the condition in which
they arrive. We need food, clothing, and first aid materials
for thousands, but we hardly have enough for a few hundred.

"We can't get needles. We have to rent a needle for a
schilling a day, and woe if you should break it."

A university professor of Vienna says in a letter to us:
"Personally, I do not mind the hunger so much, but it is so
very embarrassing that I cannot get shoe-laces and have to
walk about without."

Then the leaflet went on: "The urgent necessity for help is
also felt and stressed by the authorities of the U.S. Occupation
Army. A high American officer and an American Army
Chaplain, in co-operation with local agencies in Austria, sent
us recently more than 5,000 addresses of the most needy
people."

Then we told them that we had founded our corporation
and called it the Trapp Family Austrian Relief, Inc., in order

that our name might' warrant that every cent, every item
would reach its destination: a needy person in Austria. "We
have no overhead expenses; we do everything within our
family."

Then we suggested ways to help Austria:

"1. Send us any clothing or non-perishable foodstuffs you
can spare. We can use everything: shoe-laces, pencils, needle
and thread, woollen blankets. . . .

"2. Contribute by donations to the 'Trapp Family Austrian
Relief, Inc.,' Stowe, Vermont. YOUR DONATION AS A CHARITABLE
CONTRIBUTION IS DEDUCTIBLE FROM INCOME-TAX.

"3. Write to us and ask for addresses of needy families or
individuals if you prefer to take care of someone yourself."

And the leaflet ended:

"The other day we read the words of St. Ambrose, one of
the greatest men of the fourth century, spoken at the time of a
famine: 'If you know that anybody is hungry or sick, and you
have any means at all and do not help, then you will have the
responsibility for each one who dies, and for each little child
who might be harmed or crippled for life.' Let us also remember that other word: 'As long as you did it to one of
these My least brethren, you did it to Me.'"

Thus fortified with stationery, 100,000 leaflets, a rubber
stamp, and the best of good will, we set out for the West
Coast.

We had never done anything like it before, but then was
that not so with our music camp, our handicraft exhibition,
our concerts, or our starting to build a new house? These big
tasks had been hurled at us without allowing even enough
time to buy a handbook to look up the "how to."

We tried everything we could think of. Upon arriving in a
town, some of us went to the local newspaper to give an interview on starving Austria, while another group did the same
with the local radio station. From both parties we usually
received the greatest understanding and co-operation. At the
beginning of the concerts the leaflets were handed out, and
during the interval I made an appeal to the audience. I used to
say:

"If you want to avoid making packages, our big blue bus
will be to-morrow morning in front of the hotel——" (and
then I almost invariably named the wrong hotel, usually the

one from the day before—but the people always found the right place).

The next morning I would stand by the bus with a couple of the girls, and—what a touching sight—people would flock to us from all directions, carrying bundles or heaps of clothing in their arms. In smaller country towns pick-up trucks would drive up behind the bus and empty their contents on our seats.

It was in March and somewhere in the South-West when, after a concert, a lady stopped at the bus, took off her winter coat, and said:

" It's my only one, but I don't need it any more this year. Could you please send it to a teacher over there? I'm a teacher myself."

In another place a mother came to see me in the hotel, her face tear-stained, her hands twisting a handkerchief. A few days before she had lost her only daughter in an accident. After she had heard the appeal in last night's concert, she had worked half the night to collect all the girl's things. Now she brought them in five big boxes together with a photograph.

" Look at her," she said, " and pick me out a girl of her age in Austria, who will write to me."

When we came to the border of California, our bus was filled to the brim. At the border we were stopped and asked to show our luggage. Eyes turned to heaven, we silently pointed to the bus: " Look at the luggage!" But law is law, and the officer of the State Board of Health, or whatever it was, had to demand that we empty our warehouse. Rows of tables were arranged there for the travellers' convenience in showing their suitcases. We drove to the last row of these tables, and while emptying the bus, put everything in bags and boxes. After two hours forty-six large pieces were packed, to the admiration of the staff of that Health Board.

It was in California, in Ventura. Our appeal for Austria was received as never before. The whole town responded. We were asked to come back in a week. Different organisations made clothing drives, and when we came back to collect the contributions our bus was almost too small. It was packed to the last seat up to the ceiling, and we all had to stand in the aisle as far as Santa Barbara. The very kind Superior of the Franciscan Fathers helped us all he could. In the grounds of the Old Mission the things were packed and shipped in numerous large crates.

We were perfectly overwhelmed by the way the American people in general reacted to our appeal. And this after many years of constant drives. Starting with Finnish and Greek relief, there had been an uninterrupted chain of appeals and campaigns, and now on top of that—we came along with our unprofessional relief organisation, which consisted of a rubber stamp, a leaflet, a letter-head, and one family that was burning to help. And the miracle repeated itself after every concert. After we had said we needed food and clothing for the starving Austrians and we needed money to send to them—the people went home, got food and clothing and also some money and, like the widow's cruse, the big blue bus never went empty.

This happened to be the longest concert tour we ever had. We covered almost thirty thousand miles and gave one hundred and seven performances. On the West Coast we once had seventeen concerts in succession without a break. We had large distances to cover every day, and the days were like this: For an hour each morning our bus was filled with gifts for Austria by the townspeople who had been at last night's concert. When it was time for us to leave, Rudy, our driver of that year, and incidentally of Austrian parentage himself would blow the horn furiously.

" Three hundred and fifty miles to-day!" he would shout.

After heartfelt thanks to the generous givers, we took off and immediately started on the daily routine. In grocery stores we asked for empty boxes; in granaries, for empty feed bags. These were now packed systematically by Martina, Hedwig, Rosmarie, and Lorli. When the boxes and bags were filled, they were handed to the men. Georg and Werner tied them with double string. Agathe wrote the labels. Johanna and Maria typed lists of contents and letters announcing the parcels. They had found out that if you squeeze a typewriter between your knees at a certain angle, you can write quite well in a moving bus. Meanwhile, I was reading. The letters came in at first by the dozen, but soon by the hundred. When enough finished packages were piled up so that Rudy was walled in and no traffic between front and rear was possible any more, Rudy used to pull up at the next post office in a small country town, and the postmaster would have a red letter day in his life: that big blue bus with the word " Chartered " in front and " Trapp Family Singers " on the

ides pulling up almost to his window, girls in quaint dresses
opping out, and packages, boxes, bags, piling up on his
ounter—why—that's like Christmas! The girls helped to
veigh the load, and at the end they asked for a thousand
-cent stamps, and off they went again. The next half-hour
vas passed in complete silence, everybody licking stamps,
asting them on envelopes—the leaflet was being sent to long
ists of addresses. Then the packing was resumed, and after
wo hours, another pile of twenty or thirty bags was dumped
t another post office. And so on.

Reading the hundreds of letters was a hard task. There were
etters from people who had seen better times and never in
heir lives had thought that they would one day have to beg.
These letters were usually very long and wordy. After having
alked about everything under the sun, music or pre-war
nemories, at the very end came a final remark such as:

" My old wife and I are sitting on the floor of our com-
letely empty room. Even the doors with the door-frames and
he windows with the window-frames have been stolen." [The
limate in an Austrian winter is little different from Vermont.]
" We have nothing to eat, nothing to heat with, nothing to
vear. Sincerely yours."

There were the most touching thank-you letters coming in,
ike this one:

" But the most precious gift was the pound of coffee you
ent me. With this I have paid my debts at the shoemaker,
grocer, milk store ; I paid the rent for our room for half a
vear in advance ; I could exchange some flour, jam, and a
ittle butter for it ; and some of it I still keep in case one of us
hould get ill. How can I ever thank you enough?"

The two Catholic Army Chaplains at Vienna and Salzburg
had most generously offered their help at the very beginning.
Permission was given for us to ship everything straight to
hem. They handed it over to a small staff of volunteers, who
hecked the cases and handed the goods out. In that way it
vas possible to avoid having the things go to the black
narket or into undeserving hands.

As the trip went on, we got more and more tired, but we
earned that one can be happily tired, and the element of
happiness can outweigh the tiredness. When, on the way back,
ve stopped in St. Paul, the seminary there had collected in the
gymnasium hundreds of pairs of shoes, heaps of cassocks,

suits, etc.; and on top of it all, the seminarians helped to pac
the gifts and send them to the seminary in Salzburg. Final
they made a collection and even paid the postage.

Long after we were back from our trip, boxes and bags wit
food and clothing kept arriving at Stowe. It was more than w
could handle every day, and we started to store it in one of th
buildings in the camp. When the camp started that summe
that long barrack was full to the ceiling with clothing. Wha
we needed was hands, volunteers to help. Then a friend'
lady came one day from Rochester, New York, and simpl
took over. She recruited volunteers in the morning and othe
in the afternoon. And under the able direction of Mr
Harper the huge job of packing thirty thousand pounds
material was achieved in a few weeks.

All these are only highlights. We could go on and c
quoting names, names of towns, and names of people, wh
answered the call: " Please help!" Half a year later the b
barrack in the camp was full again; but we were absolutel
out of funds, and it does cost money to send quantities o
goods abroad. What should we do?

In our library at home we had a book about the Leopoldir
Society of Austria. That was founded in 1829 and through
the Austrian clergy and people contributed almost a millio
dollars to Catholic missions in America. There was an ide
We wrote a short letter, explaining our desperate situation
that we had many thousands of pounds of goods and couldn
send them for lack of money, and then we sent one letter
every priest in America. The whole family was occupied fo
two solid weeks in folding these 40,500 letters, putting the
into envelopes, and classifying them according to State
Again the miracle happened. Money came flowing in, mostl
in one-dollar and five-dollar cheques, and it amounted t
exactly the sum which we needed.

One day a big manila envelope arrived. Public charities i
Austria approached us with some five thousand addresses o
the most destitute and needy families, and would we or coul
we find American families who would take over one suc
address and send food and clothing from time to time?

On our little mimeographing machine we brought out sma
forms. The first page had the address of the needy family, an
in three sentences, the most necessary information. Th
second page had suggestions for four different packages: (1

To keep them alive "; (2) "To keep them clean and neat ";
3) "To keep them warm "; (4) "To make them happy."
The third page said: "Detach this side and return to our
office with your signature."

In this way we can keep track whether the offer, "Oh give
me ten names, I can easily take care of them," merely came
from the high spirits after a concert, or whether the person
really took care of his adopted brother. Up to date about
fourteen thousand families have been placed with generous
Americans.

Meanwhile, things have become a little better in the old
country. The shop windows are not empty any more. But
the question is, what is harder: not to be able to buy anything
because the stores are empty, or not to be able to buy anything because the prices are far beyond your budget? You
can only look at what you cannot get—and that makes a
people restless, and that is always dangerous. Compared with
what they were two years ago, conditions in Austria are a
good deal better; compared with what they were before the
war—conditions in Austria are still unbearably hard. Therefore, our small relief association, which has managed with the
grace of God to send about three hundred thousand pounds
of goods in a little over two years, will continue to work as
long as there is anyone left in need of relief and as long as
used clothing, old toys, canned goods, etc., find their way to
us. Everything which is now sent serves a twofold purpose!
first, it relieves the dire material need: and second, it helps
to keep up hope, without which one cannot live.

"Many a one has lost his faith in God because he first lost
his faith in man; and many a one has regained his faith in
God because he met a good man who took the bitterness out
of his heart," says Cardinal Faulhaber.

XIX. A Letter

In the summer of 1947 there went to all our friends in America
and Europe the following letter:
Dear Friends:
In the many letters arriving daily from far and near, for
which we thank you from our hearts, recurs that one anxious

question: " But how was that possible—was he sick—wha:
happened? " And so we want to tell you how it happened.

Our last concert tour was very long and strenuous. A:
usual Georg accompanied us. While driving up the Wes:
Coast from Los Angeles to Seattle, I noticed how pale he
looked, but he insisted he felt perfectly all right except for a
growing tiredness.

" But we're all tired, you as well as I," he said.

In Seattle he began to cough. I implored him to fly back to
New York to see a doctor who had once helped him wonder
fully through bronchitis.

" I'm not ill; I want to stay with you," he begged.

But the cough got worse, and in Denver, Colorado, we pu:
him on the plane.

When I didn't get any news from him for five days, I wa:
worried. Unfortunately, just at that time there was a tele:
phone strike all over the United States. I couldn't telephone
to him. So I telegraphed to the doctor, and the answer came
back: CAPTAIN VON TRAPP RECOVERING RAPIDLY FROM PNEU:
MONIA.

When I finally got Georg on the telephone, he said:

" I'm much better, but here in the hospital it's terrible. D:
come, and then let's go home. I want to go home."

But we still had concerts, and another week went by. I
received two letters and a report from the doctor, and i:
all sounded reassuring. But an anxiety had gripped me, an:
finally I flew the last 1,500 miles to New York.

As I entered the hospital room, Georg sat up in bed
stretched both arms wide, and said only: " Come!"

I held him long, pressed close to me, to gain time to pul:
myself together. My heart almost stood still with fright a:
the appalling change which in two short weeks had taker
place in him. Sunken, hollow cheeks, deep-set eyes circled
with dark shadows, bluish lips—his dear face was almost un:
recognisable, and he was as thin as a skeleton. A frightfu:
thought rose in my mind: perhaps it was not all so simple as
it had sounded in the letters.

But Georg was very happy now.

" Thank heaven you're here! Now see that you get me out
of here fast. Then let's go straight home."

At his wish I took up the telephone on his night table,

...lled the doctor in charge, and asked when I could take ...eorg home.

To my amazement, the answer was: " Any time, to-morrow ...r the day after to-morrow." He asked me to come to his ...fice that evening. He wanted to talk to me.

That reassured me again. Surely it couldn't be so bad if he ...as permitted that long trip of 330 miles. As soon as we were ... home on our mountain, the good air and the spring sun...ine, together with his favourite dishes and all that love and ...re could think of, would soon bring him back to health ...ain.

So we spent a happy day. I had to tell him every detail of ...e last two weeks. Then we made plans.

" You know, I have no pain, there is nothing the matter ...ith me any more, only I am so terribly tired and weak."

These were the last carefree hours of life together. But we ...dn't know it. Or did we suspect it somehow? Each time ...hen I stood in the doorway with a last, cheerful good-bye, ...mething " important " occurred to one of us: " Just this I ...ust really tell you." Georg was so jovial and happy, and, ...Actually he doesn't look so terribly bad, only a bit under ...e weather," thought I to myself as I sat in the taxi on my ...ay to the doctor, who would, of course, give me prescrip...ns for diet, medicine, etc.

" Thank goodness, the pneumonia is well over," I said to ...e doctor, as I sat opposite him in his consultation-room. ...mewhat hesitatingly he answered.

" Yes, but the X-ray picture shows a large shadow in the ...ng, which indicates a tumour."

" Well, then, we must cure that tumour," I said, looking ...nfidently and encouragingly at the doctor.

" But it is not a benign tumour," he answered in a muffled ...ice without looking up. I didn't understand him, and was ...ly astonished. Then suddenly like lightning, an appalling ...ought went through my head.

" For heaven's sake, doctor, it can't be cancer?"

Silently he bent his head low over his folded hands, and a ...avy silence settled over the room. . . .

New York is a very large city, and within the limits of this ...ty live more people than in all Austria. But for me in that ...nister night it was worse than a wilderness. In the wilderness at least I would have seen the starry sky, but in New York the little sky which one might still see between the sky scrapers is veiled in smoke. In my desperation I didn't even think of taking a bus or a taxi. Mechanically I simply walked on in the direction of the hotel for two and a half hours; and not a single church did I pass on the way. Quite automatically I had put my hand in my pocket and started to say the rosary. Once again this ancient prayer, which has borne up to heaven so much human suffering and heartache, proved to be a good, strong friend in need.

In my room I literally hung on the telephone. Most of the friends on whose help I counted had gone away. How I should have loved to telephone to the children or Father Wasner; but they were on the way home, and I had no idea in which city they were stopping that night. Meanwhile, it was past midnight, but there was no question of sleeping.

At last that night was over. At five o'clock in the morning I finally found an open church. At seven o'clock I took a taxi to go back to the doctor to see if there wasn't anything we could do. I remembered having heard that recently Thomas Mann, at the age of seventy-five, had successfully undergone an operation for cancer of the lung.

"Even that we have already thought of," said the doctor. "There is a marvellous specialist here in this very rare and exceedingly difficult operation. But the tumour is located in a place where one cannot operate."

"Well, what can we do then?" I choked through my tears.

"Unfortunately, nothing."

"But I can't just let him die like that!"

Silence.

And now I had to go to the hospital to fetch a completely unsuspecting Georg, and could give no sign that the doctor had given him about three months to live.

He was so glad to be out of the hospital that he paid no attention to my face.

The next day we went home. Georg was rather talkative. Interrupted by violent coughing, again and again he wanted to tell me of earlier times. Then for a longer time he was silent and gazed earnestly ahead.

Suddenly he said: "From time to time there comes a picture into my mind. I see you all on the farm, working and getting tired out, and then I look for myself, and I'm not there any more."

Was that a premonition?

We arrived in Waterbury, Vermont, the nearest railroad tation at Stowe. As the train came slowly in, I saw Rupert's laughing face greeting us through the window. He was home or a short holiday before starting his hospital work. The poor fellow knew nothing yet. But as he helped Georg down the teps of the train, his laughter gave place to real alarm.

Arriving in his bedroom, Georg said with a sigh of deep satisfaction:

"We have the most beautiful home I can imagine. Here it s best."

And now he could not do enough to assure me *how* good he felt.

While he was resting from the exertions of the trip, I told Rupert everything. On the very same day we asked a good friend of ours, a well-known doctor in the university town of Burlington, to come over. Shocked, Dr. R. heard the diagnosis of the New York doctors. Then he went to see Georg.

Long, anxious minutes slipped by. When Dr. R. finally came out of the room, I could hardly believe my eyes, so—almost pleased he looked.

"You cried too soon," he said to me. "I am absolutely unable to share the opinion of my New York colleagues. I don't believe it is cancer. The pneumonia took a lot out of him, and now he needs quiet and rest."

I could have cried for joy. I rushed to the chapel for an ardent prayer of thanksgiving, and then to Georg!

So—quiet and rest. If only there were not that racking cough, which stirred him again and again out of his sleep.

If during the past nights I had been unable to sleep for grief and affliction, now happiness kept me awake. In this night I thought of the many convents, in whose churches and chapels we had sung for cloistered nuns and monks to the greater glory of God. They were our most grateful audiences. And they had not forgotten us; at Christmas, Easter, and on east-days came greeting cards with assurances of prayer. These friends we needed now! In a short letter I told them of "the Captain's illness," and asked for their prayers.

A few days went by. Georg was tired and happy. He didn't

want to talk much. He liked it best when I sat at his bedside
held his hand, and read aloud to him. Sometimes he fell asleep
during the reading; then with my left hand I got out my
rosary. It was strange: Georg, who was always so concerned
for others and never claimed a service for himself, now did
not want to let me out of his sight for a minute. Not even at
night. He was afraid of the night. When the convulsive
coughing had again shaken him awake, he often said: " Pray
something out loud!" I prayed the ancient prayer which I
still knew from Nonnberg:

> " Oh God, we cry unto Thee,
> In the Name of Jesus,
> Through the Blood of Jesus,
> Through the most Sacred Heart of Jesus
> Most wonderfully Thou canst help us.
> Holy God,
> Holy, strong God,
> Holy, immortal God,
> Have mercy on us!"

Again and again the anxious heart appealed to Our Lady
" Maria, healer of the sick, consoler of the afflicted, pray for
us." A gentle pressure of the hand indicated to me: so, now
that's enough; now let's sleep again a little.

On the doctor's advice, Georg sat for a while in the afternoon in a comfortable arm-chair. He longed for the return of
the children. When Dr. R. called again, he was very satisfied
Since he had to go to Chicago for ten days, he gave us the
telephone number of a Dr. W., just in case, and when Dr. W.
came, he, too, spoke most hopefully about Georg's condition

In spite of the confidence of both doctors, I could not rid
myself of a secret fear. To prepare me for what was to come
the doctor in New York had pointed out to me that Georg
would become visibly weaker, finally a serious shortness of
breath would set in, and if heart failure did not intervene, he
would slowly suffocate. Like my own death sentence these
words still sounded in my ears.

Then Dr. W. himself was suddenly taken ill, and recommended to us a particular capable internist from the university
clinic in Burlington, Dr. F.

Outside the wind howled and tossed wet snow against the
window. Georg asked more and more often about the children

ren, who were still on concert tour. The big house was so
lonely and quiet. Finally, the blue bus came panting up the
hill. The poor children, they only knew that Papa was much
better. Happily they pressed all at once into the sick-room and
then—how suddenly they were struck dumb, with what difficulty they held back their tears. The horror which rose in
their eyes made me once more aware of the ghastly change. I
had wanted to ask then: "Doesn't Papa look much better
already?" but the question remained unasked. Quietly I
slipped out of the room.

The children's return worked like medicine. Georg wanted
to have them by him all the time. He wanted to hear about
the last concerts, about the success of the collections for
Austria; he wanted to see the current mail, to read letters
from Austria himself, and began to talk of the old times.

Meanwhile, from all over the country and from Europe
came answers to my plea for prayer. A real army of allies
stormed heaven.

Then came a visit from an Austrian Jesuit Father, who is
now a pastor in Boston. As I couldn't help reading the deep
emotion in Father Weiser's face, I said to Georg:

"Look, in the New Testament it says clearly: 'Is any man
sick among you? Let him bring in the priests of the church
and let them pray over him, anointing him with oil in the
name of the Lord.' Let's ask Father Weiser for the Last
Sacraments; that will certainly do you good."

Georg agreed immediately.

"All right, to-morrow morning."

We had all gathered in the chapel. While Father Weiser
was hearing Georg's confession we recited the rosary. Then
Father Weiser came to fetch the Holy Eucharist. With burning
candles we went before our Saviour, singing, into the sick-
room. It was a solemn and festive occasion. Georg was so
happy and peaceful; loudly and clearly he answered, together
with us, the priest, who said all the prayers in Latin and
German. What strength and confidence flowed forth from
these prayers! Something of Georg's peace and joy touched
all our hearts. When it was over, the children kissed their
father and quietly went out.

Afterwards I was alone with Georg. "I feel so much better,"
he said softly, taking my hand in his, and fell asleep. Quietly

he slept for several hours. Even the cruel cough was still
Immediately my heart began to sing: maybe—maybe. Tha
was the Wednesday before Pentecost.

It was the calm before the storm. The following Saturday
shortness of breath set in. Painfully he squeezed out the
words: "What's this, do I have to die now?" And he looked
at me anxiously and imploringly.

We telephoned Dr. F. immediately. He reassured us. It
was only an attack of asthma; Georg was most probably
allergic to some of the pollen from those many flowers his
children had brought with them upon their home-coming. He
gave him an injection against asthma, and we cleared the
pelargoniums and petunias out of the room.

When the new doctor saw our dreadful anxiety, he stayed
the whole afternoon in the sick-room to observe the patient
Before he left, he gave Rupert different medicines and assured
us over and over again that no one ever died of asthma, that
Georg would soon be much better. His general state of health
was completely satisfactory.

The next day was Pentecost Sunday. With hearts filled with
anxiety we prayed to the Holy Ghost, Who is also called the
"Comforter."

It was the beginning of a martyrdom. Panting heavily and
struggling for breath, Georg sat among the pillows. The
asthma medicines brought no relief, and the morphine dose
had to be increased more and more to give him a little rest at
night.

Since the beginning of the shortness of breath on the Saturday before Pentecost, the family had multiplied their prayers.
Every hour the chapel bell called us. Day and night we took
turns before the Blessed Sacrament.

Thursday after Pentecost came. In the afternoon Dr. F.
had again spent several hours with the patient. The shortness
of breath mystified him.

"If it weren't for his breathing," he said, "the Captain
could sit out here in a chair, and in a week, on the balcony."
He described his general condition, heart, lungs, etc., as sub-
stantially better than a week ago. He did not think it was
cancer, and as for the breathlessness, he thought it might be
attributed to a nervous condition. He went away more con-
fident than ever.

Then everything was as it had been in the last days, supper, evening prayer. At eleven o'clock I noticed a difference in his breathing. Suddenly I knew with absolute certainty that it was the end. I called Rupert and woke all the children except little Johannes. Father Wasner came also. After one look at the sick man he left, returning immediately with the stole and the book of Prayers for the Dying.

To assist Rupert we called the nearest doctor in Stowe, a white-haired elderly lady. She came, made a quick examination, said only. " The heart," and gave him a couple of injections. Then she sat down at the back of the room. We knelt round the bed. Slowly and solemnly the words of the Prayers for the Dying sounded through the room. We prayed the rosary together. No, many rosaries, how many, we don't know. After every single decade we said a few ejaculations aloud slowly. He was fully conscious, and in the midst of a violent struggle, he repeated from time to time: " My Jesus . . Mercy!"

It was long after midnight when the doctor listened again to his heart.

She said in an undertone: " I'm afraid this is the end."

I knew what I had to do. Many years before, we had promised each other that one would tell the other when the end was coming. Up to this moment I had waited for a miracle and clung to the confidence of the doctors. But now the word of a doctor had destroyed the very last hope. It had to be.

I got up from my knees and said very close to his ear: " Georg, the end is coming."

A terrible sob shook the breast fighting for air, and with a last effort he put his right arm around my neck, his hand sought my forehead. A farewell blessing. But that was not yet all.

" Georg, my dear Georg, you accept death willingly from the hand of God, don't you?"

That was the important, the all-deciding question which we had promised each other to ask. And in the violent spasms of his final struggle for breath, he gasped " Yes."

That was his last word.

A Saint once said: " The most beautiful word which a man can say to his God is the little word ' yes.' "

Once more Father Wasner brought Holy Communion. In full consciousness Georg received his Master and Saviour.

And now it was really there, the end. It was a hard, cruel battle.

How terribly still it was in the room when the last death-rattle was silenced. The poor breast had its peace now, the brave heart stood still. In this holy silence Georg suddenly opened his eyes. The tortured features became calm and with an expression of endless wonder Georg gazed into another world. What may he have seen there? It must have been something indescribably beautiful. After about two minutes he nodded his head a little, and the dear eyes closed for ever.

We said the rosary again beside the death-bed, and then went over to the chapel for the first Requiem Mass.

After Holy Mass we stood a moment together in the hall in front of the chapel, weary with a night's watching, sorrowful and lonely. A sad voice asked:

" What shall we do now?"

Then suddenly a scene came to my mind and I told them:

" When we were in Vancouver Island a year and a half ago, a guide described to us the customs of the Vancouver Indians in burying their dead. Do you remember his describing how they crammed their dead into a little wooden box and put this box on a forked branch in a tall tree? Then Papa turned to me and said: 'But *I* don't want to be buried that way! Let me lie a day or two among you in the living-room, while you sit round me, praying and singing. And flowers I want, a whole room full, but they must not be bought. They must all be grown on our grounds. I've already found a little place for myself not too far from the house so that you can come and visit me often. Do you think I'll have enough friends to carry my coffin? On the way to the grave you must sing ' Andreas Hofer's Farewell to Life ' and ' Meerstern, ich Dich Grüsse,' and ' Innsbruck, ich muss Dich lassen.' "

We must now fulfil his last wishes.

First we applied for permission from our Bishop. Most willingly and kindly, he gave Father Wasner the authority to consecrate a cemetery on our own grounds. Before he could do that, however, the area had to be fenced in. All the children went to work immediately to build a beautiful wooden fence. Storms and rain were over; a brilliant blue spring sky arched over the world. We thought of the flowers. In the middle of the woods, where once a little farm had stood, we knew of a few wild apple trees. The boys brought a whole wagonful of branches, and the living-room was converted into an orchard in bloom. In front of the chimney we hung a red brocade curtain. Then we brought our father down, dressed in his Austrian grey wool suit. Of all his decorations, he had taken only the Maria Theresien Cross with him. This we placed on his breast. Over his knees we spread his old U-Boat flag. Above him on the mantelpiece stood the old wooden figures as usual, Our Lord and His Apostles, smiling down on the silent sleeper, surrounded by candles and flowers. His face radiated such dignity and beauty that it reminded us of the Apostle's words: " I have fought a good fight; I have finished my course; I have kept the faith. There is laid up for me a crown of righteousness . . ."

Meanwhile, telegrams had gone out all over the world to relatives and friends. Answering telegrams came in. Two of them, particularly touching, spoke of the " brave knight of the Theresien Order, Baron Trapp." One was signed " Zita," and one, " Otto "—Empress Zita of Austria and her eldest son, Otto. I laid them beside his Maria Theresien Cross.

Throughout the whole day there were always at least two of us with him. At seven o'clock in the evening the whole family gathered around their father. Friends had arrived by aeroplane. " Pray and sing," he had wanted. From seven o'clock until midnight we prayed the rosary and after each decade we sang one of his favourite songs. At midnight we got up from our knees, solemnly Father Wasner intoned the Te Deum, and we sang, " Holy God, We Praise Thy Name." According to the promise of Our Lady, she must have taken him to his eternal home, and with this his birthday in heaven had begun. We were filled with deep, solemn joy.

Finally, the day came that was to take him from us for ever: Trinity Sunday, the funeral day. Long before daybreak I was awake. Suddenly I heard the tapping of little feet; Johannes clambered up into bed with me.

Full of joyous excitement, he said:

" Mother, I dreamt something so beautiful, I had to come and tell you. I dreamt that the funeral was already over, but we only buried an empty coffin, and our *Papali* himself carried the Cross ahead of the procession; he was tall and shining, and just beautiful. Mother, isn't that fine?"

And the little fellow snuggled up to me happily. Johannes

is not a child given to fantasy, he never invents stories, and not for a moment did I doubt that this childish dream was more than a dream.

It appeared that he had more than enough friends to carry the coffin on their shoulders past the apple trees in bloom to the small mountain cemetery. We walked behind and sang the beautiful old songs. Our Guardian Angels must have helped us to be able to do it.

By the open grave Father Wasner told of Georg's heroic life and pious death, he explained the touching ceremonies of a Christian burial, and finally said that, according to an old custom, we give our departed friend as a last gift a handful of blessed earth and a few drops of holy water.

Dear frends, you may wonder that we told you all this in such detail, but we are convinced that *he* would have it so. He was a man whose mind was set on fundamental and important things. And what is more important than to die well? In that he gave us an example that we cannot keep to ourselves. He wants to welcome all of us, his family and you, his dear friends, there where he has gone before us.

XX. The Memorable Year

There was a man in the land of Uz, whose name was Job: and that man was simple and upright, and fearing God, and avoiding evil. . . . Now on a certain day, Satan was standing before the Lord. And the Lord said to him: Whence comest thou? And he answered and said: I have gone round about the earth. . . . And the Lord said to him: Hast thou considered my servant Job, that there is none like him in the earth, a simple and upright man, and fearing God, and avoiding evil? And Satan answering, said: Doth Job fear God in vain? Hast not thou made a fence for him, and his house, and all his substance round about? blessed the works of his hands? . . . But stretch forth thy hand a little, and touch all that he hath: and see if he blesseth thee not to thy face. Then the Lord said to Satan: Behold, all that he hath is in thy hand; only put not forth thy hand upon his person. And Satan went forth from the presence of the Lord.

Now upon a certain day . . . there came a messenger to Job,

*and said: The enemy rushed in and took thy oxen and asses
and slew the servants.*

*And while he was yet speaking, another came and said: The
fire of God fell from heaven, and striking the sheep and the
servants, hath consumed them.*

*And while he also was yet speaking, there came another and
said: The enemy hath fallen upon the camels and taken them.*

*He was yet speaking, and behold another came in, and said:
The house fell upon thy children; and they are dead.*

*Then Job rose up . . . and said: The Lord gave, and the Lord
hath taken away. As it hath pleased the Lord so is it done.
Blessed be the name of the Lord.*

"The Trapps—everything they undertake seems to turn out a
success. And how closely they live together, the parents with
their ten children. What an *exceptional* family! Most families
at one time or another have to cope with sickness, and death;
with family clashes and quarrellings and the neighbours'
gossip. They must be an exceptional family!"

How many times had that been said about us and written in
newspapers and magazines, and how hard did we try to correct this impression, try to prove that we were not exceptional,
but that our times were; that only one generation ago,
families still used to live in a close unit, working, playing, and
praying together; that ours was not only a success story, but
we had our trials and troubles, too.

But somehow, that didn't sound convincing. There we were:
prosperous—healthy—lucky—united. Until the year which will
be unforgettable to us, our memorable year."

It began in May with a fresh grave on our hill.

In early June while I was on business in Boston, the message
reached me: "Come home at once. Rosmarie has disappeared." The burden had become too heavy for the sensitive young soul: a most strenuous concert tour, combined
with concentrated preparatory work for high school gradua-
tion, the anxiety during the beloved father's illness, and finally
his death. For three days and three nights we searched the
countryside, the rivers, ponds, and woods. The people of
Stowe offered their cars, their time, their sympathy. After
three days the story had to be given to the radio and newspapers. With our name that meant nation-wide publicity,
reporters crowding on the porch, searching stubbornly for

some romance, the only explanation for the disappearance. Then she was found in the woods. Months filled with untold anxiety and prayer had to pass until God sent the helper, a priest who was also a doctor and a psychiatrist and helped the young soul to find its way back to God and society.

One morning in June, little Johannes woke up at five o'clock.

"Mother, I'm so hot, and my neck aches and my legs and my arms."

His temperature was 104°.

The newspapers had mentioned several cases of infantile paralysis in the State. When the doctor finally came and discovered that it was "only" rheumatic fever—what a relief! For seven long weeks a lively little boy had to be kept quiet on his back.

This was in the early summer.

Then Hedwig developed a severe backache and was brought into the hospital by the doctor for observation. After another most anxious week, it appeared that it was not that grim ill that the doctor had feared at first.

Then came the summer camp. People arrived and were shown to their quarters. The programme went on as usual. One tried so hard to do one's best. One smiled and talked— but all the time one felt like a machine which had to be wound up. All you did was automatic; at times, even your prayer. Of course, your will turned in a general way towards God. You are resigned, you don't want to argue. You repeat over and over again: "Thy Will be done." But what you *feel* is that terrible emptiness. The sun has set in your life; it is getting cold.

One day that same August I stood outside on the kitchen square in the camp and watched aimlessly a truck and a car back up towards each other. At that moment Lorli came running to take something off the truck. I screamed as loudly as I could. It was too late, the drivers didn't see her. How lucky we were—only a couple of ribs were broken.

When in September another baby had come and gone, not able to live on account of my bad kidneys, I didn't seem able to recover. When the whole family went to Fall River, Massachusetts, for Rupert's wedding, I was in bed, too ill to be even sad or sorry or worried. I was only relieved: now I wouldn't spoil his great day with my tears. When I had ecovered to a certain extent, I wanted to take part in the oncert tour, and left together with the others in November. After a few weeks long fainting spells set in, accompanied by onvulsions and high blood pressure. I was put into a hospital n the Middle West. I was seriously ill. After the best doctors ad tried everything, I was told that all there was left for me o do was to pray. On Christmas Eve I received the Last acraments. In January I improved slightly and was allowed o travel home. There was nothing medicine could do for me ow. I could only wait. It might take many more months.

After the " seven fat years " the " seven lean years " had ome upon the Trapp Family, all compressed in ten months. Now they had to cope with sickness, breakdowns, death. At imes it looked hopelessly complicated.

But must it not have looked that way to Job, the man in the and of Uz who had lost all his material goods, his children, is health, and the confidence of his friends? And what did ob do? After he had said: " The Lord gave and the Lord aketh away, blessed be the name of the Lord," he prayed for he friends who had turned against him.

And how does Holy Scripture usually end a story which is vritten as an example for us? " Go and do thou likewise."

XXI. Cor Unum

here is a beautiful story in the Gospels: There was once a nan who was paralysed; and that's all we know of him. We lon't know whether he wanted to be cured, whether he ever sked for it. We don't know what his thoughts were. But this nan had friends, and they had made up their minds to have im cured. They put him on a litter and carried him to the ouse where on that day the famous prophet, Jesus of Naza- eth was preaching. There was such a crowd around the house, hat they couldn't get in. But they were so determined that othing could make them change their plan. They climbed up o the flat roof with their sick friend, and through an opening, hey let down the litter directly at the feet of Our Lord. Then he Gospel says so beautifully. " And when Jesus had seen *heir* faith, He said to the sick one: ' Arise, take up thy bed nd walk.' "

This is one of the most consoling stories, as it shows wha
we can do for our friends, and what our friends can do fo
us. When the news of my serious sickness became know
letters and telegrams came in great numbers from all ove
Austria and America, assuring us that many people wer
storming heaven. And again it happened: When He saw *the*
faith, He said to the sick one. " Arise . . . and go." Against a
hope, I recovered fully. According to the doctor's words, th
cannot be attributed to medicine. Whatever the paralyse
man's thoughts may have been before—when he took his be
and went home, he knew that he had been cured through th
faith of his friends. How he must have loved them ever after

Then came the big day in May when we were summoned t
the court-house in Montpelier—the five years of waiting wer
over. It happened to be the Feast of Corpus Christi, and sinc
early morning we had been in a festive mood. What a mixe
group it was, waiting there in the court-room: Italian
Croatians, Syrians, English, Irish, Polish people, and w
Austrians. The clerk called the roll. Then the judge entere
the room. We all rose from our seats. Then we were aske
to raise our right hand and repeat the solemn oath o
allegiance to the Constitution of the United States of America
After we had ended: " So help me God," the judge bade u
sit down, looked at us all, and said: " Fellow citizens," H
meant us—now we were Americans.

After Armistice Day when the boys were still in Europe, the
had gone for a short visit to Salzburg and found that our ol
home there had been confiscated by Heinrich Himmler; tha
it had been made his headquarters for the last period of tha
cruel war; that the chapel had been turned into a beer pa
lour; and what had been Father Wasner's room had becom
Hitler's quarters when he came there. Gruesome stories the
heard, such as this:

One day when Hitler was there, chauffeurs and orderlie
were waiting outside on call. One of these soldiers humme
the melody of a Russian folk-song. Hitler heard this, jumpe
to the window and yelled:

" It is beneath the dignity of a German soldier even t
hum a Russian folk-song "; and he had them all shot on th
spot, without taking the trouble to find out who the singe
was.

That house was haunted for us all. How could we ever live
again happily on such bloodstained ground? When it was
given back to us after the war, we prayed that we might be
able to sell it. Our prayer was answered. The house was sold
to a religious order in America which wanted to establish a
seminary in Europe. The place is now called Saint Joseph's
Seminary. It has a chapel again.

With the money we paid our debts, mortgage and all.
What a relief that was! With the rest we wanted to build
two additional wings on the house, one with a large chapel,
and the other with enough room for guests so that eventually we could have our Song Weeks at home, winter and
summer.

After having learned the hard way how *not* to build a house,
we engaged a contractor this time. All we had to do was sit
back and watch those powerful bulldozers eat their way into a
deep cellar twice as long as the one we had dug inch by inch,
and in one-tenth of the time. When the new wing was roughly
finished, the family and the men who had worked on the
house had a festive dinner. Then we had to stop building for
the time being because the money was used up. Some day
there will be another dinner when the new wing is completely
finished.

Martina had a bosom friend, Erika, from whom she was
inseparable during her school years. Ever since we had come
to America, it was understood that Erika would some day
come to visit us. This plan, interrupted by the war, was resumed afterwards, but it took years until finally Martina
rushed through the house waving a telegram and shouting:

" *Erika arrives by plane in Boston to-morrow!* "

Two weeks later a happy young couple entered my room
—it was Werner and Erika, who wanted to go on through
life together. There was a beautiful engagement feast. The
newspaper man, when he learned in an interview that Father
Wasner had in his speech compared Erika to Rebecca, who
had also left her home and her family to follow a beloved
husband into a strange country, said dreamily:

" Rebecca—oh, yes, I saw the movie "—wherewith we
hastened to explain that it was Rebecca of the Old Testament,
who had married Isaac.

The wedding shortly after Christmas was celebrated in the

new chapel. When the bride threw her bouquet over her shoulder, Martina was the lucky one who caught it, and there is one of the Canadian boys who agrees most heartily that for this reason Martina has to be the next bride.

One day last year we felt very strongly that our home had to be given a name. We all sat down together and tried to think of one right away. At first, it seemed to turn into one of those evenings where you can't stop laughing. The suggestions got funnier and sillier all the time.

Father Wasner, who had joined us, finally said:

"The new name should have a meaning. It should stand for what the place wants to be." That made us serious again, and it made us contemplate: what *does* the place want to be? Father opened his New Testament, and his eyes fell on the words of the Acts of the Apostles which describe the life of the first Christians in Jerusalem: "They were one heart and one soul"—"COR UNUM ET ANIMA UNA." This Father Wasner read aloud to us, and there was a great silence. It was the answer to what we had been looking for: our new name and our new motto.

We all felt the greatness of this hour, and willingly we accepted the new challenge. Werner, who usually listens rather than speaks, spoke then and summed it up for all of us.

"Let us take this first Christian community for our example. Let us have no private property, but share everything together as they did. And let us feel obliged, every one of us, to keep a quiet half-hour in which we shall daily meditate on the life of Christ, that we may imitate it better and better."

That was the beginning of "Cor Unum," and the end of the "Trapp Family." It was a great and memorable moment in which we learned that the Trapp Family Singers had by now become an institution which did not depend any more on the members of the family. It had been our mission to present the best music to the multitudes near and far. More and more often it happened that people, old and young, who liked our music, wanted to be "adopted" into the family. The family ties have proved to be elastic, and so the family has grown and is still growing.

Our hill has become a holy hill for us since it contains that hallowed space with a lone grave, covered with flowers, ramed by mountains, overshadowed by a large wooden cross. From there silently, the head of the family watches over his own.

There we go through the year together, celebrating the feasts and the fasts as we used to in the old home. Many of the old folk customs have been transplanted to the new world, much to the joy of the friends of Cor Unum.

As the weeks, the months, the years go by, we see more and more that only one thing is necessary to be happy and to make others happy, and that one thing is not money, nor connections, nor health—it is Love.

Now read the further adventures
of the Trapp Family Singers

THE TRAPP FAMILY ON WHEELS

The Trapp family story, on which the Academy Award-winning film *The Sound of Music* is based, has inspired millions throughout the world with its charming picture of Christian family life enduring in a world of cruelty and war.

The book you have just read is a half-million-copy bestseller in paperback, and the film *The Sound of Music* has broken all box-office records wherever it has played.

Now Fontana Books takes pride in bringing you the paperback edition of Maria von Trapp's sequel *The Trapp Family On Wheels*. In this new book, the Trapp family sings its way around the world—South America, Germany, Italy, their old home at Salzburg in Austria, Sweden, Hawaii, and a triumphant tour of Australia and New Zealand.

"Readers who enjoyed the first book will not be disappointed in its sequel. This little band of singers travels all over the world giving pleasure. Their gaiety and happiness is engagingly transmitted."
Books of the Month

Fontana books . . .

paperbacks by famous authors

available wherever famous books are sold

Other great books that are now great films

DOCTOR ZHIVAGO

by Boris Pasternak

Russia's greatest modern novel, awarded the Nobel Prize for Literature. David Lean's epic film, winner of five Academy Awards, is based on Boris Pasternak's novel, which has already sold over half-million copies in Fontana paperback alone. "Will come to stand as one of the great events in man's literary and moral history." New Yorker.

THE AGONY AND THE ECSTASY

by Irving Stone

Over 2 million copies sold of this famous bestseller. Irving Stone's masterpiece of the life of Michelangelo is as powerful as the mountainous genius of the greatest artist of all time. "Anyone who wants the facts about Michelangelo can turn confidently to *The Agony and the Ecstasy*." Daily Telegraph.

BORN FREE

by Joy Adamson

The great animal story enjoyed by over 50 million people throughout the world. *Born Free*, and its sequel, *Forever Free*, detail a unique relationship between humans and lions that has astounded naturalists. The film, starring Virginia McKenna and Bill Travers was the Royal Film Performance for 1966.

Fontana books

paperbacks by famous authors

available wherever famous books are sold

Famous authors
in Fontana religious books

WILLIAM BARCLAY

The Mind of Saint Paul
Prayers for Young People
The Plain Man Looks at the Beatitudes
More Prayers for the Plain Man
The Plain Man's Book of Prayers
The Plain Man Looks at the Lord's Prayer

GEORGE BERNANOS

The Carmelites
The Diary of a Country Priest

C. S. LEWIS

Surprised by Joy
Letters to Malcolm: Chiefly on Prayer
Miracles
The Screwtape Letters
Screwtape Proposes a Toast and other Pieces
The Four Loves
Reflections on the Psalms
The Problem of Pain
Mere Christianity

J. B. PHILLIPS

A Man Called Jesus
The Young Church in Action
The Book of Revelation (trans.
The Gospels in Modern English
Making Men Whole
Letters to Young Churches